Teaching in Transnational Higher Education

Teaching in Transnational Higher Education examines current trends and challenges that face students, teachers and institutions of higher education around the globe. This book comes at a pivotal moment when many universities are offering their courses in offshore locations. Students can now attain reputable, diverse degrees without leaving their home country.

The book clearly defines and takes an in-depth look at the various types of transnational education, including: institutions that have campuses abroad, teach specific courses abroad, and form partnerships with diverse institutions to teach jointly.

Teaching in Transnational Higher Education serves as a forum for debate on insightful topics such as:

- the modification of teaching to adapt to the needs of diverse students;
- the use of technology in the classroom;
- the view of higher education as a marketable service;
- the importance of cultural awareness and understanding in a transnational classroom;
- the complexities of assuring quality education across borders.

The authors choose to highlight a broad sampling of transnational programs including those in Zambia, China, and the United Arab Emirates. Interviews with students and teachers participating in these programs of study make this an enjoyable and unique portrait of higher education that is invaluable to those who teach and learn around the world.

Lee Dunn is a lecturer and academic developer in the Teaching and Learning Centre at Southern Cross University, Australia.

Michelle Wallace is an Associate Professor in the Graduate College of Management at Southern Cross University, Australia.

Teaching in Transnational Higher Education

Enhancing Learning for Offshore International Students

Edited by

Lee Dunn and

Michelle Wallace

 Routledge
Taylor & Francis Group

NEW YORK AND LONDON

First published 2008
by Routledge
270 Madison Ave, New York, NY 10016

Simultaneously published in the UK
by Routledge
2 Park Square, Milton Park, Abingdon, Oxon OX14 4RN

Routledge is an imprint of the Taylor & Francis Group, an informa business

© 2008 Taylor & Francis

Typeset in Sabon by EvS Communication Networx, Inc.
Printed and bound in the United States of America on acid-free paper by Walsworth
Publishing Company, Marceline, MO.

Library of Congress Cataloging in Publication Data
Teaching in transnational higher education : enhancing learning for offshore
international students / edited by Lee Dunn and Michelle Wallace.
p. cm.
Includes bibliographical references and index.
ISBN-13: 978-0-415-42053-2 (hardback)
ISBN-13: 978-0-415-42054-9 (pbk.)
1. Transnational education. I. Dunn, Lee, 1940– II. Wallace, Michelle, 1949–
LC1095.T43 2008
378.03--dc22
2007033472

ISBN 10: 0-415-42053-9 (hbk)
ISBN 10: 0-415-42054-7 (pbk)
ISBN 10: 0-203-93062-2 (ebk)

ISBN 13: 978-0-415-42053-2 (hbk)
ISBN 13: 978-0-415-42054-9 (pbk)
ISBN 13: 978-0-203-93062-5 (ebk)

Contents

PART II
Perspectives on Teaching 55

PART III
Perspectives on Learning 133

Preface

The development of this book has been prompted by our own experiences teaching in transnational programs, managing and developing staff who teach in transnational programs and reflecting on issues of quality, learning and teaching, identity and culture in a number of contexts that include the transnational.

One of our most influential experiences was a team teaching opportunity 'off-shore', which enabled us to develop a dialogue with each other based on our different perspectives of shared experiences. This dialogue encompassed our realization of the unique nature of the transnational teaching and learning experience (of course we were seasoned teachers but in the transnational context novices again) and gave us the opportunity to question a lot of 'givens' from our professional meta-perspectives of academic staff developer and human resource development scholar.

We threw ourselves into the literature and engaged in some tentative empirical research with students. This grew to the development of a small body of our own publications and relationships with others researching in the transnational higher education field. We found an emerging literature on many aspects of transnational higher education but no collections focusing on learning and teaching in the transnational context. The development of a book was the logical next step.

We present this edited volume as the 'first word' on transnational learning and teaching and look forward to a continued dialogue on this developing topic.

Lee Dunn and Michelle Wallace

Acknowledgments

We acknowledge Southern Cross University and our respective organizational units, The Teaching and Learning Centre and the Graduate College of Management for their recognition of our research and publication endeavours. We also acknowledge early, modest internal research grants from the Graduate College of Research, which enabled us to begin our transnational research journey. We would like to thank Victor Marsh, PhD for his editorial support.

Contributors

Christine Bateman is Director of Education UK Marketing and Communications at the British Council. She has responsibility for the Prime Minister's Initiative for International Education and manages a global marketing campaign for UK education. She has over a decade of experience in international education and has extensive knowledge of international markets and education issues. Prior to her current role, Christine worked as a specialist adviser on transnational education within the British Council.

Maureen Bell is a Senior Lecturer in the Centre for Educational Development and Interactive Resources at the University of Wollongong. From 1997 to 2007 Maureen was coordinator of the University of Wollongong Foundations of University Teaching course. Her research interests include higher education teaching practice, peer review of teaching, peer observation of teaching, and internationalisation of the higher education curriculum. In 2007 she received a citation from the Carrick Institute for Learning and Teaching in Higher Education (Australia) for her contribution to the professional development of university teachers. Maureen is a Fellow of the Higher Education Research and Development Society of Australasia.

Chelsea Blickem is an Academic Advisor within the Centre for Teaching & Learning at Unitec New Zealand. A particular area of interest is assessment, and the development of language and academic literacies in all programmes. Until March 2004 Chelsea was Programme Director for the Certificate in Intensive English at Unitec. In 2001 Chelsea was a key member within the School of Languages, Unitec, which facilitated the delivery of the Certificate in Intensive English offshore in Beijing, China.

Maria Bjorning-Gyde (Fusion Teaching Ltd) has taught EFL since 1987 in Sweden, New Zealand and China. Her main areas of expertise include teacher training, course design and management. Maria works as an independent trainer and consultant, delivering the Trinity CertTESOL in Hong Kong and China and professional development programs for Secondary School teachers in Hong Kong and China. She is involved in a number of writing projects which focus on teaching and learning in a Confusion cultural context.

Jude Carroll is a Teaching Fellow based in the Oxford Centre for Staff and Learning Development at Oxford Brookes University in the United Kingdom. She has lived and worked in the United States, several European countries and in Africa. She is published in the area of plagiarism and international students.

Anne Chapman is an Associate Professor in the Graduate School of Education at The University of Western Australia. She teaches in the areas of qualitative research methods in education, youth culture, and language and literacies. Her main research interests are the internationalisation of higher education and the social semiotics of classroom learning. Her current research focuses on the dynamics of educational communities and student identity in the context of the internationalisation of Australian universities.

Michael R. Davidson is Research Development Advisor at the University of Ulster in Northern Ireland, where he works with PhD students and their supervisors and research-only staff. Previously he was Director of Studies for the PGCHE at the University of Nottingham, where his work was recognized with a Lord Dearing Award. Before coming to the UK, Michael co-ordinated an Academic Development Centre at Rhodes University, in South Africa.

Shelda Debowski is the Director of Organisational and Staff Development Services at the University of Western Australia. In a previous academic role at Murdoch University she taught a number of courses in China. Shelda has published several papers on working in transnational teaching contexts. Shelda is the President of the Higher Education Research and Development Society of Australasia.

Catherine Doherty lectures in language and socio-cultural studies in the Faculty of Education, QUT. She came to teacher education with experience in adult literacy and community education, migrant English programs and curriculum and policy roles. Her research focuses on how cultural identity interacts with pedagogy, curriculum design and globalisation processes, such as online networking.

Francis Doogan (Fusion Teaching Ltd) has taught EFL since 1990 in New Zealand, Japan and China. His main area of expertise and interest is teacher training. Francis now works as an independent trainer and consultant, delivering the Trinity CertTESOL and professional development programs for Secondary School teachers in Hong Kong and China. Francis is involved in a number of writing projects which focus on teaching and learning in a Confucian cultural context.

Allison Doorbar manages JWT Education globally. She was instrumental in conducting benchmark research into International Student Decision Making a decade ago and has worked extensively in this area. She has led many market research assignments for education clients including projects for institutions, government organizations and agencies as well as for individual institutions and private providers. Allison led the research commissioned by the British Council into the transnational education market, the findings from which are featured in this book.

Lee Dunn is a lecturer and academic developer in the Teaching and Learning Centre at Southern Cross University. She has published in the areas of assessment of student learning and transnational higher education.

Martin East is a senior lecturer in the School of Language Studies at Unitec New Zealand. He holds a PhD in language teaching and learning from the University of Auckland. His research interests include globalisation and its impact on language learning. He has also been instrumental in developing the New Zealand component of a China/NZ degree program.

Sandra Egege joined the Student Learning Centre of Flinders University in 2002 as an academic advisor, after several years tutoring in Philosophy. Her main research areas focus on Innateness and Culture and cultural influences on cognition. She is particularly interested in teaching critical thinking to international students and is currently researching the efficacy of overt teaching of critical thinking in developing critical thinking skills.

Margaret Hicks is Associate Professor and Associate Director Teaching and Learning in the Flexible Learning Centre at the University of South Australia. She has worked in universities for over sixteen years and in the area of academic development for the last ten years. In her current role she provides leadership for academic developers and learning advisers. Her research interests include academic development in higher education, student learning in higher education and preparing teachers for university teaching.

Futao Huang is a Professor in the Research Institute for Higher Education, Hiroshima University, Japan. He earned his PhD in China. He publishes widely in Chinese, Japanese and English in the areas of transnational higher education and internationalization of higher education in a globalised age.

Kylie Jarrett was part of the Academic Development team at the Flexible Learning Centre of the University of South Australia, at the time of this writing. Her specialisation was Transnational Education, which involves working with teachers from UniSA and those in partner organisations teaching UniSA courses. She is currently Lecturer in Multimedia at the National University of Ireland Maynoothylie.

Anne Jelfs is eLearning Development Manager within the Institute of Educational Technology at the UK Open University. Anne has worked for over twelve years in distance education and she has published refereed journal articles in this area. Her other interests are in the quality assurance of distance education and her PhD was on stakeholders' conceptions of quality in distance higher education.

Salah Kutieleh joined the Student Learning Centre at Flinders University in 1996 as an academic advisor to international students and has been the Head of the Centre since 2004. His research interests include the impact of teaching culturally-specific notions on international students' learning, their approaches to learning, the cultural roots of plagiarism, student attrition, and postgraduate supervision. He is a psycholinguist and a former international student.

Betty Leask regularly researches, publishes and consults in the area of internationalisation in higher education, including internationalisation of the curriculum and professional development for transnational teaching. Her current role is Dean of Teaching and Learning in the Division of Business at the University of South Australia (UniSA).

Grant McBurnie is senior associate in the School of Global Studies, Social Science and Planning at RMIT University, Australia. His writings on international education have been published in several languages and by international organisations. Grant is currently involved in a ten-country comparative study of the governance of cross-border higher education funded by the Australian Research Council.

David Pyvis is a Associate Professor in the Faculty of Media, Society and Culture at Curtin University of Technology, where he is involved in various programs delivered onshore and 'offshore' in Mauritius and Malaysia. He has many years' experience of teaching in 'offshore' programs, conducting classes on research methods for postgraduate students in Singapore and Hong Kong. His main research interest is in quality issues in transnational education.

Rachel Scudamore is an educational developer, based at the University of Nottingham in the UK. Rachel's main interest is using technology to support learning, particularly finding ways to ensure that teaching issues are to the fore in developing and implementing online learning resources. She is Director of the PESL project (Promoting Enhanced Student Learning). Until recently, Rachel was Course Director for the University's Postgraduate Certificate in Higher Education, the programme for new lecturers at Nottingham.

Nick Shackleford is the Head of the School of Language Studies at Unitec, New Zealand. Nick's research interests include language policy, management of language programmes, English for specific purposes and transnational education. He has been active in establishing relationships with universities in China and Japan in support of the school's exchange and international programmes.

Lois Smith currently holds the position of Chair, Centre for Language and Culture at the University of Wollongong in Dubai (UOWD). Lois has six years' experience working in the transnational educational environment of UOWD, and has taught ESL. Her research interests focus on higher education in an international context, both from the students' and from the teachers' perspective.

Lejla Vrazalic is Chair of the College of Undergraduate Studies and Associate Professor at the University of Wollongong in Dubai. She was one of the Co-ordinators of the Program for the Enhancement of Learning and Teaching. Her interests are in HCI, e-commerce and educational development. Lejla has received many university and national awards for her outstanding contributions to teaching and student learning.

Michelle Wallace is an Associate Professor in the Graduate College of Management at Southern Cross University. She is published in the areas of human resource development, gender and transnational teaching and learning.

Ting Wang is a Lecturer in Educational Leadership and Coordinator of Offshore Chinese Postgraduate Programs in the School of Education and Community Studies at the University of Canberra, Australia. She has published articles in several international journals and presented refereed papers at a number of international conferences. Her research interests include transnational education, leadership in cross-cultural settings, professional development of educators and comparative studies.

Gill Whittaker is a Learning and Teaching Fellow at the University of Bolton, UK, with a research focus on one-to-one engagement in learning and teaching. Gill has developed mentors and supported numerous mentoring projects across the UK and has developed a range of courses on mentoring reflective practice to undergraduates and serving teachers. Gill has taught on successive courses in Zambia since 1998. Gill is currently developing a mentoring system to support continuing professional development across the University.

Christopher Ziguras is Associate Professor of International Studies RMIT University. He has published extensively on international education policy, transnational higher education, trade policy, skilled migration and health behaviour. Previous appointments include: Research Fellow at the Monash Centre for Research in International Education (1999–2001); Deputy Director of the Globalism Institute (2002–04); and Head of RMIT's School of International and Community Studies (2004–05).

Craig Zimitat was Senior Lecturer at the Griffith Institute for Higher Education. He is now Deputy Director at the Learning and Teaching Development at the Centre for Advancement of Learning and Teaching at the University of Tasmania. His work primarily revolves around institutional and academic staff development for elearning. Craig's other academic interests focus on first year experience, learning through technology and medical education.

Introduction

Transnational higher education is an emerging area of scholarship. It is described as the situation where 'the learners are located in a country different from the one where the awarding institution is based' (UNESCO-CEPES 2000). While it has much in common with distance education, transnational higher education usually has a face-to-face component that includes both 'foreign' and 'local' teachers. This book is for those who teach and support students in transnational higher education.

Transnational higher education takes a number of forms. Some institutions have branch campuses in other countries, some franchise their courses overseas and some work with partners in another country to deliver their courses jointly. The chapters in this book reflect this diversity.

The book has been arranged in four sections, which explore issues that have emerged in transnational higher education and some of the implications of transnational education for teachers, learners and institutions. It is clear that certain themes resonate across the chapters. These include the tension between trade and capacity building, debates around whether curriculum should be delivered undiluted or whether it should be adapted for transnational students and issues of cultural hegemony and relativism. The book does not purport to be fully inclusive of all transnational perspectives or to explore transnational higher education in every country in which it is offered. Rather it offers perspectives on some systems, some programs and some educators' and students' perspectives as a 'first word' in what is a generative and lively avenue of scholarship.

Readers will find that authors have used a range of terminologies to describe the operational aspects of transnational higher education. The country or institution which is the base for the awarding degree is called the 'foreign', 'mother', provider' or 'home' country, while the country or institution in which the degree is being offered to transnational students may be called 'host' or 'local.' Joint programs are 'joint' or twins'. We have honoured individual author's use of terminology rather than standardizing it.

Part I, 'Current and Emerging Issues in Transnational Higher Education', offers perspectives on the issues of transnational higher education. From one perspective transnational higher education can be viewed as part of a liberalization of trade and a 'service' that can form part of free trade agreements. In Chapter 1, Ziguras and McBurnie offer a view that education services are important sources of income for exporting countries, overview the western provision of transnational higher education and explore the concerns of the critics of trade liberalization in relation to higher education. They explain that, while trade agreements have achieved less in terms of traded education, the principles on which trade agreements have been based have been widely adopted by governments.

The role of transnational higher education as part of capacity building for developing countries is another, less discussed perspective. In Chapter 2, Bateman and Doorbar present a UK perspective based on research undertaken through the British Council. What is striking about this research is the potential for far reaching developments in transnational education that include not only course delivery but also staff development, research collaboration and capacity building of local universities. While transnational higher education has been hitherto delivered by western, developed countries, this chapter also gestures towards a vision where some developing countries develop transnational capacities themselves.

China has become one of the largest importers of transnational higher education since the mid-1990s. In Chapter 3, Huang presents an overview of the higher education context in China and explores government policy. He then focuses on the significant role of joint programs between Chinese and foreign education providers, while expressing the view that they have not yet contributed substantially to China's mass higher education provision.

The role of technology and electronic delivery in transnational higher education cannot be underestimated. In Chapter 4, Jelfs explores the capacity building versus moneymaking aspects of transnational education as mediated by the use of technology. She expresses concerns about interactive technologies being used for one-way transmission of course content and the potential for online education to result in degree mills. However, she also views the use of interactive technologies, whereby students can publicly express course concerns, as empowering and enhancing equity. The development UK and European quality benchmarks are also seen as a positive check on exploitative practices.

While each of the above chapters has, in their own ways, alluded to issues of culture, Chapter 5 tackles them head on. Ziguras examines the argument that western-developed transnational higher education has the potential to undermine the national cultures of developing nations and explores the debate as to whether the 'market' or governments should determine transnational provision of higher education. In examining issues of culture and power in transnational higher education partnerships, he focuses on the de-coupling in some transnational arrangements of course development, delivery, assessment and certification and the potential of such practices for cultural dissonance and dislocation.

Part II, 'Perspectives on Teaching', focuses on issues for transnational teachers and moves through issues of culture to very practical teaching strategies. Chapter 6 continues the discussion of cultural issues raised in Part 1, particularly by Chapter 5. Wang explores arguments around western cultural imperialism and cultural assumptions but cautions against utilizing outdated cultural stereotypes as the traditional cultures of many countries are also in transition. She advocates intercultural understanding and uses as her case study a post-graduate leadership program to explore issues of cultural dissonance and intercultural dialogue and capacity building.

In contrast, Egege and Kutieleh, in Chapter 7, argue that intercultural awareness and sensitivity that lead to adaptation of the curriculum and pedagogy fly in the face of the need for consistency and over-emphasize 'difference'. They argue that cultural differences between students do not necessarily lead to cognitive differences and that most culturally based learning preferences are built upon past experiences. They contend that good teaching based on well founded principles and explicitly articulated academic expectations offer students what they want; a transformative western education.

Chapter 8 offers a very specific approach to language learning. Bjorning-Gyde, Doogan and East challenge the communicative language teaching model commonly used to teach English as a second language and question the use of western language pedagogies in this context. From their teaching experience with Chinese students they present a 'fusion' model of language teaching that combines practice in Chinese classrooms with that of western classrooms.

Debates around culture are very apparent in discussion of what is construed as academic dishonesty. In Chapter 9, Carroll explores student plagiarism in the transnational context and examines how plagiarism can be managed from both institutional and individual teacher perspectives.

Chapter 10 offers a very different perspective on culture. Here Whittaker, working with Zambian teachers, questions the authenticity of utilizing a reflective practice approach, which calls on analytical perspectives, when confronted with real life social disadvantage that the teachers are powerless to influence. This highly reflective and affective chapter offers a reality check for those advocating that western pedagogies do not need to be adapted.

Chapter 11 details a staff development program undertaken by a UK university at a branch campus in Malaysia. Davidson and Scudamore offer a personal account of the cultural issues involved in running development activities for a very diverse range of staff. They discuss the adaptations, both cultural and practical, in the mode of delivery.

Finally, in Chapter 12, Leask offers a very practical perspective on the skills needed for successful intercultural engagement in the transnational classroom. From empirical research she discusses the key characteristics of transnational teachers and the need for a curriculum that is both internationalized and localized.

Part III, 'Perspectives on Learning', considers transnational higher education from the learners' point of view. In Chapter 13, Zimitat provides a snapshot of how one Australian university is achieving internationalision of the undergraduate curriculum. Student perceptions of curriculum changes show varying degrees of success and interesting differences between domestic and international students.

Bell, Smith and Vrazilic, in Chapter 14, examine how a university that conducts a transnational program in Dubai embeds two of the university's desired graduate attributes: one being an appreciation of the value of cultural diversity in a multicultural, global environment and the other a capacity for teamwork. The United Arab Emirates has a young, highly multicultural population and the university's undergraduates reflect the mix of diverse nationalities. The authors investigated the use of small group activities as the curriculum vehicle to achieve the two graduate attributes. Student perceptions of the strategy are reported vividly and while much has been achieved, challenges still remain.

In Chapter 15, Doherty examines the realities of combining domestic and transnational cohorts in a fully online MBA program. Problems arose when some members of each group felt that their rights had been infringed. There were tensions between local identities and the global realities of the online course exacerbated by some aspects of the contractual agreement between the Australian university and its Malaysian partner.

Chapman, in Chapter 16, follows with a case study of one student undertaking a professional doctorate taught transnationally in Hong Kong. The Educational Doctorate was designed to be participative, democratic and collaborative. A local learning community was deliberately nurtured while the lecturers communicated mainly via email with some visits to Hong Kong. The student valued the early development of a learning community, but was disappointed that the University did not take responsibility for further fostering the collegial learning which diminished with time. However, the student also found that he was forced to become an independent learner when his supervisor was mostly only available by email. Towards the end of the research component of the EdD he recognises the value of becoming proactive.

In Chapter 17, we report a survey of undergraduate students in Singapore and the People's Republic of China. Our study examines why these transnational students study for a foreign degree, how they balance their studies with the rest of their life responsibilities and how they prefer to spend their study time. We found differences between men and women, full-time and part-time students and between Singapore and PRC students.

The final section of the book, Part IV, 'Implications for Institutions', broadens the discussion to include implications for institutions that offer transnational higher education. In Chapter 18, McBurnie warns of the damage that can be done to country and institutional reputations when international, national and regional Quality Assurance regulations and guidelines are not properly implemented. He provides a useful three-step framework for effective institutional approaches to achieving quality programs.

Debowski follows in Chapter 19, with an educational manager's detailed look at the 'risky business' of managing the quality of a transnational educational strategy. She identifies five areas of risk and recommends an integrated approach to managing these complex programs.

In Chapter 20, Blickem and Shackleton describe the reality of a program planned and conducted in the early stages of New Zealand transnational education, prior to the strengthening of national Quality Assurance requirements. The authors describe how a succession of difficulties within the partnership itself, and the external blow of the SARS epidemic led to the demise of the program. They report a range of corporate learnings from the experience.

In Chapter 21, Pyvis reports a study of a franchised program in Mauritius. The study investigated whether the program delivered on the Mauritian Government's hopes for economic and social renewal through 'quality overseas provision of education' with 'world class standards.' The study concludes that institutions should recognise that there are a 'legion of risks' to be addressed.

Hicks and Jarrett, in Chapter 22, discuss the University of South Australia's 'whole of institution' approach to the induction, orientation and professional development of staff in transnational higher education programs. The authors are concerned with how to achieve equal relationships between teaching staff of the provider institution and those of its local partner. Readers will appreciate the practical guidelines and examples of good practice that are included in this chapter.

Our chapter concludes Part IV. In Chapter 23, we have drawn together threads and themes from the literature and the previous chapters in this book to argue for an inclusive holistic approach to managing transnational higher education. We argue that inclusive communities of practice could promote authentic intercultural learning. We recognise financial and workload constraints and recommend that these communities be nurtured and combined with the normal operational tasks of teams that plan, teach and support transnational education.

REFERENCE

UNESCO/Council of Europe (2000) *Code of Good Practice in the Provision of Transnational Education*. Bucharest: UNESCO-CEPES.

Part I

Current and Emerging Issues in Transnational Higher Education

1 The Impact of Trade Liberalization on Transnational Education

Christopher Ziguras
RMIT University

Grant McBurnie
RMIT University

INTRODUCTION

International trade is simply the commercial exchange of goods and services across national borders, but including education within such a definition is by no means simple. Labour unions and student groups around the world are adamant that education is a social good which should not be treated as a commodity or be included in agreements governing international trade, yet it often is. In this chapter we explain how transnational education has come to constitute a traded service like any other in global, regional, and bilateral trade agreements.

The monetary value of education services has been estimated at US$30 billion (WTO 1998). Most of this value is generated by internationally mobile students, and the Organization for Economic Co-operation and Development (OECD 2005) estimates that by 2003 there were 2.12 million tertiary students studying outside their countries of origin, a rise of nearly 50 per cent since 1998. In calculating expenditure on international education, economists take into account the tuition fees paid by students, as well as their travel and living expenses. Even exchange students, who do not pay fees to their host institution, have an economic impact through their spending while in the host country, and as such they contribute to the host country's export earnings. Income to educational institutions from their overseas operations is also included in a country's export earnings figures. The largest exporter, the United States, estimates the economic value of international students at US$13.5 billion (IIE 2006). Australia and New Zealand have fewer students overall, but have much higher proportions of international students in their universities than the United States, and for them the income from international students constitutes a very significant export industry. In Australia, international students enrolled at Australian domestic or overseas operated campuses in 2002 spent a total of A$5.2 billion (US$2.8 billion at 2002 average exchange rate), around half of which was spent on tuition fees and half on goods and services purchased in Australia (Kenyon and Koshy 2003). In New Zealand, in 2004, fee-paying international students are estimated to have contributed NZ$2.2 billion (US$1.5 billion at 2004 average exchange rate) (International Enrolments In New Zealand, 2006).

While mobile students are well covered by official data, governments currently keep little consolidated information about mobile programs (transnational education courses) or mobile institutions (international branch campuses). It is clear from available sources that there are several hundred thousand students studying foreign education programs while remaining in their home country (McBurnie and Ziguras 2007). There is a strong concentration in the Asian region, where British and Australian universities are the most active providers. In the first half of this decade, the number of students—chiefly from Asia—enrolled in Australian transnational higher education programs grew from 23,891 in 2000 to 63,906 in 2005, representing around a quarter of Australia's international university students across this period (DEST 2001, Table 77; 2006, Table 3.7.7).

The impact on some countries is enormous. For example, one quarter of Hong Kong tertiary students and a third of Singapore tertiary students are enrolled in transnational education programs (Garrett and Verbik 2003). At the same time, several traditional net importing countries (including Malaysia, Singapore, Dubai, Qatar and others) have declared their goal of becoming net exporters and regional education hubs by attracting international students to their shores. The presence of prestigious foreign providers (delivering transnational education) is a part of the drawcard. Clearly, the economic implications of transnational education are significant for all of these countries, and national trade policies are one way for governments to try to steer the direction of development of such markets.

Trade policy is the way in which states develop strategic approaches to governing trade, both to influence their domestic economies and also their nation's position within the global political-economic system (Dicken 2003). Trade policy development, as Hart (2002) has observed, is 'a matter of solving trade and investment problems within a framework of domestic and international rules as well as competing domestic and international political pressures' (2002: 5). Trade agreements are formal contracts between governments setting out the rules and conditions under which trade will be conducted between the signatory parties. Interestingly, the legalization, or codification, of trade in education through the General Agreement on Trade in Services (GATS) and other trade agreements has elicited much greater opposition than the growth of commercial international education ever did. These agreements can be multilateral, such as the GATS, which is administered by the World Trade Organization (WTO); regional, such as Mercosur in South America; or bilateral, such as the Singapore–New Zealand Free Trade Agreement. There are various types of arrangements, characterised by the level of economic integration they involve. The four key types, in ascending order of integration, are:

1. Free trade area: restrictions between members are removed, but each is free to pursue its own policies towards non-members.
2. Customs union: combines removal of restrictions between members with a common customs regime (tariffs and non-tariff barriers) towards non-members.
3. Common market: allows the free movement of the factors of production (labour, capital, goods and services) among members, in addition to having the qualities of a customs union.
4. Economic union: a common market in which broader economic policies are harmonised and subject to supranational control (Hart 2002: 523–7, Dicken 2003: 146–7).

While the differences between trade, trade policies and trade agreements appear clear, they are often confused in the education literature. To say, as many critics of trade liberalization do, that education is not a commodity, and therefore cannot be traded clearly, flies in the face of facts. Nothing is inherently a commodity, but rather a thing becomes a commodity when it is exchanged for money. While an objection to the treatment of education as a commodity is an understandable ideological position, it is incorrect to say that education *cannot* be treated as a commodity because it possesses some innate quality that cannot be the subject of commercial exchange. To say, in the context of GATS, that education is a complex service that *should not* be treated the same as cars and bananas, is another matter. Similarly, the absence of a trade agreement does not mean that trade is not taking place, nor will the signing of a trade agreement necessarily lead to an increase in the volume of international trade of any one service or good.

THE POLITICS OF LIBERALIZING TRADE IN EDUCATION

Proponents of trade liberalization argue that there are four key benefits: improved market access and conditions for suppliers; improved choice for consumers; improved quality of services due to increased local competition; reduction of risk due to operating under a predictable, rules-based, transparent international trade regime. We look at these in turn in relation to transnational education.

Improved market access and conditions for suppliers is a straightforward, self-interested argument from exporters. For some countries, as illustrated above, the exporting of education services is a major revenue generator, bringing in billions of dollars in foreign exchange. It is also a persuasive argument for net importers that harbour ambitions to become net exporters. The United States, Australia and New Zealand have been the most vocal advocates of trade liberalization in education, all having conducted significant studies into the barriers to free trade in education (GATE 1999, APEC 2001) and have called for countries to increase their openness to foreign education providers through the WTO negotiation rounds (WTO 1998, 2000, 2001a, b; see also McBurnie and Ziguras 2003, Ziguras et al 2003). These countries' interest in growing international education markets is clear; the United States is by far the largest exporter of education, while Australia and New Zealand have higher proportions of international students in their universities than any other country and education ranks among both countries' top export industries. Within the United States, it should be noted, most of the educational establishments are uninterested or opposed to trade liberalization, and the liberalization agenda is being driven by for-profit education providers, the testing industry, and the Department of Commerce (AUCC et al 2001, Altbach 2005). Britain, which is also a major exporter, is constrained in its advocacy for trade liberalization by its membership in the European Union. While flows of students and institutions have been liberalized extensively within the EU, externally the UK is represented by Brussels, which is ambivalent on educational trade matters due to the diversity of views among the EU membership.

Improved choice for consumers is an argument particularly stressed by major exporting nations. In its negotiating proposal to the WTO, Australia notes that trade liberalization will have the effect of 'facilitating access to education and training courses that in qualitative and quantitative terms are not otherwise available in the country of origin' and that 'education services negotiations should aim to give consumers (students) in all countries access to the best education services wherever they are provided and through whatever mode of supply they are provided' (WTO 2001a: 3). Similarly, when countries allow foreign providers to operate on their soil, the host government will declare that this is for the benefit of its citizens, in terms of widening choice and educational opportunity. New Zealand's proposal to the WTO argues that 'increased access for Members to education where it has previously been limited is a vital component in the development of human capital' (WTO 2001b: 1).

The Australian statement refers to 'providing a competitive stimulus to institutions with flow-on benefits to all students' (WTO 2001a: 1). These are 'demonstration effects', which may result from foreign provision exposing the local system to other curriculum, pedagogical styles, administrative and managerial systems, and research approaches. In some countries the presence of transnational education has played a role in the development of quality assurance systems; these may be developed initially as a filter mechanism for dealing with foreigner providers and subsequently applied to monitor and improve the standards of local providers. Further, the licensing of foreign providers may spur the host government to offer degree-granting powers to hitherto sub-degree local private providers.

Supporters of trade liberalization stress the benefits of a predictable, rules-based, transparent international trade environment. Inter alia, this reduces risk for the exporter and should therefore enhance the stability of the service provision. In terms of transnational education, the argument would be that a liberal trade agreement would reduce various of the risks—legal, financial and sovereign—inherent in offshore provision, thereby helping to prevent the collapse of programs or branch campuses, and reducing the risk to students of disruption to their education.

Critics of trade liberalization advance a number of concerns in relation to higher education. Domestic providers and trade unions express concern that their wages and conditions may be undermined by a liberalized trade regime. Education unions, and in particular their global umbrella group Education International, have been among the most active critics of freer trade in education, primarily concerned that the entry of for-profit providers would lead to competitive pressures that gradually erode working conditions and funding levels in existing institutions (Education International 2004). For the unions, the demonstration effects of the new, more commercial providers, may damage the domestic system as a whole. The Canadian Association of University Teachers declared its concerns that under a full GATS commitment:

> Senates, collective agreements and academic freedom will fall victim to the drive for the sale of educational services. They are, after all, in the way of unimpeded trade. In the end, university autonomy will suffer, if not be totally jeopardized. Our profession will be casualized. Words and ideals like long term commitment, social responsibility and knowledge for the common good will be disastrously eroded – or extinguished (Booth 2000: 1).

A wider concern is the perceived potential for trade liberalization to erode the government's prerogatives to regulate the size, level (undergraduate and postgraduate) and disciplinary mix of the local system if this interfered with the profit-driven goals of individual education exporters. Both economic liberals and protectionists agree that profound changes can result from opening a highly state-regulated national education system to new private providers that are able to move nimbly to target areas of demand where students are willing to pay tuition fees. The protagonists differ on whether such changes are beneficial or harmful. A related concern is the possibility that GATS commitments may interfere with the right of the government to target subsidies to domestic public providers, without being obliged to also subsidise private and/or foreign providers.

Trade liberalization raises fears about quality, not because the new entrants are of lower standard than existing providers, but because they are often of lower status. Education is a positional good, in that the worth of a qualification is judged by its position in relation to other qualifications; within each city and nation, prestige hierarchies have been apparent as long as the educational institutions themselves. More recently, the advent of formalized rankings of various kinds responds to a widespread interest in finding more objective rankings than prestige. Parents, employers and government officials have all been keen to have access to objective comparative data on educational outcomes that may either support or challenge historical status hierarchies. The shift from informal reputation to formal rankings is becoming increasingly obvious on a global scale with the advent of rankings such as those conducted by London's *Times* newspaper and Shanghai Jiao Tong University. Within national systems, students seek to study in prestigious institutions and institutions seek the 'best' students. While some new entrants into a national system may be foreign elite institutions that position themselves among the best local institutions, more commonly foreign providers are seeking to recruit those students who were not able to access prestigious local institutions. They are liable to be branded 'bottom-feeders'—that is, institutions that cater to poor quality students. As Ruch (2001) has observed, of the reaction to US for-profit universities, many of the concerns about the quality of new tuition-funded providers are based on the status of the students these institutions seek to recruit rather than any informed judgement about the merits of the educational programs being delivered.

Developing countries are especially vulnerable to negative consequences of trade liberalization according to many international organizations and developing country governments. For example, the Association of African Universities expressed concern at 'the ambiguities, silences and lack of clarity in GATS provisions, the lack of transparency in GATS deliberations, and insufficient knowledge and understanding of the full implications of GATS for higher education, especially in developing country contexts.' It resolved to 'caution against the reduction of higher education, under the GATS regime, to a tradable commodity subject primarily to international trade rules and negotiations, and the loss of authority of national governments to regulate higher education according to national needs and priorities' (Association of African Universities et al 2004: 6). It called on African governments to treat GATS with caution until further research was undertaken about its possible effects, and a better understanding could be reached on how trade in education services 'can best serve national and regional development needs and priorities on the African continent' (2004: 6).

NUTS AND BOLTS: WHAT DO FREE TRADE AGREEMENTS MEAN IN PRACTICE?

All trade agreements apply the principles of *market access* and *national treatment* to trade in services, and to illustrate what these mean in relation to transnational education we will consider the GATS, which is an extensive multilateral agreement binding all of the WTO's 150 member countries. Each WTO member country voluntarily commits to uphold these principles in relation to particular services. Relatively few countries have made commitments applying to education services, while most have made commitments on financial services and telecommunications where cross-border trade is more extensive.

Unrestricted market access in education services exists when foreign services and service providers are not subject to any quantitative limitations, limitations on forms of legal entity under which educational institutions may be established, or limitations on foreign equity participation. A commitment to national treatment binds governments to 'accord to services and service suppliers of any other Member, in respect of all measures affecting the supply of services, treatment no less favourable than that it accords to its own like services and service suppliers' except where conditions and qualifications are specified the schedule of commitments (WTO 1995). Whether foreign services and service providers are subject to 'formally identical treatment or formally different treatment', they must not be treated in such a way as to modify the conditions of competition in favour of domestic providers. This means that foreign education providers may be subject to different requirements than domestic providers, but the effect must not be to disadvantage foreign providers over their domestic competitors. In the GATS, education services are distinguished according to level (primary, secondary, higher, adult, and other), and governments choose which of these to commit to liberalizing, if any. Like all services, education is also classified according to the 'mode of supply', which relates to the location of the supplier and consumer of the service.

Mode 1, cross-border supply, refers to the supply of a service 'from the territory of one Member into the territory of any other Member' (WTO 1995 Article I). In education this mode includes transnational 'distance', 'correspondence' or 'online' education in which an educational institution from one country is teaching a student who is resident in another country, where teachers and students remain in their own countries and communicate through post, fax, the Internet, etc. Mode 2, consumption abroad, refers to the supply of a service 'in the territory of one Member to the service consumer of any other Member'. This relates to students travelling abroad to study in another country. This is the only mode of supply that does not impact upon transnational education. Mode 3, commercial presence, refers to the supply of a service 'by a service supplier of one Member, through commercial presence in the territory of any other Member'. This relates to the establishment of branch campuses of foreign educational institutions (for example, Knight 2002: 193, FADTRC 2003: 45). Mode 4, presence of natural persons, involves provision of a service 'by a service supplier of one Member, through presence of natural persons of a Member in the territory of any other Member'. In education, this refers to teachers, academics, administrators or marketing staff travelling across national borders to provide educational services (including the administration and marketing thereof) in the student's home country. Short courses may be provided purely through the presence of natural persons, but in most cases the movement of natural persons in education is used to complement cross-border supply and/or commercial presence.

The distinctions between these modes of supply matter when governments commit to liberalizing some forms but not others. In practice, the implications of commitments to free trade in education are complex and subject to legal interpretation in each country, given the range of regulatory frameworks and types of institutions involved. For example, China has made no commitment to market access or national treatment for cross-border supply of higher education, so it reserves the right to restrict access to foreign programs offered in China, either by distance education or in collaboration with local universities. However, it has committed to both market access and national treatment for consumption abroad, meaning that it cannot restrict the ability of Chinese students to study abroad. For commercial presence China has committed to market access, allowing foreign campuses to be established with majority foreign ownership permitted, but it has not committed to national treatment in this mode of supply, so the government is able to discriminate between domestic- and foreign-owned campuses if it wishes to. In relation to the movement of natural persons, China has committed to allowing individual educators to provide services in China if they hold relevant qualifications and are invited by a local institution. These broad commitments provide legally binding constraints on Chinese regulations related to cross-border education, but knowing the GATS commitments alone does not reveal much about the varieties of regulation applying to different forms of delivery (for a more detailed account, see Ziguras 2003).

Further complicating the impact of trade agreements, most countries are in practice much more open to foreign education providers than they commit to being under international treaties. Since the early 1990s, many countries have embarked on 'unilateral' liberalization, meaning that they have opened their systems to private and foreign providers unilaterally and voluntarily, often without binding it in an international agreement. For example, Malaysia is very open to foreign programs and has been actively recruiting branch campuses for a decade, but it has not 'bound' this open approach legally by enshrining it through the GATS or any bilateral free trade agreements. This means that Malaysia retains the option of closing off some of the rights of foreign providers in the future. When countries make commitments within a trade agreements they very rarely commit to a level of openness that was not already in place. So rather than trade agreements prizing open markets and thereby growing the volume of transnational education provision, they instead provide greater certainty to educational institutions that the regulatory environment will not become greatly less open in the future. In this way trade agreements decrease the level of risk faced by institutions operating transnationally, but they have done little on their own to change governments' policies.

The only instance we are aware of in which a trade agreement dramatically challenged a government's approach to transnational providers is Greece's dispute with the European Commission. Greece's case is unusual, and arises because of a clash between the EU's free trade principles and Greece's constitutional prohibition of private higher education (Alderman 2001, McBurnie and Ziguras 2007). Despite the millions of words of warning written about the harmful effects of the GATS and bilateral free trade agreements on education, similar clashes over a nation's right to regulate are difficult to locate.

CONCLUSION

It is now 12 years since the GATS came into effect, and in that time hundreds of bilateral trade agreements have also been implemented, most of them covering education services to some extent. Looking back, it is difficult to escape the conclusion that trade agreements have achieved less than anyone expected. They have not caused wholesale privatization of education systems, eroded national quality assurance systems, or led to an influx of low quality global education brands, but neither have they prized open markets previously closed to transnational providers. While these international legal agreements have proved relatively insignificant, the principles on which they are based have been adopted widely by governments. In many countries, the principle that new institutions—whether privately owned, publicly listed or religious, for-profit or not-for-profit—should be allowed to enter education markets and compete for students with established providers. Similarly, the notion that governments should not discriminate between local and foreign providers has been broadly accepted. Liberalization based on these principles has occurred more extensively in other service industries, to the extent that in most economically advanced economies it is difficult to remember a time in which governments protected a small number of domestic providers against new domestic and foreign entrants to their markets. Now we accept and benefit from the deregulation and global integration of banking, telecommunications, transportation, and media. The education sector has moved more slowly in most countries, but the same principles of economic liberalization have assisted the growth of transnational education in many countries in which supply of tertiary education was previously highly restricted.

REFERENCES

Alderman, G. (2001) 'The Globalizationof Higher Education: Some Observations Regarding the Free Market and the National 'Interest', *Higher Education in Europe* 26 (1): 47–52.

Altbach, P.G. (2001) 'Higher Education and the WTO: Globalization Run 'Amok', *International Higher Education*, 23: 2–4.

—— (2005) 'The Political Economy of International Higher Education Cooperation: Structural Realities and Global Inequalities', NUFFIC Conference: 'A Changing Landscape', The Hague. Online. Available: http://www.nuffic.nl/nederlandse-organisaties/nieuws-evenementen/evenementen-archief/past-event-1/Downloads

APEC (2001) *Measures Affecting Trade and Investment in Education Services in the Asia-Pacific Region*, Singapore: Asia Pacific Economic Cooperation.

Association of African Universities, UNESCO and Council on Higher Education (South Africa) (2004) 'Accra Declaration on GATS and the Internationalization of Higher Education in Africa', *International Higher Education*, Summer: 5–7.

AUCC, ACE, EUA and CHEA (2001) *Joint Declaration on Higher Education and the General Agreement on Trade in Services*. Association of Universities and Colleges of Canada, American Council on Education, European University Association, Council for Higher Education Accreditation. Online. Available: http://www.unige.ch/eua/En/Activities/WTO/declaration-final1.pdf.

Booth, T. (2000) *Academic Freedom as Just Another Commodity*. Canadian Association of University Teachers. Online. Available: http://www.caut.ca/en/bulletin/issues/2000_sep/pres.htm.

DEST (2001) *Students 2000: Selected Higher Education Statistics*. Department of Education, Science and Training. Online. Available: http://www.dest.gov.au/sectors/higher_education/publications_resources/statistics/selected_higher_education_statistics/students_2000.htm.

—— (2006) *Students 2005: Selected Higher Education Statistics*. Department of Education, Science and Training. Online. Available: http://www.dest.gov.au/sectors/higher_education/publications_resources/profiles/students_2005_selected_higher_education_statistics.htm.

Dicken, P. (2003) *Global Shift: Reshaping the Global Economic Map in the 21st Century*, London: Sage.

Education International (2004) *Globalization, GATS and Higher Education*, Brussels: Education International.

FADTRC (2003) *Voting on Trade: The General Agreement on Trade in Services and an Australia–US Free Trade Agreement*, Canberra: Senate Foreign Affairs, Defence and Trade References Committee.

Garrett, R. and Verbik, L. (2003) *Transnational Higher Education, Part 1: The Major Markets—Hong Kong & Singapore*, London: Observatory on Borderless Higher Education.

GATE (1999) *Trade in Transnational Education Services*, Washington, D.C.: Global Alliance for Transnational Education.

Hart, M. (2002) *A Trading Nation: Canadian Trade Policy from Colonialism to Globalization*, Vancouver: University of British Columbia Press.

Institute for International Education (IIE) (2006) *Opendoors*. Online. Availble: http://opendoors.iienetwork.org/?P=89211 (accessed 12 June 2007).

Kenyon, P. and Koshy, P. (2003) *The Economic Benefits to Australia from International Education*, Canberra: Commonwealth Department of Education, Science and Training.

Knight, J. (2002) 'The Impact of GATS and Trade Liberalization on Higher Education', in S. Uvalic-Trumbic (ed.) *Globalization and the Market in Higher Education: Quality, Accreditation and Qualifications*, Paris: UNESCO.

McBurnie, G. and Ziguras, C. (2003) 'Remaking the World in Our Own Image: Australia's Efforts to Liberalise Trade in Education 'Services', *Australian Journal of Education* 47 (3): 217–34.

—— (2007) *Transnational Education: Current Issues and Future Trends in Offshore Higher Education*, London: RoutledgeFalmer.

Ministry of Education (2007). International Enrolments in New Zealand 2000–2006. Online. Available: http://minedu.govt.nz/web/downloadable/dl11293/-v1/economic-impact-report.doc (accessed 2 November 2007).

OECD (2005) *Education at a Glance: OECD Indicators 2005*, Paris: Organization for Economic Co-operation and Development.

Ruch, R.S. (2001) *Higher Ed, Inc.: The Rise of the For-Profit University*, Baltimore and London: Johns Hopkins University Press.

WTO (1995) *General Agreement on Trade in Services*, Geneva: World Trade Organization.

—— (1998) *Communication from the United States: Education Services*: World Trade Organization Council for Trade in Services.

—— (2000) *Communication from the United States—Higher (Tertiary) Education, Adult Education and Training*, Geneva: World Trade Organization Council for Trade in Services.

—— (2001a) *Communication from Australia: Negotiating Proposal for Education Services (S/CSS/W/110)*, Geneva: World Trade Organization.

—— (2001b) *Communication from New Zealand: Negotiating Proposal for Education Services (S/CSS/W/93)*, Geneva: World Trade Organization.

Ziguras, C. (2003) 'The Impact of the GATS on Transnational Tertiary Education: Comparing experiences of New Zealand, Australia, Singapore and Malaysia', *Australian Educational Researcher* 30(3): 89–110.

Ziguras, C., McBurnie, G. and Reinke, L. (2003). Implications of the GATS: Are foreign universities entitled to Australian funding? 17th IDP Australian International Education Conference, 21–24 October, Melbourne. Online. Available: http://www.idp.com/17aiecpapers/sessions/article345.asp (accessed 2 November 2007).

2 The Growth of Transnational Higher Education
The UK Perspective

Allison Doorbar
JWT Education

Christine Bateman
British Council

DEFINITIONS OF TRANSNATIONAL EDUCATION

Transnational education (TNE), as defined by the British Council, refers to education provision from one country offered in another. Transnational education includes a wide variety of delivery modes including distance and e-learning, validation and franchising arrangements, twinning, and other collaborative provision.

Within the university sector in the UK, the term 'transnational education' is not widely used. Most universities use the umbrella term 'collaborative international provision' or more commonly describe TNE by its component parts, e.g. 'franchised provision'and 'distance learning'. Similarly, research conducted by the British Council has revealed that key target audiences involved in the local delivery of TNE, as well as students and other stakeholders, are also not familiar with the term TNE and typically use 'distance learning' to describe the program that they are undertaking or involved with.

EXPANSION OF TRANSNATIONAL EDUCATION

The UK has a long history of delivering education transnationally. As one of the early developers of large-scale distance learning programs, the UK has been well positioned to offer courses to students in many countries outside the UK.

The introduction of full fees for international students by the British Government in the early 1980s brought about a more business-like culture in relation to international education. Since then, UK Higher Education (HE) institutions have developed a stronger, more entrepreneurial approach, have adapted well to change and taken advantage of new opportunities. For example, many UK twinning programs in Malaysia stem from UK providers responding to changes in government policy in the 1980s and the Asian currency crisis in the 1990s. A significant reduction in government scholarships from Malaysia and other economic changes meant that for many of the large numbers of Malaysians who had traditionally come to the UK to study, this was no longer a possibility. Delivering more programs in Malaysia, which allowed for a shorter period of study time in the UK (typically one or two years), provided an effective solution to this challenge and enabled Malaysians to continue to have access to British programs that would not have otherwise been available to them. At the same time it enabled UK providers to maintain their strong relationships with Malaysia.

Since the late 1990s, a 'third phase' of TNE has emerged. There has been unprecedented growth in transnational education, instigated by the drive of overseas governments to develop knowledge economies (Bohm *et al* 2004). The consequence of this is a rapidly changing and far more competitive environment for transnational education. New models are emerging as a part of this. There has been a significant expansion of overseas campuses, as leading international universities are enticed by favourable conditions, e.g. Nottingham Malaysia campus. There is also a renewed focus on TNE between research universities, as universities look for mutually beneficial opportunities to increase both their brand profile and research capabilities. Furthermore, the private sector is playing an increasingly greater role. It is arguably the private sector that will make the biggest difference in terms of significantly increasing the number of education places globally.

Continued demand is predicted in Transnational Education. Countries where this is likely to be most significant include China and India. TNE in China has already grown substantially in recent years, with new university campuses being built at the rate of one per week. The main focus in China now is on developing quality. TNE development in India has been much slower, due to government attitudes and legislation.

Potentially, the greatest demand for TNE over the medium to long term will come from sub-Saharan Africa. Taking into account population size and the very low participation rates in higher education (currently less than 10 per cent), there is likely to be demand from an additional 150 million students over the next few decades.

CHALLENGES IN DATA AND THE MOST COMMON GEOGRAPHICAL AND SUBJECT AREAS

While there are no definitive figures for the UK for students enrolled in UK TNE programs—it is an optional data return for the statistical collection from the Higher Education Statistics Agency (HESA)—British Council research suggests that there are currently more than 250,000 people studying for UK degrees outside of the UK. In addition to this, we estimate more than half a million people enrol for UK professional examinations each year (marketing, accountancy, etc.).

In 2003, five Asian countries (China, India, Malaysia, Hong Kong, Singapore) made up 58 per cent of TNE activity for the UK, and it is predicted that those countries will account for 65 per cent of global demand by 2020. To give some examples of the number of UK programs delivered transnationally:

- China currently has 77 UK HE institutions, offering a total of 346 programs. It is estimated that the number of students in China pursuing British transnational education programs will approach 40,000 by 2006/07.
- Singapore currently has 148 transnational education courses provided by British education providers. Singapore has a target to attract 150,000 international students by 2012, and the Singapore Government's explicit inclusion of transnational education within this policy means that the outlook for UK education in Singapore remains strong. In other words, in order to facilitate its growth as an international education destination, and meet its international enrolment targets, the Singapore Government is looking for transnational education provision to meet that demand.
- Malaysia currently has about 30,000 students involved in British transnational education programs, and India about 15,000. These, again, are only estimates, because it is difficult to ascertain an accurate assessment of the total picture.
- Hong Kong, as of March 2006, had an incredible 568 UK courses registered, and about 43,000 students currently enrolled.

Currently the main subject areas in demand are business and related studies, computer studies, and arts and humanities.

THE DRIVERS, MOTIVATIONS AND VIEWS ON TNE

British Council commissioned research in 2006 (Tang and Nollent 2007) to look at the motivations of the UK sector in delivering transnational education. The research revealed that all UK higher education providers have a strong interest and are engaged to some extent with transnational education.

The main motivation for UK universities undertaking TNE is internationalization. Jane Knight defines internationalization as 'the process of integrating an international/intercultural dimension into the teaching, research and service functions of the institution' (http//www.obhe. ac.uk/products/reports/archived.html?year=2005).

Much of the transnational education provision from the UK has developed at the department/faculty level and, often, quite opportunistically. As universities look more strategically at their international engagement, rationalization of TNE provision is occurring in some institutions and being scaled up in others. There is also an increase in central TNE roles and/or departments as institutions tighten up on quality controls and try to ensure a better 'strategic fit'.

This trend is consistent with wider changes within the UK education sector. Universities are moving away from international strategies, defined through student recruitment, to something far broader, encompassing teaching and research partnerships and ensuring that UK students also have exposure to an international dimension in their education. Transnational education is one part of this broader international remit.

The research also highlighted differences between different types of institutions. For research-led universities, the prime motivation for undertaking TNE is to build research links. This in turn strengthens the universities' brands, increases the number of world-class academics, and enhances the diversity of the student body—all of which lead to a greater international profile as well as faster growth and financial benefits.

For other universities, the student focus is a more significant driver— enabling more students to benefit from higher education, widening participation and exposing students to an international experience.

Financial issues are also important for UK universities as the international arena becomes more volatile. Since 2003/04, most UK universities have seen more modest growth in terms of international students coming to the UK. Vastly increased domestic provision in many of the UK's major source countries, including TNE, has had an impact—particularly in countries like China. International students now expect, and have, more flexibility. The length of time spent in the UK by international students has decreased substantially, with more and more students choosing to come for just one or two years of study. The implication for most UK providers is that *some* TNE delivery is essential to ensure continued flows of international students to UK campuses.

MODELS OF DELIVERY

There are many different models of TNE delivery adopted by UK providers. The reasons for universities' choices of models are varied but the common perception is that no one size fits all. The predominance of a model may relate to the university's mission, the geographical areas where it operates, financial imperatives, or the perceived acceptability of models in relation to quality.

We can also see how demand for different models of delivery is changing as competition increases. For example, distance learning and 'flying faculty' programs have traditionally been a major part of the UK's TNE offering—particularly in East Asia. These programs have usually been at the postgraduate level, where students are typically mature and are seeking part-time professional development programs that allow them to study and work at the same time. Although still popular, the cost of sending out UK staff to teach makes these programs increasingly 'non competitive', as part-time local provision becomes more extensive. In addition to this, international campuses also provide a competitive threat, offering international qualifications, excellent facilities, and reputable local and international faculty.

UK institutions have taken limited steps to set up overseas campuses. While overseas campuses present a significant opportunity, they also present a significant risk and are a major financial- and resource-draining undertaking. University of Nottingham has campuses in Malaysia and China. Westminster, Liverpool, Middlesex and Heriot-Watt have also invested in overseas campuses. Overseas campuses are often developed in collaboration with a financial partner, rather than another institution.

Joint awards, dual degrees, and combined models are becoming one of the dominant models of TNE delivery. As higher education capacity grows internationally, there is less need to 'import' qualifications from foreign providers. Joint and dual awards provide a way of providing mutual recognition of systems and academic input, leading to a more collaborative/international award with high relevance in the global marketplace.

The UK Government and the British Council have invested in two programs: *UK India Education Research Initiative* (UKIERI) and *British Degrees in Russia Project* (BRIDGE)—both of which are based on development of joint programs, as opposed to 'exporting UK degrees'.

For UKIERI, the UK has pledged £12 million through contributions by key government departments and the British Council. The private sector has also contributed £4 million with the Indian Government matching funding for science-related collaboration. By 2011, the following will have been achieved:

- 50 new collaborative research projects, including 5 'major' projects linking centres of excellence, will have been established;
- 40 new UK award programs delivered collaboratively in India with 2,000 Indian students enrolled;
- 300 additional Indian research students, postdoctoral researchers and staff will have worked in the UK;
- 200 UK researchers worked in India, and 200 UK undergraduate students supported for studies in India;

- and 2,000 Indian research students completed research degrees in the UK through collaborative delivery.

The BRIDGE Initiative, funded through the Department for Education and Skills and managed by the British Council, started in July 2003 and aims to increase collaborative working between UK and Russian universities, leading to the development of dual degrees.

The project is funded through England's Department for Education and Skills (DfES) and is managed on a day-to-day basis by the British Council. There are now a total of 17 active BRIDGE partnerships, including eight Masters programs, one undergraduate award, and eight continuing professional development programs.

With both BRIDGE and UKIERI, the aim has been to change the nature of the relationship among the UK and Russia and India. It recognises that partnerships need to be of mutual benefit to be sustainable over the long term.

QUALITY ASSURANCE

Ensuring high quality of delivery is critically important to the UK. Every time a course is perceived as poor quality it damages the UK brand. Competition alone will undoubtedly drive up standards. Initiatives like BRIDGE and UKIERI help to develop mutual understanding and recognition of quality assurance issues across both countries.

WHO ARE TRANSNATIONAL EDUCATION STUDENTS?

In 2004 and 2005 the British Council commissioned JWT Education to undertake an extensive market research study to better understand this rapidly growing market and the significant potential it represents for UK providers. Up to this point there had only been very limited research undertaken to understand the motivations and key decision-making factors for students pursuing British TNE programs. This research set out to:

- provide a detailed profile of the target audience (age, employment, income, funding, previous experience and expectations);
- understand why students choose TNE (versus studying for a local qualification or studying abroad);
- understand perceptions and the importance of the country the qualification is from (in relation to TNE programs);
- identify the key decision-making factors used in the selection of TNE programs;

- understand the importance of terminology in the promotion of TNE programs;
- and identify key information sources for students.

The study involved both qualitative and quantitative work. The qualitative phase was conducted in the five key markets for the UK—Singapore, Malaysia, Hong Kong, India and China—and comprised interviews and groups conducted across a range of target audiences, including students, their influences (e.g. parents) as well as other key stakeholders, such as local partners, agents, employers, and government. The quantitative phase involved interviews with more than 1,700 students studying in four of the key markets.

The research revealed some interesting findings, as presented in the following paragraphs, one of the most significant being just how diverse and complex this sector is. Aside from the fact that hardly anyone interviewed had ever heard of the term TNE, there is so much diversity in everything: the modes of delivery, the influence of the UK institution granting the qualification, the experience of the students, and the perceptions of the different stakeholders, with obvious implications.

For example, two students undertaking a degree from the same UK institution in the same market could be having vastly different experiences in terms of the quality of the local partner providing some, if not all, of the tuition; the quality of that tuition; and their exposure to the UK institution granting the degree. Yet both students will graduate with the same qualification. This has clear implications to the UK's brand and more significantly the brand of the individual institution. In fact, in some interviews, students actually expressed surprise that any leading university would allow such diversity in the delivery of its courses and choice of partners.

In attempting to better understand who pursues TNE programs, we tried to segment the market. It was evident from the research that the market can be divided into three main groups of students: undergraduates, postgraduates, and third-country students. The undergraduate segment comprises three main sub-segments: students who could not get a place at a local university; those who could not afford to study overseas; and those who did not want to go overseas to study. Many of these students want to obtain a foreign qualification that is affordable. The prominence of these factors changes by country. For example, in a mature market like Singapore, those students pursuing undergraduate TNE degrees are doing so either because they could not get into one of the local universities, which for most is their first choice, or because they could not afford, or choose not, to study overseas. Most of these students complete their whole undergraduate degree in Singapore. For them, TNE is either their second or third choice. This is in contrast to other markets, e.g. Malaysia, where TNE is many students' first choice and where many plan to complete only the first one or two years of their degree in Malaysia, and the balance in the UK. An obvious consequence of this is that perceptions about the quality of TNE vary significantly, with some students considering it to be as good as, if not better than, a local university, and others ranking it third, with a local university and an overseas university in selected countries both considered more desirable options.

The postgraduate group of students typically tend to be 30 and older and are looking, like most postgraduates everywhere in the world, to enhance their career opportunities through postgraduate study. They also seem to comprise three sub-segments: a group who want to purse a highly specialised qualification that is not available at their local university; a group who want to pursue part-time postgraduate study—this audience is typically working full-time, and part-time study is not available at their local universities; and a group who are looking for something that is a little bit different, a qualification that will give them a competitive edge in the marketplace. They feel that a foreign qualification may do that.

Last, there is the group of third-country students—students pursuing a UK TNE qualification but in a third country rather than in their home country. This group currently tend to be mainly in Singapore and Malaysia. This audience wants a UK qualification but for a variety of reasons—usually cost, safety or proximity—wants to study somewhere other than the UK.

Fifty-nine per cent of the students in the study were studying undergraduate programs. However, there were some major differences between markets, with nearly all TNE students in Singapore pursuing undergraduate programs, in contrast to Hong Kong, where most were studying at the postgraduate level, again highlighting the significant differences that exist between markets (at least currently). Interestingly 82 per cent were attending classes at a local institution (with this maybe supplemented by online delivery and distance), but still most TNE students appear to be receiving some form of classroom tuition. Furthermore, a strong preference for this was evident in the research, with almost no students indicating a desire to undertake an exclusively online TNE qualification. This may well change in the future, as access to the Internet improves, and the target audiences' familiarity and comfort with it grows.

The importance of the UK institution's reputation in influencing a student's choice of TNE program seemed to vary between markets. While obviously important to all students to some degree, reputation was much more important to students in Malaysia and Singapore than it was to students in Hong Kong and China. In Singapore, the reputation of the local institution was very important to students, to the degree that students were willing to pay a premium to go to what they considered to be a better local institution, even though they would graduate with the same qualification. This was not nearly as important to students in the other markets. For students in both Malaysia and China, ultimately obtaining a UK qualification seemed to be very important to them, with 75 per cent and 95 per cent, respectively, of students from these countries saying that they intended to go on to study in the UK.

Given the importance that TNE students attach to both obtaining a UK qualification, and a qualification from a reputable institution, it is going to be increasingly important for the Education UK brand to target these audiences and for individual institutions to effectively manage the promotion and delivery of their brands to these groups.

CONCLUSION

UK interest and engagement in transnational education will continue into the foreseeable future. However, the models and drivers for UK engagement are likely to change. Already we have started to see things move substantially, with the increasing number of overseas campuses, and new models of delivery from the private sector. The emerging world of transnational education also seems to depend far more on partnerships among institutions, the private sector and governments.

Within the UK, there has been a shift towards a more strategic view of internationalization; this can be seen across institutions, government and agencies. This is an important change for the UK, with the recognition that the environment for international education is becoming more complex and that a strategic approach is central to ensure the future competitiveness of UK higher education.

REFERENCES

Böhm, A. and Follari, M., Hewett, A., Jones, S., Kemp, N., Meares, D., Pearce, D. and Van Cauter, K. (2004) *Vision 2020, Forecasting International Student Mobility: A UK Perspective*, Report to the British Council, UK.

BRIDGE (nd) Available at: http:www.britishcouncil.org/learning-bridge-project.htm (accessed April 2007).

Knight, J. (2005) *Borderless, Offshore, Transnational and Cross Border Education: Definition and Data Dilemmas*, Observatory on Borderless Higher Education. Online. Available at: http://www.obhe.ac.uk/products/reports/archived.html?year=2005 (accessed April 2007).

Tang, N., and Nollent, A. (2007) *UK-China-Hong Kong Transnational Education*, Report to the British Council: Sheffield Hallam University, UK.

UKIERI (nd) Available at http://www.ukieri.org (accessed April 2007)

3 Regulation and Practice of Transnational Higher Education in China

Futao Huang
University of Hiroshima

INTRODUCTION

With growing marketization and globalization since the 1990s, new forms of higher education activities have emerged. Transnational, or borderless and cross-border education, activities have played an increasingly important role in national higher education in many countries. In some, especially in developing countries in Asia, transnational higher education activities have largely affected higher education reforms and even restructured the national higher education system. China provides no exception.

Though there is a wide variety of transnational provision in China, this article mainly deals with the joint-degree programs and institutions in partnerships with universities of foreign countries, including those of Hong Kong. Both the joint-degree programs and joint institutions have become an increasingly important and integral part of China's higher education. By examining these joint programs, this chapter provides a clear example of how a developing country is dealing with the incoming foreign provision of higher education at both policy and institutional levels.

BACKGROUND

Recent developments in China's higher education

Since the 1990s, there has been an increasing demand for higher education. Like many developing countries in Asia, as the public sector was unable to meet this demand, the government sought to increase the involvement of the non-government sector in higher education. As a result, there has been a dramatic increase in access to higher education, mainly through:

- Increasing access to existing public institutions;
- Expanding access through diversification of the sources of supply, by establishing a range of non-government institutions, and
- Growing numbers of students enrolling in joint programs provided by Chinese-foreign partnerships operating in various institutions.

The strategy for increasing access to higher education through diversifying routes has resulted in the massification of China's higher education in recent years. Since the late 1990s, the enrollment has kept increasing steadily. By 2004 the total enrollment in higher education amounted to nearly 20 per cent of the cohort aged 18 to 21, indicating China had already achieved mass higher education (China Education Yearbook Editorial Board 2005: 95), according to Trow's (1973: 57) definition of the development of higher education through the elite-, mass- and universal-access stages.

The current Chinese higher education system consists of three major types of institutions (China Education Yearbook Editorial Board 2005, Ministry of Education 2007: 208). There are 1,731 regular higher education institutions (of which 684 are four-year universities and 1,047 are junior colleges not awarding bachelor's degrees), 505 adult education institutions, and 228 non-government regular and adult institutions. The proportion of non-government students grew from 0.7 per cent in 1998 to 4.3 per cent in 2003—a rate of growth even faster than that of the regular institutions (SIES 2003, China Education Daily 2004).

Most regular institutions and some adult institutions belong to the public sector. Regular institutions are vertically administered and financed by one of the three types of administrative authorities: The Ministry of Education (MOE), Central level ministries and agencies, and Provinces and province-level municipalities. Most of the adult institutions are run by provinces and municipalities, with few being administered by MOE and Central level ministries and agencies.

However, it is worthy of note that even if there has been a striking rise in the number of students in the non-government sector in recent years, by 2004, only four of them were qualified to confer bachelor's degree and none of them could provide any post-graduate programs. The vast majority of them are two-year institutions of short-circle programs and almost totally depending on students' tuition and fees.

Terminology and typology

There are numerous terminologies used to describe transnational provision in different countries. In China the term similar to 'transnational education' is *Zhongwai hezuo banxue* meaning 'foreign co-operation in running schools (meaning higher education institutions)'. In the SEC's *Interim Provisions for Chinese–Foreign Cooperation in Running Schools* of 1995 (Chapter 1, Provision 2), it is defined as occurring when:

> Those foreign corporate, individuals, and related international organizations in cooperation with educational institutions or other social organizations with corporate status in China, jointly establish education institutions in China, recruit Chinese citizens as major educational objectives, and undertake education and teaching activities.

With the exception of compulsory education, military and religious education, as well as some other special limitations imposed by government, Chinese-foreign cooperation in running institutions has been involved in a wide range of educational activities. Modes of study include part-time, full-time, intensive, on-campus, off-campus, formal and informal.

At an undergraduate level, there are currently four major types of joint degree programs being provided in Chinese campuses (Huang 2006).

- 1+3 Type: similar to preparatory study for formal study in foreign universities. Chinese students study for one year in local campuses, mainly in areas of language learning and basic subjects. After one year's study and being admitted, these students can go to foreign campuses for advanced studies. All academic credits can be transferred into foreign partners' institutions and students can be awarded bachelor's degrees of foreign partners' institutions after completing three years studies. In addition, students can also continue their master's degree programs in foreign campuses.
- 2+2 Type: Chinese students finish their educational programs in Chinese institutions and foreign campuses for two years respectively. In this type, Chinese students are asked to study the majority of their course, including some professional programs provided in foreign partners' institutions, during their first two years in Chinese institutions. Then they move to foreign campuses to finish the second two years studies.
- 3+1 Type: Chinese students complete the majority of educational programs offered in the foreign partners' institutions in Chinese campuses. Then they go on their studies in foreign campuses in the final year and will be awarded degrees from foreign institutions on completion.
- 4+0 Type: Chinese students study without going abroad. They spend their four years in local campuses without going to foreign universities, but educational programs are jointly provided by both Chinese institutions and foreign institutions in China.

Government policy and regulation

Clearly, the Chinese government has welcomed and encouraged international input and transnational provision in the national education system, since it helps China's higher education open its door more widely to the outside world, brings with it international quality standards and expertise, and also, to some extent, promotes massification of higher education. For example, in the *Regulations of the People's Republic of China on Chinese-Foreign Cooperation in Running Schools*, promulgated by the State Council in March 2003 (State Council 2003, Provision 3 Chapter 1), it is stated that:

> The State encourages Chinese-foreign cooperation in running schools to which high-quality foreign educational resources are introduced. The State encourages Chinese-foreign cooperation in running schools in the field of higher education and vocational education, and encourages Chinese institutions of higher learning to cooperate with renowned foreign institutions of higher learning in running schools.

Licensing and status

In contrast to many other countries in Asia, foreign religious organizations and individuals are not included in the regulations and, as a result, are not permitted to provide any forms of educational activities in China. In the same *Regulations* of 2003, it is strongly emphasized that neither provision of compulsory education service, nor special education services such as military, police and political education services, is approved (Provision 6, Chapter 1), nor are any religious education or activities permitted (Provision 7, Chapter 1). According to government policy, no transnational activities can be provided absolutely and solely by foreign institutions themselves without any form of cooperation with, or involvement of, Chinese institutions located in China. Therefore, the major option for foreign providers wanting to offer courses in China is to deliver courses through a local partner. They are not allowed to apply to be licensed as a private Higher Education Institution (HEI; i.e. open a branch campus). Moreover, it is only the local Chinese partner that can submit an application for registration, licensing, or granting corporate status. The application to the relevant educational administrative body in the central government is then examined and approved by the government at the appropriate level for the type of transnational institution (State Council 2003, Provision 10, 11, 12, 13, Chapter 2). Especially at higher education level, in most cases, they are expected to jointly operate an institution with Chinese public institutions, though there has been an increase in the number of private institutions being involved in such activities in recent years.

Accreditation and quality assurance

With respect to requirements for establishing such institutions, it is emphasized that transnational institutions or programs must be accredited and approved in accordance with the same criteria that are used to accredit and approve Chinese institutions, directly decided and supervised by the Ministry of Education. Admission of students for undergraduate degree-conferring programs must be strictly based on the national admission plan for individual higher education institutions. The entry requirements for Chinese-foreign partnerships in operating institutions to pursue post-graduate studies must meet the standards and procedures of Chinese host institutions and, at the same time, cannot be lower than the requirements of foreign partner countries. It is emphasized that the complete or major teaching activities should be conducted at the Chinese campus. Courses from overseas providers leading to professional qualifications must meet requirements of professional licensing bodies, in the same way as local providers. They must also be accredited in the home country. In the twinning, or split-degree programs, the Ministry of Education asked that the proportion of incoming foreign educational programs should make up more than one third of the total and core programs. In other words, the proportion of professional core programs and teaching hours should constitute more than one-third of the total program/curriculum and total teaching hours respectively and this applies to public and private institutions.

In addition to the approval framework by central government and local authorities, in 2004 the Ministry of Education decided to exercise a review and check on all the Chinese-foreign partnerships in operating institutions and program provision. According to the government document (MOE 2004a), all the joint institutions and programs that were established and offered after 1995 and prior to the *Implementation of Regulations* of 2004 should be reviewed and rechecked. A variety of methods have been implemented in the process of review, including documentation examination and field visits. Some of major foci include:

- Whether the joint institutions or programs are legal or not; especially, are they concerned with compulsory, political or any other fields that are forbidden by government?
- Is there any religious education provided? Is there any foreign religious organization, institution, or person involved with the joint institutions and programs?
- Does an institution meet the minimum requirement formulated in the law or in the related government regulations?
- Is the agreement of joint operation in running any institution, and offering any program, legal and based on the government regulations?

- Are the governance and administrative arrangements in the joint institution or program legal and do they meet government regulations?
- Are the rights of faculty members and students well-protected in a joint institution and program?

Currently, the process of review is still proceeding. Some of the results have been published through websites and in newspapers. By doing so, the government expects to provide more detailed information concerning joint institutions and programs and make them more accountable.

Operation and administration

In the *Regulations* of 2003 (Articles 21 and 23) strong leadership by the Chinese side is once again stressed. It affirms that:

> Chinese members on the board of trustees, the board of directors or of the joint managerial committee shall not be less than half of the total number.

And:

> The president or the principal administrator of a Chinese-foreign cooperatively-run school shall be a person with the nationality of the People's Republic of China and shall be subject to approval of the examination and approval authorities.

In *Interim Provisions* (SEC 1995, Provision 5, Chapter 1) it is explicitly described that no profit can be pursued in such transnational programs:

> Chinese-foreign cooperation in education shall abide by the Chinese law and decrees, implement China's guideline for education, conform to China's need for educational development and requirement for the training of talents and ensure teaching quality, and shall not seek profits as the objective and/or damage the state and public interests.

However, in the *Regulations* (2003, Provision 3, Chapter 1), it is mentioned that Chinese-foreign cooperation in running schools is beneficial to public interests. The regulations do not forbid profit-making, stating only that a reasonable tuition fee should be charged, according to cost-recovery principles, and in consideration of the local standard of income and the students' financial situations.

Compared with *Interim Provisions* of 1995, some specific changes can be found in the *Regulations* of 2003. For example, it is expected that not only vocational education, but also transnational programs in the field of higher education, should be encouraged. Besides, it is stressed that the State encourages Chinese institutions of higher learning to cooperate with renowned foreign institutions of higher learning in running educational programs (*Regulations 2003*, Provision 3, Chapter 1) in order to improve the quality of teaching and learning and introduce excellent foreign educational resources. Furthermore, even some for-profit activities are likely to be recognized.

By issuing such regulations mentioned above, on the one hand, the Chinese government ensures that China's sovereignty can rest with the Chinese side, with the educational market in China supervised and adjusted by government. On the other hand, the internationalization of China's higher education can be greatly facilitated by the introduction of excellent foreign educational ideas and services.

Growth of joint programs and institutions

Growth of transnational programs can be roughly divided into two phases: the informal, incidental and laissez-fair phase prior to 1995 and then, with the promulgation of Contemporary Regulation (SEC 1995), the more structured, systematic and well-regulated phase after 1995.

From the late 1980s, some Chinese universities were already undertaking partnerships with foreign universities to provide joint training courses and programs for faculty development, but no degree-conferring programs in co-operation with foreign countries were permitted prior to the mid-1990s. After the issue of the *Interim Provisions* of 1995, there has been a surprisingly rapid expansion in the number of these joint programs, especially programs with the authority to confer foreign degrees, or both Chinese and foreign degrees. For example, in 1995, there were only two joint programs that could lead to a foreign degree. According to an incomplete data set (MOE 2005), it is estimated that by the end of 2002, there were 712 joint institutions and programs in collaboration with foreign partners. Of these, there were 82 institutions offering short-cycle programs, 69 institutions providing undergraduate programs and 74 institutions delivering graduate programs. The number of joint programs had increased nine-fold from 1995 to 2002.

By region, these joint institutions are mostly located in big and wealthy cities and provinces like Shanghai (111), Beijing (108), Jiangsu province (61) and Zhejiang province (33). These joint degree-conferring programs are mainly provided in China's famous, public universities and the top three providers are the USA (154 programs), Australia (146 programs) and Canada (74 programs), indicating that the countries undertaking transnational education in China are mainly developed, English-speaking countries.

With regard to fields of study, since 1995, the joint programs in international management have continued to constitute the largest proportion of all (55 per cent) including the MBA, marketing, accounting, financial management, human resource management, and travel management. This has been followed by engineering (15 per cent), economics (9 per cent), education (7 per cent), science (5 per cent) medicine (4 per cent), law (2 per cent) and literature (2 per cent). Clearly, professional or practical educational programs comprise a big share of the total programs. On the one hand, it indicates that the government policies, which encourage more practical and urgently needed joint programs in China, have been largely implemented in practice, and on the other hand, it reflects the great demand in China for training manpower equipped with advanced knowledge of international management.

By June 2004, the number of joint programs provided in Chinese higher education institutions in collaboration with foreign partners had reached 745, and joint programs qualified to award degrees of foreign or Hong Kong universities amounted to 169 (MOE 2004b). Similar to the data of 2002, the majority of them are concerned with professional education. For example, in addition to programs concerning engineering, computing, information science and English language, a great many belong to the fields of business and management studies that prepare professionals for work in multinational corporations, or in firms engaged in international commerce. Almost all of them are provided in China's most prestigious universities. Many of them enjoy a higher level of international academic influence and are often equipped with better infrastructure and well-regarded staff members than other Chinese universities (Huang 2003). As for foreign partners, by 2004 the number of joint degree-conferring programs with Australian universities had surpassed those with U.S. institutions (MOE 2004a).

Also by 2004, among those degree-conferring programs in partnership with foreign countries and regions, nearly 70 per cent of these joint degree programs lead to master's degrees with only two joint programs awarding PhDs from American universities—in engineering and in optical science (MOE 2004a).

Several factors have led to the substantial increase in the number of transnational programs in Chinese universities. For example, by encouraging the involvement of foreign universities with China's higher education, the Chinese government hopes that more students can be admitted to higher education institutions. At the same time, both Chinese host institutions and foreign partners are expected to make a profit and generate sources of income from this co-operation. Joint programs, particularly those leading to a qualification of a foreign or of a Hong Kong university, charge tuition fees up to, or more than, five times those of local institutions.

More importantly, it is widely believed that integrating foreign educational programs into Chinese campuses will provide a practical and also a very efficient way to improve academic quality and standards, as well as facilitate internationalization of Chinese higher education. By undertaking joint programs with prestigious foreign partners, individual higher education institutions in China can have a full and direct understanding of current educational missions, ideas, curriculum management, and delivery of educational programs in foreign universities. Moreover, by introducing those programs that are urgently needed but cannot be provided by Chinese institutions, China can train more graduates with international perspectives in a faster and more efficient way. It is worth noting that the final aim of the Chinese government is to develop and expand China's capacity to meet its educational and skills needs through its own institutions in this era of globalization.

A special mention should be made that the establishment of branch campuses by foreign universities or corporations is still not permitted at the time of writing, despite one example that seems to indicate the presence of a branch campus. The University of Nottingham, Ningbo, China, was established by the University of Nottingham (UK) in partnership with Zhejiang Wanli University, a private university. In this university, a majority of programs are imported and taught by faculty members from the University of Nottingham. This case shows that the Chinese government is prepared to allow a partnership with a foreign institution to create a higher education establishment with the status of a corporation in China. However, it must be strongly emphasized that the University of Nottingham, Ningbo, China, which is considered as one of China's most admired new model universities, with the status of corporation, is not a branch campus of the University of Nottingham but a completely independent university owned by Zhejiang Wanli University. Together with the educational programs from the University of Nottingham, China-based degree programs are also taught entirely in English. Students will receive the same awards as those conferred by the University of Nottingham upon graduation.

CONCLUSION

Transnational education in China is characterized by Sino-foreign partnerships in educational programs, and the operation of universities involved in transnational higher education is now part of the national higher education system. It is generally believed that importing foreign degree programs, new educational ideas, curricula and media of instruction, as well as importing governance arrangements from many leading Western universities, will lead to improvement of academic quality and standards in Chinese higher education.

Joint programs and foreign institutions have come to play a growing and significant role in China's higher education. In particular, these joint degree programs are currently considered an important supplementary part of the curriculum of Chinese higher education institutions. At this stage, and due to the fact that only a very few of China's non-government institutions are conferred with an authority to award degrees, these joint degree programs are usually provided in the public sector. They are mainly concerned with management, engineering, and other professional and academic programs at a graduate level, and are strictly regulated by the central government.

It should be pointed out that because of expensive tuition fees, and especially as the majority of these joint programs are involved with profitable activities, there is no clear evidence that they have led to a wider access to higher education or contributed substantially to China's mass higher education, as expected by the government.

There are many issues concerning these joint programs and institutions: the ambiguity of the legal arrangement of the joint degree programs and institutions; concerns about the commercialization of education in China, as well as about academic quality; and, as yet unclear, the impact of English-taught programs and English products on nationally based undergraduate education and teaching. However, a variety of key factors as discussed earlier—the implementation of supportive policy by government, the increased demand for higher education that cannot be met solely by the national or public sector, and active involvement of individual institutions being driven by an entrepreneurial spirit—will inevitably lead to a further expansion of transnational providers in Chinese campuses.

REFERENCES

China Education Daily (2004). May 27.

China Education Yearbook Editorial Board (2005) *China Education Yearbook 2005*, Beijing: People's Education Press: 95 (in Chinese).

Huang, F. (2003) 'Transnational Higher Education: A perspective from China,' *Higher Education Research & Development* 22(2): 93–203.

—— (2006) 'Transnational Higher Education in China-A Focus on Degree-Conferring Programs,' in Futao Huang (ed.) *Transnational Higher Education in Asia and Pacific*, International Publication Series 10, Research Institute for Higher Education, Hiroshima University: 21–33.

MOE (2004a) 'Notice on the Review and Check of Joint Programs and Institutions.' [Jiaoyubu guanyu zuohao zhongwai hezuo banxue jigou he xiangmu fuhe gongzuo de tongzhi] Online. Available at: http://www.jsj.edu.cn (accessed 16 March 2005).

MOE (2004b) 'List of Joint Programs Leading to Degrees of Foreign Universities and Universities of Hong Kong.' Online. Available at: http://www.jsj.edu.cn/mingdan/002.html (accessed 16 September 2005).

MOE (2005) 'Basic Situation of Joint Programs and Institutions' [Zhongwai hezuo banxue jiben qingkuang] Online. Available at: http://www.jsj.edu.cn/ (accessed 6 June 2003).

MOE (2007) Online. Available at: http://www.edu.cn (accessed 23 March 2007).

SEC (1995) Interim Provisions for Chinese-Foreign Cooperation in Running Schools and Regulations of the People's Republic of China on Chinese-Foreign Cooperation in Running Schools. Online. Available at: http://www.jsj.edu.cn/ (accessed 9 July 2003).

State Council (2003) Regulations of the People's Republic of China on Chinese-Foreign Cooperation in Running Schools. Online. Available at: http://www.jsj.edu.cn/ (accessed 20 October 2003).

Shanghai Institute of Education Science (SIES 2003). *Zhongguo minban jiaoyu Ivpishu* (*Green Book of Private Education in China*). Shanghai: Education Press.

Trow, M. 1973, 'Problems in the Transition form Elite to Mass Higher Education', in *Policies for Education*, Paris: OECD: 57.

4   Buyer Beware (Caveat Emptor)

Anne Jelfs

Institute of Educational Technology, Open University

INTRODUCTION

There has been increased use and development of information technology as a tool to disseminate teaching and learning across the world. The Internet has become a part of many people's daily lives, which in turn has led to the development of educational materials for presentation on the 'web' and, increasingly, universities are integrating global provision in their repertoire of education.

In this chapter I look at the problems and opportunities that this increased use of technology can offer transnational education whilst dealing with expectations that are not always fulfilled. For example, the Internet as a delivery medium is not always available if there is a problem with electricity supply. At the same time there are many new developments—e.g. iPods, and mobile technologies such as tablet PCs and mobile phones—in media for delivery. There are also new ways of teaching and communicating that impact transnational teaching, such as 'blogs' and 'wikis'. Briefly, a blog is a web log that is usually developed by an individual, and a wiki is a website that allows all users to edit or change the content. All of these developments impact on the delivery of transnational education.

The chapter looks at transnational education and the concerns about quality, quality assurance and overseas provision. For this chapter the term 'transnational' will be used to define any provision made by a university to students who are physically located in another country **to** that of the host university. This is in contrast to place-based universities that have international or overseas students studying and residing with them, even if some of that provision is via the Internet.

According to Garrett and Verbik (2004), transnational higher education has become a major global phenomenon and is predicted to grow significantly over the next twenty years. At the same time, some providers of education on a worldwide basis are increasingly treating education as a commodity and students as the customers (The Futures Project 2000). In fact, the claim is that education has become 'market driven' where university management want to capture the market, which is often in less-developed countries than their own. The Futures Project (ibid) claims that over a thousand universities in the United States now provide virtual or online courses and web-based distance education has created new arms of existing universities and colleges.

It is useful to make the distinction between transnational education and distance education. Distance education is the provision of courses and degrees at a distance, regardless of the students' location. Therefore, a student can be located in the home country. A main player in distance education is the UK Open University (UKOU), and it can be argued that distance education can be seen as a legitimate form of learning that the UK Open University started, and that it expanded the previously poor relation of correspondence courses. Perraton (2000) confirms this by saying that correspondence education had low status and was used by some universities mainly as a way of raising revenue to subsidize the on-campus students (86).

This chapter is organised around four topics: the global markets for transnational education; the development of electronic provision of education; communication between providers and students; and buyers' expectations.

GLOBAL MARKETS

Globalization has led to multinational and transnational corporations operating in a market not bounded by national and geographical considerations. This leads to opportunities for transnational corporations such as McDonalds and Disney to operate on a worldwide scale. With access to technology we can buy books from Amazon.com or trade through eBay.com. We are all consumers, as well as buyers and sellers, in this globalization of commerce. However, due to globalization and growth in transnational corporations, they can now operate in education. Lemaitre (2002) says there are benefits and opportunities of providing education to global markets and that education is missing from most analyses of globalization 'not considered part of the transnational corporate world (even though transnational higher education is becoming an important part of the total exports in many countries') (31).

As stated earlier, any market consists of buyers and sellers that trade in its commodity, and here the commodity is higher education. To compete effectively in the marketplace, an educational institution needs to differentiate itself from its competitors (Joseph and Joseph 1997). Differentiation is reliant on distinctiveness and an assumption that what is being received is not only 'different', but of high quality. Joseph and Joseph (1997) factor analysed higher education students' feedback questionnaires and found seven factors that students said they wanted from a university when making choices of one institution over another. These factors were: program issues; academic reputation; physical aspects/ cost; career opportunities; location; time; and, 'other' (e.g. family). The most important ratings were given to academic reputation, and to the notion of an 'elite' university. This again returns to the question about what to buy and where from. For many students the notion of an 'elite' university is based on the Oxbridge model in the UK and the Ivy League universities in the US. These universities trade less in offshore education, but there are plenty of providers willing to imitate their brand names.

Transnational education is attractive to some providers as it offers opportunities for increased market expansion. For students it provides the opportunity to obtain a foreign qualification at a considerably reduced cost (McBurnie and Ziguras 2001). At the same time, for mature students studying in their home country, this means being able to stay with their families and continue to work whilst studying part-time. In fact, constraints on enrolment are now no longer a matter of geography, but of access to the Internet and the ability to pay the enrolment fee and the costs of communication (Perraton 2000). Globalization has many attractions to growing universities and the developing technologies offer more opportunities to deliver education online. Universities in the north are fully aware that new technologies make it possible for them to reach new audiences, but also that their status and relationships are changing as they compete in new ways for students, with each other, and with developing corporate universities and agencies (Perraton 2000:145–6). In some importing countries, transnational provision provides a significant proportion of the higher education offering (Hatakenaka 2004).

It is claimed that transnational delivery offers important advantages to both source and host countries, and to institutions and students, through boosting domestic higher education capacity, and as a source of additional income (Garrett and Verbik 2004). It is even claimed that transnational delivery of UK programmes will greatly expand by 2010, more so than students moving to the host institution for the duration of their degrees.

In the UK, more than 100 institutions are providing distance learning courses, in addition to face-to-face provision (Hatakenaka 2004), and international student enrolment in the United Kingdom (UK) was more than 340,000 in 2004/05 (Atlas of Student Mobility 2005). The UK is the second largest host of international students after the United States, at 12 per cent of the world's share in 2006. Also, the value of transnational provision to UK higher education institutions was £99 million in 2001/02 (Universities UK), so distance education and transnational education form substantial contributions to UK higher education funding.

The recognition of qualifications is acknowledged by many university accreditation units, and is something that is recognised by higher education quality assurance agencies worldwide. So, transnational education is an important export, but there is no single quality assurance body that is responsible for ensuring the export is of value for money, of good quality, and provides the student with a recognised degree.

Now that more institutions can offer higher education in other countries, there is greater need to have robust quality assurance systems or guarantees of acceptable levels of provision (Jelfs 1999). These third party assurors are considered in some depth by the Observatory on Borderless Higher Education (online), although there is still no global standard. However, access to transnational education is also reliant on access to the technology that delivers the education. Access to the electronic provision has many restrictions, including the digital divide phenomenon (Ardito *et al* 2006), where access to a qualification is based on access to digital equipment.

DEVELOPMENT OF ELECTRONIC PROVISION OF EDUCATION

For many potential students worldwide, access to appropriate technology infrastructures is limited. There is currently growth in the number of countries that have broadband access to the Internet, but there are many that have no such communication tools, or access to computing equipment is limited by intermittent electricity supply. Without good infrastructures, both students and teaching staff will be frustrated by the lack of access to materials and study support.

There are many concerns about the provision of transnational education and how to supply courses to students. To ensure the potential for transnational teaching, the materials and the teaching staff have to be of the same standard as the place-based institutions. One suggestion is that courses offered as transnational education should be well-tested courses that are pedagogically rigorous, that have already achieved good results, and are well received by the place-based students. However, if tutors have a perceived notion that online teaching requires increased hours spent working online and developing new materials, this could impact their willingness to take part in transnational teaching, which would require, therefore, additional training and support.

A number of concerns are raised with the electronic delivery of education, including the ability to plagiarize. Plagiarism is always a concern, and assessment that students previously produced in hard copy can now be produced in electronic versions, therefore making it easier to exchange between students. Assessment that is electronically delivered does, however, have a lot of positive elements to it. Assessment can be emailed to the tutor for grading, and the grades entered into the appropriate database, before emailing the annotated version back to the student. Data can be collected on the assessment results and, with the use of computer log data, it is possible to see if particular sections of the material/course/website are being accessed, and, if necessary, draw inferences from the data (McKnight and Demers 2003).

COMMUNICATION BETWEEN PROVIDERS AND STUDENTS

Many of the proponents of transnational teaching suggest that to counteract the language difficulties between host nation and delivering nation, there be the opportunity for students to work in an asynchronous way. These asynchronous tools include email, discussion forums, conferencing, and new communication tools such as blogs and wikis. These new developments of electronic delivery of transnational education are still primarily English language-based. This may put some students at a severe disadvantage in their attempts to secure an overseas qualification. Turoff *et al* (2004) found very significant contribution rates for asynchronous group discussion among students for whom English was not their first language. Turoff *et al* thought that the equal participation of students was because those students who did not have English as their first language could re-read messages before replying. They also found that these students were spending two or three times more in reading mode, and re-read more of the discussion, than the American students. It is questionable whether this a good or bad thing, where students have to read text over and over again.

There is also the concern of getting students to communicate if they have problems, not just with the technology, but also academically. For example, Frank *et al* (2004) found that, when they compared communication levels between students and the teaching staff at two institutions, those students at the University of the South Pacific used email to contact their peers, but not their lecturers. Whereas, in contrast, students at the Central Queensland University who were working in groups were more likely to ask questions to staff that were relative to group formation and assignment queries. It could be that this is a cultural explanation of communication.

In the classroom, one of the expectations in the student-centred approach that many university courses adopt is communication—that is, communication with tutors and other students. However, students and teaching staff have to have established communication protocols, such as how regular the contact will be—how often the student can expect the teacher to log-on and reply to queries, etc., and how these expectations are shaped and guided. Students may not have the skills to use the technology and may need training and, if so, who will provide this? Tutors may be reluctant to provide additional support for information literacy training unless it is part of the course. It might be that students' needs will be provided for as part of a separate course or by a different provider inside or outside the institution. This type of support might not always be available for students through the education provider, and student motivation to complete the course may decline. For a disreputable provider this might not be a concern, because drop-out from the course would mean income from the course fees without the complication of providing student support. There is evidence that without student support and integration into a social world there is a possibility of student withdrawal from the course (Tinto 1993; Simpson 2003).

FULFILMENT OF BUYERS' EXPECTATIONS

If buyers have to beware, surely someone should be helping students decide which courses are a value for their money and are of sound quality?

> But some things *are* better than others, that is, they have more quality. But when you try to say what the quality is, apart from the things that have it, it all goes *poof*! (Pirsig 1974: 178)

In the UK, the higher education quality assurance agency first became aware of concerns about institutions' overseas collaborative arrangements in 1993/4, and most problems seemed to have been with private education providers (Brown 2004). A number of agencies throughout the world have considered the practicalities of a set of criteria, guidelines or code of practice for distance education and transnational education providers on a global or regional basis. Setting up such guidelines has its own problems and difficulties. However, some attempts have been made. For instance, the British Association of Open Learning (BAOL), the Council for the Accreditation of Correspondence Colleges (now known as the Open and Distance Learning Quality Council), and the European Association for Distance Learning (formerly known as the Association of European Correspondence Schools), have all developed guidelines or codes of practice to assure the quality of the materials or education provision of their courses (Jelfs 1999). BAOL has developed a *Quality Kitemark* to assure the quality of the qualification providers. It is based on the quality of the necessary systems to provide a satisfactory experience. Further studies in the use of 'kitemarks' as standards in provision found that an approved 'kitemark' had many perceived advantages, as it could be included in the institution's headed paper, or quoted in the prospectus and advertising literature. It was found to be advantageous in the world of 'branding, and market segmentation', where institutions want to stand out from the crowd (Jelfs 1999), and a 'kitemark' with renowned approval could be one way of gaining more of the market share.

The Commonwealth of Learning has shown an interest in developing quality assurance guidelines. As an intergovernmental organisation that was established in 1987 by the Commonwealth Heads of Government, it works on behalf of member states across all sectors of education, from basic literacy to continuing education. It aims to use distance education methods to assist member Commonwealth countries to meet the demands for access to a quality education and training. It is not only in the British Commonwealth and Europe, but also in the US, that the importance of ensuring the quality of distance education is being considered and reviewed. In the US, the Distance Education and Training Council (DETC) accredits institutions for achieving certain standards. It accredits a wide range of institutions, from military colleges to those allied to medicine. Institutions can voluntarily approach DETC after two years of unaccredited operating experience, and are accredited through self-evaluation reports.

If it is assumed that qualifications are indeed a 'vital currency', then prospective students need information about the quality of the courses they may wish to follow, and employers need to know about the standards achieved by graduates who they may recruit. Both students and employers needed impartial and readily available information on which to base their choices about where to study or where to recruit. Parker (2004) suggests that increased access to education can also mean access to poorly designed and executed courseware, whilst at the same time academics are concerned about academic rigor (Chua and Lam 2007).

There are obviously concerns in many of the major countries, either concerns about quality of courses (Calvert 2003) or concerns about the quality of the international provision of education (Evans 2003). There has been a growth in the number of quality assurance agencies to combat these concerns. The Global Alliance for Transnational Education (GATE) provides quality assurance certification for transnational education programmes. GATE defines itself as having the primary purpose of addressing and improving the quality of education that crosses national borders. To achieve this aim, GATE has developed a code of practice containing a set of principles for transnational education. An institution can request GATE to review its transnational education programme, after which certification can be achieved. GATE suggests that certification offers not only individuals, but also governmental agencies, a check on the quality of the education being exported or imported.

As Garrett (2004) points out, there is usually a positive image of the host country's transnational provisions as bringing much needed capacity and expertise, and a negative image of many foreign providers as second-rate and characterized by a money-making focus on the most popular and lucrative programmes. Many universities are moving from traditional higher education teaching and learning to an electronic presentation with little previous knowledge, just because it has become so easy to put materials 'online'. One conclusion is that there are differences between teaching students at a distance and traditional face-to-face higher education teaching, which can make the transition to a global provider problematic. Too often, potentially interactive technologies are used to present one-way lectures to students in remote locations (Jonassen *et al* 1995). This is in contrast to Perraton's views that the impact of '[b]roadcasting and the Internet have, in different generations, been heralded as forces that can transform education' (Perraton 2000: 139).

There is also the problem of the appearance of 'degree mills' on the Internet, and the dubious legality of some awarded degrees (Santos 2002). The fact that non-official higher education is not subject to the national mechanisms of quality assurance in the host country raises problems of transparency and control (Santos 2002). In the UK, the Trading Standards department is encouraged to follow up suspect operations, and the British Council is informed of suspect providers in their regional locations. There are concerns in the UK on the proliferation of 'fake' degrees. Peter Williams, of the Quality Assurance Agency in the UK, noted at the end of December 2005 that a lot of companies with British-sounding names sell degrees online. He feels that this in turn affects the reputation of UK higher education in the international arena. Perhaps the success of UK institutions in providing a high quality education has by itself encouraged this problem. Alan Contreras, of the Office of Degree Authorization in the US said: 'These problems come from the stellar reputation of British higher education worldwide' (Dowd 2005). The problem can be blamed on the poor legislative system that allows these types of degrees to become available worldwide when, as long as they don't make incorrect claims of accreditation, they can offer the courses to unwitting students.

However, new technology in the form of blogs and wikis also empowers students, as they provide arenas for discussion or identification of bogus courses. This returns to the discussion about access to the technology and the ability to be able to interact through this technology with other groups. Potential students may continue to rely on word of mouth about high- and low-quality education providers; it is just that now this word of mouth is electronic and online.

CONCLUSIONS

There has been considerable growth in transnational education and part of that growth can be attributed to the developments in technology and electronic delivery of education. There has also been growth in marketing legitimate university courses, but as demonstrated by the concerns in the UK, many providers are not offering legitimate degrees. It is very easy to word advertisements as if they were from reputable university providers, so buyers need to be aware of this.

Currently there are no international guidelines or codes of conduct that can safeguard buyers. Many organisations such as GATE make serious attempts at safeguarding buyers; but with the ease at which disreputable providers can set up their websites, charge fees, and then provide bogus qualifications, it is far too easy. It is therefore still a case of 'buyer beware'.

REFERENCES

Ardito, C., Costabile, M.F., De Marsico, M., Lanzilotti, R., Levialdi, S., Roselli, T., Rossano, V. (2006) 'An Approach to Usability Evaluation of E-learning Aplications', *Universal Access in the Information Society* 4: 270–283.

Atlas of Student Mobility (2005). Available at: http://www.atlas.iienetwork. org/?p=48047 (accessed 30 March 2007).

Brown, R. (2004) *Quality Assurance in Higher Education: The UK experience since 1992*. London: RoutledgeFalmer.

Calvert, J. (2003) 'Quality Assurance and Quality Development: What will make a difference?' In G. Davies and E. Stacey (eds) *Quality Education @ a Distance*. Boston: Kluwer Academic Publishers, 17–28.

Chua, A. and Lam, W. (2007) 'Quality Assurance in Online Education: The Universitas 21 Global approach'. *British Journal of Educational Technology* 38 (1): 133–52.

Dowd, H. (2005) 'UK Kudos Hit by Fake Degrees'. *Times Higher Education Supplement,* 23 December 2005. Available at: http://www.thes.co.uk/ search/story.aspx?story_id=2026901 (accessed 13 June 2007).

Evans, T. (2003) 'Globalisation and Reflexivity: Some challenges for research into quality education mediated by ICTs'. In G. Davies and E. Stacey (eds) *Quality Education @ a Distance*. Boston: Kluwer Academic Publishers, 3–16.

Frank, J., Toland, J. and Schenk, K. (2004) 'The Effect of Culture on Email Use: Implications for distance learning'. In C. Howard and K. Schenk (eds) *Distance Learning and University Effectiveness: Changing educational paradigms for online learning*. Hershey, PA, USA: Information Science Publishing, 213–233.

Garrett, R. (2004) 'Transnational Delivery by UK Higher Education, Part 2: Innovation and competitive advantage'. *The Observatory on Borderless Higher Education*. Available at: http://www.obhe.ac.uk/products/reports/ pdf/HESA_TNE_briefing_note.pdf (accessed 18 January 2007).

Garrett, R. and Verbik, L. (2004) 'Transnational Delivery by UK Higher Education, Part 1: Data and missing data'. *The Observatory on Borderless Higher Education*. Available at: http://www.obhe.ac.uk/products/reports/ pdf/UKTNEpt1.pdf (accessed 18 January 2007).

Global Alliance for Transnational Education (GATE;1997) *GATE Certification Manual*. Washington, DC: Global Alliance for Transnational Education. Available at: http://www.edugate.org (accessed 13 June 2007).

Hatakenaka, S. (2004) 'Internationalism in Higher Education: A review'. *Higher Education Policy Institute*. Available at:http://www.hepi.ac.uk/downloads/12Internationalism%20in%20Higher%20Education%20A%20Review.pdf (accessed 13 June 2007).

Jelfs, A. (1999) 'Quality Assurance for Distance Education: Distance education 'kitemarks''. *Continuous Improvement Monitor*. Available at: http://llanes.auburn.edu/cimjournal/Vol1/No4/vol1no4.pdf (accessed 18 October 2007).

Jonassen, D., Davidson, M., Collins, M., Campbell, J., and Bannan Haag, B. (1995) 'Constructivism and Computer-Mediated Communication in Distance Education'. *The American Journal of Distance Education* 9 (2): 7–26.

Joseph, M. and Joseph, B. (1997) 'Service quality in education: a student perspective'. *Quality Assurance in Education* 5: 15–21.

Lemaitre, M. J. (2002) 'Quality as Politics'. *Quality in Higher Education* 8 (1): 29–37.

McBurnie, G. and Ziguras, C. (2001) 'The Regulation of Transnational Higher Education in Southeast Asia: Case studies of Hong Kong, Malaysia and Australia'. *Higher Education* 42: 85–105.

McKnight, R. and Demers, N. (2003) 'Evaluating Course Website Utilization by Students Using Web Tracking Software: A constructivist approach'. *International Journal of E-learning*, July–September, 13–17.

Observatory on Borderless Higher Education. Available at: http://www.obhe.ac.uk/products/briefings.html (accessed 18 January 2007).

Parker, N.K. (2004) 'The quality dilemma in online education'. In T. Anderson and F. Elloumi (eds) *The Theory and Practice of Online Learning*, 385–421.

Perraton, H. (2000) *Open and Distance Learning in the Developing World*. In D. Keegan and A. Tait (eds) *Routledge Studies in Distance Education*. London: Routledge.

Pirsig, R. M. (1974) *Zen and the Art of Motorcycle Maintenance: An Inquiry into Values*. London: Bodley Head.

Santos, S. M. (2002) 'Regulation and Quality Assurance in Transnational Education', *Tertiary Education and Management* 8: 97–112.

Simpson, O. (2003) *Student Retention in Online, Open and Distance Learning*. London: Kogan Page.

The Futures Project (October 2000) 'The Universal Impact of Competition and Globalization in Higher Education'. *The Futures Project: Policy for Higher Education in a Changing World*. Available at: http://www.futuresproject.org

Tinto, V. (1993) *Leaving College: Rethinking the Causes and Cures of Student Attrition* (2nd ed.). Chicago: University of Chicago Press.

Turoff, M., Discenza, R., Howard, C. (2004) 'How Distance Programs Will Affect Students, Courses, Faculty and Institutional Future'. In C. Howard, K. Schenk, and R. Discenza (eds) *Distance Learning and University Effectiveness: Changing Educational Paradigms for Online Learning*: 1–20.

Universities UK. Available at: http://www.UniversitiesUK.ac.uk (accessed 30 March 2007).

5 The Cultural Politics of Transnational Education

Ideological and Pedagogical Issues for Teaching Staff

Christopher Ziguras

RMIT University

INTRODUCTION

Should an international branch campus of an Anglophone university insist that its students speak only English on campus? Should lecturers travelling overseas to teach in transnational programs be required to undertake cultural awareness training? Should Western universities teach in Asia the same way they would in their home country, or as Asian universities do? Do Western programs spread a neo-liberal political philosophy in developing countries that justifies elite privilege while ignoring the majority of learners? Questions such as these are raised, not just because of the obvious cultural distance between the producers and the consumers of transnational education, but also because of the more subtle power dynamics that shape international higher education markets. The term 'cultural politics' draws attention to both the cultural dimensions of politics and the political dimensions of culture, and this chapter will focus on the interplay of these in the transnational classroom, in national policies towards foreign education providers, and in public debate around the internationalization of higher education systems.

NATIONALIST CRITIQUES OF CULTURAL HEGEMONY THROUGH EDUCATION

The critique of cultural imperialism in international education dates from the 1970s, and especially in the work of Martin Carnoy (1974) who argued that European colonial powers, and subsequently the United States, had deliberately implanted forms of education in Africa, Asia and Latin America that would support the imperial powers' continued political and economic interests. During the Cold War this involved a range of American educational initiatives aimed at building support for capitalist economic policies and eroding support for socialist movements in countries within the United States' sphere of influence. As was common in Left critiques of the 1970s, Carnoy's analysis over-emphasizes the commonality between the anti-colonial and the anti-capitalist, thereby painting a world in which (just) two sets of cultural values play out: a ruling class culture in which capitalist and colonial states justify their exploitation with a veneer of bourgeois liberal individualism, but ranged against them are a proliferation of liberation; and anti-capitalist movements that seek to free the masses from oppression. Education is used both to pacify opposition to imperialist domination and to create the illusion that social inequality is in fact meritocratic, but reform requires revolutionary changes: 'Our analysis makes clear to us the fundamental necessity to change the economic and social structure before the system of public schooling can be changed' (Carnoy 1974: 361). It is useful to recount Carnoy's now rather dated critique here because it helps to contextualize the way in which some contemporary critics see transnational education—a form of cultural imperialism benefiting only the Western ruling class.

The contemporary critics of cultural imperialism in international higher education are less concerned with the actions of individual governments and more concerned with the growth of global markets. Foremost among these is the international organization representing education trade unions, Education International, which has regularly expressed concern that the growth of a global marketplace in higher education will harm developing countries, in particular fearing 'the cultural and linguistic hegemony of a few industrialized countries globally, undermining national cultures' (Education International 2004: 4). Education International's stance is typical of a widespread opposition to commercial transnational education, seeing foreign programs and providers as 'a threat to national sovereignty and culture and as a serious attack on the core values of the system of higher education' (Stella 2006: 260–1).

These critiques are routinely presented through three rhetorical moves. The first is to describe a familiar binary opposition between national, public, culturally appropriate education on the one hand, and foreign, commercial, culturally imperialist education on the other. Education International (2004) paints the interaction between local and foreign education providers as part of a broader clash of values:

> At the centre of the current debate is a fundamental clash of values. On the one hand, there are those who would see international education simply as another commercial venture and who view emerging trade treaties as ways to expand and lock-in private market forces. On the other hand, others assert that education is above all a human right and a public good, and that market forces alone cannot guarantee the maintenance and enhancement of an accessible

and high quality higher education system. In the emerging global economy where the neo-liberal values of privatization and market competition are dominant, it is crucial for those of us committed to public education to reaffirm certain fundamental values and principles (Education International 2004: 5).

This is a softer, but still unsophisticated, neomarxist critique, rhetorically pitting public 'goods' and human 'rights' against market 'forces' and private 'competition'. The second plank of the contemporary critique is to argue that the public culture of developing countries is being penetrated by foreign education providers' alien values. While elsewhere Education International is a staunch defender of academic freedom and institutional autonomy, when it comes to cross-border activity, Education International advocates government control over university curricula to ensure that universities fulfil a nation-building role:

> Many developing countries have no control over the contents of the curricula offered by foreign providers. Such curricula may not be culturally or socially relevant, and may not meet the economic needs of developing nations. The quality of foreign universities may not match those of local institutions, and may not take account of national cultures (Education International 2004: 15).

And:

> A balance must be struck between the convenience of using a few languages as the international medium of teaching, research and publication, and the need to sustain linguistic diversity, bearing in mind universities' role, *inter alia*, as carriers of the national culture. While transnational arrangements may have as part of their motivation the achievement of economies of scale, this is not to be achieved by a centralized approach to the content of higher education or the development of homogeneous higher education 'products' (Education International 2004: 28).

Transnational programs and institutions are seen to be carriers of homogenous global cultural forms that threaten national cultures and languages. The third move is to call for governments in developing countries to protect their nation by blocking or restricting the activities of foreign providers. The flow of knowledge and culture through commercial international education is unidirectional, they argue, advocating instead that internationalization should occur through cooperation between public universities in different countries, rather than competition from new private and transnational providers. Education International affirms that:

Transnational arrangements must not be used to produce, promote or justify a standard or homogenized version of higher education. Within transnational arrangements, there must be clear and effective protections for national or regional cultures, and for the interests and expectations of students and staff (Education International 2004: 27).

And:

The continued internationalization of higher education should be based on co-operation and exchange rather than competition and commerce. It should promote cultural and linguistic diversity and understanding, broaden educational opportunities and access, enrich the educational experience of students and staff, facilitate international development, and enhance the free flow and exchange of knowledge and ideas (Education International 2004: 31).

Therefore, Education International recommends an interventionist and protectionist role for the state, which it says should screen the courses and curricula offered by foreign providers to verify 'whether they are relevant and supportive of the culture of the receiving country' (Education International 2004: 16).

Nationalist opposition to transnational higher education is still popular among academics and their unions, but has been losing favour with government policy makers. In the past decade, most developing countries have been gradually moving away from restrictive and protectionist economic policies and towards liberalising their domestic economies and increasing their openness to international trade and investment. As the two most populous developing countries, China and India, learned, even with the best intentions, extensive state ownership and restrictions on markets and on international trade and investment were not successful in reducing poverty. The challenge now in most developing countries, as in the advanced economies, is to develop public policy that combines public provision with market regulation so as to ensure that the public can benefit from the best features of each. Faced with these challenges, the ideological opposition to domestic and international markets espoused by Education International and the anti-globalization movement offers little practical policy advice.

National higher education systems are often highly regulated in developing countries, with comprehensive government regulation of the number and type of providers, the scope and quality of their offerings, and recognition of their qualifications. Transnational programs often manage to escape such restrictions by being based outside the regulatory purview of the government in the institution's home country and in the country in which it is operating. Consequently, transnational providers are often freer to respond to unmet demand for education than are domestic institutions. Restrictions on public funding available to public universities, and restrictions on tuition-funded private colleges and universities in the students' home countries, have limited their ability to keep pace with demand, enhancing the competitive advantages of foreign programs over local alternatives.

The fundamental political question is whether the number and character of transnational programs should be determined by the state, as Education International advocates, or by the market. The trend over the past decade, encouraged by international agencies such as the World Bank and the Organization for Economic Co-operation and Development (OECD), has been for governments to allow private and foreign providers to grow in response to student demand, thereby supplementing public provision and expanding the volume and diversity of programs offered. Governments have been very reluctant to take on the task of assessing the cultural relevance of foreign programs, instead leaving this to quality assurance agencies, and more significantly, to the institutions and students involved.

The code of good practice for transnational education, developed by UNESCO and the OECD to guide governments and providers, clearly establishes an expectation that transnational providers 'are responsible for the quality as well as *the social, cultural and linguistic relevance* of education and the standards of qualifications provided in their name, no matter where or how it is delivered' (UNESCO and OECD 2005: 14, emphasis added). Educational institutions operating across borders are asked to ensure that the programs they deliver across borders 'take into account the cultural and linguistic sensitivities of the receiving country' and the code suggests that 'a commitment to this effect should be made public' (UNESCO and OECD 2005: 14). There is a tension between the common regulatory requirement that an offshore program be the same as, or identical to, that which authorities in the home country have accredited, and the pedagogical principle that the program be tailored to suit the culture and context in which students are learning. Consequently, programs are usually described as having 'equivalent' or 'comparable' outcomes for students, even though the student experience may differ considerably (Stella 2006: 269).

IMPEDIMENTS TO CULTURAL AND
CONTEXTUAL ADAPTATION

The simplest way to develop programs able to be taught simultaneously to students in different countries is to produce a standardized, globalized curriculum that it is largely independent of the local context of the student (Ziguras and Rizvi 2001). The success of global online education, in particular, relies on being able to develop curriculum that, in the words of Bates and de los Santos (1997: 49), 'is relevant to learners wherever they happen to reside'. Globalized curricula are generic, universalized programs produced in one location for global consumption. This relies on removing specific references to local experiences and examples that may confuse or distract remote students, and focusing on universal approaches that can be applied in any context. Observers have long noted that transnational higher education has usually involved Western educators simply exporting a locally developed curriculum, albeit with local references removed (Wells 1993, McLaughlin 1994, Kelly and Tak 1998). Removing location-specific content is often necessary to avoid confusing offshore students, but by trying to universalize a course, lecturers run the risk of abstracting the curriculum from real-world contexts, and thereby elevate to the status of 'universal' many locally and culturally bound ways of thinking, communicating and working. The question we are faced with in this chapter is why, despite the widespread agreement on the desirability of adapting and tailoring transnational programs to suit the specific student group, does it seem to happen so rarely?

International distance education and partner-supported programs, which make up the vast bulk of transnational enrolments, are generally 'demand absorbing' forms of higher education, in that they cater to unmet demand for higher education from students who miss out on places in established local institutions (or where similar programs are not offered locally) and who are not able to study overseas. These programs are offered in a highly competitive environment where the fees involved may be substantial by local standards. In order to be competitive in catering to this demand, successful programs must be affordable, have a reputable local partner, and concentrate on providing those services and qualities which students value most. It is for this reason, as Philip Altbach (2000: 5) has noted, that transnational higher education 'does not really contribute to the internationalization of higher education worldwide. Knowledge products are being sold across borders, but there is little mutual exchange of ideas, long-term scientific collaboration, exchange of students or faculty, and the like'. This narrow focus is typical of tuition-funded higher education world-wide; in the absence of government subsidies and endowments, most students will choose lower-cost institutions that focus on their learning needs rather than expensive institutions that fund activities that may have broader benefits but do not significantly improve students' experiences.

Addressing the 1998 conference of the Global Alliance for Transnational Education, the Vice-Chancellor (President) of an Australian university explained the rationale for this stripped-down version of higher education delivered at the University's 'retail outlets':

> [W]e provide no sporting facilities, no spacious landscaped lawns and gardens, no facilities for cultural, political, religious or hobby activities beyond a computer games and table tennis room. We don't even administer the campuses or employ the staff. The management of the campuses is outsourced entirely to our for-profit joint venturer, who is also the employer of the local academic staff ... (Chipman 1998: 10).

This university's outlets also have small libraries in comparison with traditional university campuses; despite these apparent disadvantages, they enrol significant numbers of students who pay fees only slightly lower than the nearby 'full-services' traditional university campuses. Students choose this university, their student feedback tells them, because of the year-round teaching which allows students to enter and exit programs flexibly and complete earlier; the small-group teaching which provides for a greater familiarity with teachers and other students; and ready access to computer facilities and online materials. In short, the students:

> do not feel they are paying for anything they have no wish to use.... they are getting the benefits of access to the academic products, academic services and academic standards of a stereotypical modern university, including a credential undifferentiated from one earned in one of our 'traditional' campuses, in a way they find more convenient, and more cost-effective in terms of their own money and time (Chipman 1998: 11).

It is difficult for prospective students to know how relevant and accessible a foreign program's curriculum and pedagogy is; such nuanced aspects of program quality remain relatively opaque even for those students who extensively research the range of foreign programs offered in their location, or who have access to first-hand, word-of-mouth accounts of the program. Students often know much more about the local partner institution, and will often select a program on the basis of the perceived quality of the local partner, which brings us to the question: *who* should ensure that transnational delivery is culturally appropriate, and *how* should they do this?

In understanding the diffusion of responsibility involved in transnational education, the candour of the Vice-Chancellor in discussing the decoupling of course design, teaching and assessing from other services that institutions normally provide, these three can be provided 'at a fraction of the cost of the stereotypical modern university' (Chipman 1998: 9).

Most transnational programs are offered through collaborative relationships in which a local partner institution provides a range of services to students on behalf of the institution, which awards the qualification. This involves what some commentators refer to as 'unbundling' or 'disaggregation of the supply chain' in which the various services that need to be supplied as part of an educational enterprise (including marketing, administration, teaching, provision of library facilities, assessment) are disentangled from one another and delivered by one or another organization as specified by a partnership agreement between the two organizations. This approach is very similar to the packaging of curriculum employed by multi-campus for-profit universities in the USA (Farrel 2003).

Reviewing the literature on teaching in transnational education, Leask (2006) identifies four types of cultural knowledge required for effective transnational teaching:

- understanding of local culture(s) including the political, legal and economic environment;
- understanding of how the teacher's own culture affects the way they think, feel and act;
- understanding of how culture affects how we interact with others;
- and understanding of social, cultural and educational backgrounds of students.

In practice it seems such understanding is rare among new teaching staff, and uneven among experienced teaching staff. It is very common for fly-in-fly-out lecturers to be sent abroad to teach students in an off-shore program with very little preparation and without detailed understanding of their students or the local context in which they are teaching (Gribble and Ziguras 2003). Over time, through experience and considerable trial and error, many seasoned lecturers begin to tailor their content and teaching style, but this is made difficult by the intensity of much fly-in-fly-out teaching which often involves fewer contact hours than in the home country, taught over a much shorter time-frame. It is common for both students and lecturers to have little time for reflection. Having studied a group of Melbourne-based lecturers teaching in Singapore, Hoare (2006: 172) concluded that they:

> [d]eparted [Melbourne] not as 'empty vessels' but as individuals with all the preconceptions, values, beliefs and general cultural baggage that we all carry. In some instances they shared much of this baggage with their colleagues and in others they stood alone. Whatever the case, they were people with 'good intentions' however they were generally not well supported toward the development of an effective biculturalism by their normative experiences, their community of practice, or their employer. When they attempted to transmit their culture of teaching and learning in Singapore, they met with varying levels of conflict and resistance which ... shook them into cultural

awareness. They learned a lot in a relatively short space of time, and they often learned in a difficult, 'thrown in the deep end' transgression-induced manner.

Hoare's detailed observations echo broader studies that have found that lecturers teaching offshore have very little pre-departure or ongoing training for the task (Gribble and Ziguras 2003, Dunn and Wallace 2006). As Leask (2004) and Stier (2003) have noted, visiting academics are cultural outsiders in the offshore location, compared with their students and local teaching staff. Many find teaching in such an unfamiliar environment disconcerting, and for some it is the first time their own 'taken for granted culture becomes visible to them or they realize that other people hold stereotypes and prejudices about them' (Stier 2003: 80). This explains why Leask (2006) found that lecturers in another Australian university's transnational programs were more concerned about cultural issues than their students were. Nevertheless, the Singaporean students in Hoare's (2006) study clearly had a sense that, early in the program, something was not quite right. But they may not describe their concerns as 'cultural', rather, that there was a need for their Australian teachers to have greater comparative understanding of a wide range of differences between teaching sites. Hoare (2006) argues for a considered movement from teacher-centred to student-centred pedagogies, which is rendered overt through discussion with students early in the program (e.g. 'How do we work together to render this program worthwhile for you?'). There is clearly a need for institutions to better prepare and support their staff teaching offshore, and while practices vary widely between institutions some, like the University of South Australia (UniSA 2006), are beginning to do this very well.

Most transnational delivery involves locally employed teaching staff, and it is these teachers who are in the best position to localize foreign educational materials and act as cultural intermediaries between foreign academics and offshore students, which can enable them to facilitate a process of staged acculturation (Coleman 2003: 365). Clearly, locally employed teachers are in an excellent position to be able to assist in developing curriculum in ways that reflect the culture and context in which their students are learning (Leask 2004). However, locally employed teaching staff, like casual teaching staff on the home campuses, are often under-qualified or inexperienced, and commonly have little input into the core curriculum. The marginalization of these teachers, who have extensive contact with students, is a problem everywhere, but especially in transnational education, where the locally employed teachers are remote from the lecturer, usually employed by a different organization (the local partner institution), are usually working full-time elsewhere, and are paid only for their time with students. It is common for local teachers and fly-in-fly-out lecturers to never meet each other, let alone teach alongside on another (Hoare 2006), but such interaction is crucial to enable productive cross-cultural teaching relationships to develop.

CONCLUSION

Over time, most local partner institutions seek to develop their own academic programs and decrease their reliance on foreign universities, and this involves the recruitment of highly qualified academic staff who are centrally involved in curriculum development. The major lasting legacy of transnational education will be the capacity-building role they have provided in assisting small private colleges to develop the scale and experience needed to be able to upgrade their status and operate independently (McBurnie and Ziguras 2007: 80–3).

REFERENCES

Altbach, P.G. (2000) 'The Crisis in Multinational Higher Education', *International Higher Education* 21, Fall: 3–5.

Bates, A.W. and de los Santos, J.G.E. (1997) 'Crossing Boundaries: Making Global Distance Education a Reality', *Journal of Distance Education* 12 (1/2): 49–66.

Carnoy, M. (1974) *Education as Cultural Imperialism*, New York: Longman.

Chipman, L. (1998) The Changing Face of Transnational Education: The Future of Higher Education in a Global Context—Opening address to the 1998 Global Alliance for Transnational Education Conference, *'The Changing Face of Transnational Education: Moving Education—Not Learners'*, Paris. Washington: Global Alliance for Transnational Education.

Coleman, D. (2003) 'Quality Assurance in Transnational Education', *Journal of Studies in International Education* 7 (4): 354–78.

Dunn, L. and Wallace, M. (2006) 'Australian academics and transnational teaching: an exploratory study of their preparedness and experiences', *Higher Education Research and Development* 25 (4): 357–69.

Education International (2004) *Globalization, GATS and Higher Education*, Brussels: Education International.

Farrel, E.F. (2003) 'Phoenix's Unusual Way of Crafting Courses', *Chronicle of Higher Education* 49 (23): 10.

Gribble, K. and Ziguras, C. (2003) 'Learning to Teach Offshore: Pre-departure Training for Lecturers in Transnational 'Programs', *Higher Education Research and Development* 22 (2): 205–16.

Hoare, L. (2006) *So Near and Yet So Far: An Ethnographic Evaluation of an Australian Transnational Education Program*, Melbourne: The University of Melbourne.

Kelly, M.E. and Tak, S.H. (1998) 'Borderless Education and Teaching and Learning Cultures: The Case of Hong Kong', *Australian Universities' Review* 41 (1): 26–33.

Leask, B. (2004) *Transnational Education and Intercultural Learning: Reconstructing the Offshore Teaching Team to Enhance Internationalisation*, trans. Translator, Adelaide: Australian Universities Quality Agency.

—— (2006) *Keeping the Promise to Transnational Students: Developing the Ideal Teacher for the Transnational Classroom*, trans. Translator, Perth: IDP Education Australia.

McBurnie, G. and Ziguras, C. (2007) *Transnational Education: Current Issues and Future Trends in Offshore Higher Education*, London: RoutledgeFalmer.

McLaughlin, D. (1994) 'Contrasts in learning in Asia and the Pacific', *Pacific-Asian Education* 6 (2): 41–50.

Stella, A. (2006) 'Quality Assurance of Cross-border Higher Education', *Quality in Higher Education* 12 (3): 257–76.

Stier, J. (2003) 'Internationalization, Ethnic Diversity and the Acquisition of Intercultural 'Competencies', *Intercultural Education* 14 (1): 77–91.

UNESCO and OECD (2005) *Guidelines for Quality Provision in Cross-Border Higher Education*, Paris: United Nations Educational, Scientific and Cultural Organization and the Organization for Economic Co-operation and Development.

UniSA (2006) *Teaching Resources: Transnational Teaching*. University of South Australia. Online. Available HTTP: http://www.unisanet.unisa.edu.au/learningconnection/staff/practice/transnational.asp

Wells, M. (1993) *The Export of Education: Exploitation or Technology Transfer*, Sydney: Research Institute for Asia and the Pacific, University of Sydney.

Ziguras, C. and Rizvi, F. (2001) 'Future Directions in International Online 'Education', in D. Davis and D. Meares (eds) *Transnational Education: Australia Online*, Sydney: IDP Education Australia.

Part II

Perspectives on Teaching

6 Intercultural Dialogue and Understanding
Implications for Teachers

Ting Wang
University of Canberra

INTRODUCTION

Australia today is the third-largest exporter of higher education services internationally, with international students comprising well over 20 percent of total student enrolments in Australian universities. About two-thirds of international students study on university campuses within Australia, while the remainder are enrolled offshore (Harman 2006). Transnational programs are an established and integral part of the internationalization activity of many Australian universities. Despite a growing body of literature on transnational education in recent years, some scholars argue that the current understanding of offshore students' learning situations is often general, fragmented, and sometimes confusing (Gribble and Ziguras 2003). There is a profound need to consider the learning and teaching situations that lay at its heart (Tsolidis 2001), and to develop intercultural competence and intercultural learning in transnational education (Allan 2003; Greenholtz 2000; Leask 2004).

China is one of the most important markets for Australia's international education sector. The largest numbers of international student enrolments in 2005 were from China (AEI 2006). Chinese students enrolled in Australian offshore programs also increased rapidly in recent years. This chapter is part of a larger project that investigated the perceived influence of an Australian offshore graduate course upon Chinese educational leaders' conceptions of leadership and learning and their leadership practice over a one year period from 2002 to 2003 (Wang 2004). While some of the key findings have been reported elsewhere (Wang 2005, 2006, 2007), this paper, with reference to the interview data, focuses on the intercultural learning experiences of Chinese participants and the implications of intercultural dialogue and understanding for teachers in transnational education settings.

THEORETICAL FRAMEWORK

The current scene in education administration in East Asia, including China, is full of 'cultural borrowing' (Cheng 1998; Walker and Dimmock 2000) and the vital importance of avoiding 'cultural imperialism' is increasingly emphasized (Bush and Qiang 2000). The importation of substantive ideas from one cultural context to another can be beneficial, but is fraught with risk and should be undertaken with sensitivity and care (Ribbins and Gronn 2000). Research into international programs suggests that we should address issues like cross-cultural pedagogy, cultural sensitivity and awareness, and cultural dissonance (Allan 2003; Tsolidis 2001). It is established that developing countries like China have pre-existing administrative cultures and traditions, which are different from the core assumptions of European and American societies. This couples with an understanding that the participants in international programs may hold different assumptions about learning, pedagogy, leadership, and the purpose of education from those who teach them. There might be a danger that academics from Western nations who conduct leadership development courses in developing nations may operate from unquestioned assumptions that paradigms and practices from the Western cultures are automatically appropriate to contexts, which have different cultural traditions. Such practices have been viewed as contemporary forms of cultural imperialism.

The traditional cross-cultural lenses frequently take the form of mapping differences between cultures to enhance cross-cultural understanding (Hofstede 1980, 1991). The five dimensions Hofstede identified are high/low power distance, individualism/collectivism, masculinity/femininity, uncertainty avoidance, and short term/long term orientation. These dimensions are suggested as choices between pairs of empirically verifiable alternatives that allow the identification of patterns within and between cultures to emerge, and facilitate their meaningful ordering (Hofstede 1980, 1995). Some scholars have warned of the dangers of describing groups in essentialist terms of contrasting beliefs and values as a form of 'generalization' which should be treated with 'scepticism' (Putnis and Peterlin 1996: 74). Osland and Bird (2000) argue that while this sophisticated stereotyping is helpful to a certain degree, it does not convey the complexity found within cultures. Culture is embedded in the context and cannot be understood fully without taking context into consideration. This comparative approach is limited by its tendency to conceptualize culture as a static reality, rather than a dynamic and multi-faceted phenomenon.

In an era of constant and discontinuous change, such generalizations have limited utility. The traditional cultures of developing nations are themselves in a state of disruption as global forces penetrate their boundaries. The strange mix of socialist collectivism and market forces in contemporary China clearly illustrates the fluidity and complexity of Chinese culture. Collard and Wang (2005) argue that contemporary cultures embody conflicts to a greater extent than the snapshots provided by cross-cultural analysis. The reality is more fluid and multi-layered. It is more like a multimedia production where images shift and transmute as different cultural forces, dominant traditions, pre-existing sub-cultures and international forces collide.

The concept of intercultural understanding offers a way forward for transnational education. It frames cultural interaction in dialectical terms as a conversation or interview rather than a frozen snapshot. It also recognizes the power of human agency by privileging reflective dialogue over submissive cloning. It understands that interactions between individuals from different cultures entails inherited frameworks infused with differing perceptions and values. However, dialogue offers possibilities for building emergent understandings and new frameworks rather than submission to imported wisdom. It permits adaptation, fluidity, nuanced change, and even resistance (Collard and Wang 2005). Unlike traditional cross-cultural approaches, which tend to emphasize stereotyped differences between static cultures, intercultural dialogue acknowledges cultural dissonance and allows dynamic interactions between hybrid cultural forces. It seeks to enhance intercultural sensitivity, mutual understanding, and reciprocal relationships during this interactive process. Teachers and students in transnational programs become partners in intercultural construction. Traditional cross-cultural approaches are not appropriate in this setting and that ongoing dialogue offers more opportunities for change and even resistance to the accepted inherited cultural frameworks that people bring to transnational teaching and learning. Therefore, this research is not a cross-cultural study in the traditional sense, which implies a comparative approach. It employs a more culturally sensitive approach, which recognizes that a complex interaction between Chinese and Western cultures is occurring in the participants of this study.

RESEARCH METHOD

The research design of the study was a pre- and post-comparison case study inspired by the phenomenographic approach (Marton 1981, 1986). Phenomenography is an approach to research that has been used to help understand the key aspects of the variations in the experiences of groups of people (Marton and Booth 1997). Fifty-two educational leaders from Zhejing Province, China, enrolled in the offshore course of Master of Educational Leadership conducted by an Australian university in 2002. The sample comprised 20 participants, 15 males and 5 females, approximately proportional to the gender ratio in the cohort.

Eight school principals, six university administrators, and six system officials participated in this study.

An in-depth and semi-structured interview technique was used to explore participants' responses to open-ended questions. Two sets of interviews were conducted in April 2002 and April 2003 to examine the perspectives of 20 participants on their experiences and conceptions of learning and leadership prior to and after undertaking the course. The average time for each interview was approximately one hour. All documents distributed to participants were translated from English into Chinese and all interviews were administered in Chinese. Each interview was audio-taped, transcribed verbatim, and translated into English. The 200 pages of transcripts were coded based on emergent themes and categories. The responses were sorted into conceptual categories on the basis of similarities and differences. The transcripts were also summarized as a series of vignettes that focused on individuals' conceptions and self-reported leadership practice. The data analysis was conducted by moving between the full transcripts and the vignettes. Quotations presented in this paper were translated from Chinese into English.

FINDINGS AND DISCUSSION

Addressing cultural dissonance

Tensions between different cultural forces in transnational programs can be illustrated by the experiences of the participants in this study. Awareness of one's own and other cultures, and understanding of differences, are essential steps in cultural learning. However, this is acquired via an affective rather than a cognitive process and through experiential, more than intellectual, learning (Cushner 1990). Cultural awareness involves looking inward, reflection and praxis (Allan 2003). In this study, participants' personal experiences of Western approaches of learning and teaching make them reflect on their previous assumptions and practices. As commented by one male school principal, 'Confrontations and clashes with different perspectives and practices from Western countries were evident in class'. Another female system official claimed that 'this program provides us with opportunities to reflect on our work practice and previous understandings about learning and leadership.' She was able to 'use the program as a platform and reflect on many issues, and then come up with new understandings'.

Findings indicate that most participants were impressed by their real experience of 'studying overseas without going abroad'. A male system official commented that 'we personally experience how foreign teachers deliver a course. Their teaching approaches are different from us, which make us reflect on our way of teaching'. He viewed this intercultural experience as 'worthwhile and impressive'. Another school principal found his experience 'fresh' because Australian teachers 'pay less attention to knowledge transmission, but attach much importance to the whole learning process and developing student abilities and wisdom'.

While valuing their different educational and cultural experiences, participants were aware of cultural dissonance. For instance, a senior system official indicated Australian academics' lack of knowledge about Chinese education and preferred 'more intercultural interactions, more in-depth discussions about Chinese emergent issues, and more consultations in class'. A university administrator described his struggles in making sense of Western concepts and theories due to differences in cultural background and ways of thinking. He concluded that despite the tensions, Chinese students and Australian teachers 'were getting closer' in their interpretations:

> In terms of understanding of certain concepts, we may have different interpretations and beliefs from those of foreign teachers due to cultural differences. Sometimes it seemed that we were talking about the same concept, but it was hard for us to understand them, or vice versa. We tried to understand their interpretations with our understandings, come up with our interpretations, and then internalize what they have explained. We try to seek common grounds in understanding certain concepts.

Participants claimed that they shared some Western educational ideas, such as student-centred learning, developing student creativity, participatory decision-making and distributed leadership. However, there were many systemic and environmental constraints in their workplaces. Most often they had to conform to the prevalent social norms and continue to respect old practices. There was generally a big gap between their 'theories espoused' and 'theories-in-use' (Argyris and Schon 1978).

It is significant to note how Chinese participants addressed the tensions between different cultural forces. They enrolled as students of a Western offshore program, attended the course delivered by Australian academics, studied Western course materials, and were exposed to Western approaches of learning and teaching, Western culture, values, philosophies and ideologies. In order to fulfill the requirements of the course and develop professionally, they were supposed to accommodate the needs of Western academic norms and transfer the knowledge learned to their workplaces. But in order to develop in the Chinese context, they needed to continue to be mindful of the way things are done in China. Cultural dissonance seemed to be unavoidable in such transnational programs. People may generally escape cultural dissonance by retreating to the dominant culture in which they are living. In practice, after the course participants continued to be subjected to the strong forces of the Chinese culture and context, this mediated the influence of Western culture and ideas.

ENHANCING INTERCULTURAL SENSITIVITY

The study shows that participants reportedly held comparatively traditional perceptions about leadership and learning because of Chinese cultural, social and economic influences. They reported that their learning experiences and exposure to alternative perspectives helped them to expand their conceptions, enhance their intercultural sensitivity and awareness, and develop an international perspective. At the same time, they reiterated that the unique Chinese culture and local contexts would also continue to influence their conceptions and choice of strategies of learning, teaching, and leading in practice.

Respondents maintained that China is different from Western countries 'in terms of historical, social and cultural background, and economic development'. It was therefore believed to be important to 'adapt leadership practice to the local context and followers'. It was considered inappropriate and questionable to 'adopt Western leadership ideas indiscriminately without considering the contemporary Chinese context'. A senior system official emphasized an active mediation between his cultural heritage and insights from other nations:

> I think it is very important to have intercultural communication. We need to absorb and make full use of some advanced Western ideas and practices while keeping the essence of our culture. Having some understandings of Western culture and education will be helpful for us to look at Chinese education from an international perspective.

This official insists that the Chinese should not surrender their cultural heritage before the allure of Western leadership theories. He is searching for an enriched perspective, which will assist the evolution of Chinese education from a national to an international perspective. Another academic made his points explicit in the following response:

> Obviously, we have our own ideas, philosophies, and characteristics. We need to take Chinese culture and contexts into consideration. However, if we think there are more similarities than differences between Chinese culture and Western culture, we would adopt a more tolerant and open attitude to Western ideas. Undoubtedly, we can draw beneficial experiences from the development of Western countries.

It can be seen that the identification of similarities and differences becomes the learning compass, which enables practitioners to discriminate between what may be adopted and rejected from other cultures. It also suggests that the delivery of offshore programs is not simply a direct transfer of Western theories and ideas to a developing country. To some extent, the delivery is actually a process of dissonance, interaction and integration between different cultures, values, philosophies, and beliefs. It is a process of intercultural dialogue rather than indiscriminate 'cultural borrowing' (Walker and Dimmock 2000), or imperative 'cultural imperialism' (Bush and Qiang 2000). Most importantly, it can be a rewarding learning process for both learners and course deliverers.

DEVELOPING INTERCULTURAL DIALOGUE

The findings reveal that it is problematic to transplant Western theories to non-Western countries without considering local contexts and cultures. It is up to the practitioners from developing countries to reflect on and adapt Western ideas to local contexts. When Western ideas, which are contradictory to Chinese traditional culture and political ideology, are promoted, it is probable that cultural dissonance occurs and misunderstanding, resistance and open defiance are likely to be encountered in practice. For example, a school principal believed she would only accept the Western ideas or concepts, which she regards as useful and applicable:

> In a Chinese classroom, if a Chinese teacher adopted the same teaching approach employed by our Australian teacher, he might not be welcome by students at all, because it may not fit so well in the Chinese context.

Respondents claimed that efforts should be made to integrate the essence of Chinese leadership ideas with alternative Western leadership perspectives. For example, a senior system official emphasized a balance between scientific management and participatory decision-making in leadership practice:

> Local context, cultural background, and qualities of followers need to be considered when adapting Western leadership theories. We may rationally propose that we should have flattened organisational structure and democratic management. But in reality this can hardly be achieved. We need to consider the qualities of organisational members. If their qualities are not up to the desirable standard, enforcing shared leadership or flattened structure may bring trouble to an organization.

The most sophisticated comments on intercultural interaction and capacity building came from a Director of a local Educational Bureau:

> Australian academics have introduced many theories and practices in Australia and other Western countries. There are also many theories and best practices in China....We have lots of best practices, but our efforts in analysing, synthesizing, summarizing practices and coming up with theories are far from enough. We should not only learn and adapt theories from Western countries, but also propose new theories applicable to Chinese contexts. If Australian academics help with Chinese educators in this regard, they will make great contributions to capacity building and creativity promotion of Chinese educators.

As stated previously, Western course developers and deliverers need to take precautions to avoid cultural imperialism or the indiscriminate imposing of Western theories upon the recipients. Leadership developers from Western countries may act as culture and knowledge brokers in introducing alternative perspectives and practices rather than as radical-change agents in bringing about immediate transformation in recipients' leadership conceptions and practices.

IMPLICATIONS AND CONCLUSION

The responses from this cohort of participants indicate that to ensure a genuine intercultural dialogue, it is inappropriate for Western academics to regard themselves as the privileged holders of Western ideas who can impose radical prescriptions for the situations of developing countries. It is advisable that they be flexible reflectors, ready to cater to the needs of learners from different cultures, and critical helpers of their capacity building. It is therefore important for them to develop their intercultural competence and intercultural learning. They should endeavor to respect and value the knowledge that the students have, and construct the course as a reciprocal learning situation. At the same time, it is necessary for learners from recipient countries to give up resistant attitudes towards alternative perspectives or feelings of superiority about their own culture, and attempt to adapt to the best of the ideas and essence from other cultures. In this sense, intercultural dialogue and understanding is actually a significant aspect of this leadership development program, which may also apply to other international programs.

This study suggests that intercultural dialogue is a complex and multi-dimensional process. It is more complex than 'cultural borrowing' from another culture which is perceived to be more advanced by many political authorities. Nor is it always a stubborn resistance to outside forces. It is a process of interaction where individual players consciously mediate between cultures and choose to amalgamate knowledge and values from both in unique ways. The result is a group of educated practitioners with more sophisticated repertoires than agents from both the indigenous and foreign cultures. Such individuals may be examples of an emerging international culture composed of diverse origins which is more complex than that of any one nation or culture. It can be seen from this study that the result of intercultural contact is not a cultural loss on the part of recipient country (Gronn 2001). It is rather a dynamic process of cultural dissonance, interaction, dialogue, and integration based on mutual understanding and benefit. The study highlights the need for intercultural understanding and critical accommodation of Western ideas, and cultural sensitivity of transnational education.

REFERENCES

AEI (2006) *People's Republic of China: market data snapshots,* Canberra: AEIThe Australian Government International Education Network.

Allan, M. (2003) 'Frontier Crossings: Cultural Dissonance, Intercultural Learning and the Multicultural Personality', *Journal of Research in International Education,* 2(1): 83–110.

Argyris, C. and Schon, D. (1978) *Organizational Learning: A Theory-of-Action Perspective,* Reading, MA: Addison-Wesley.

Bush, T. and Qiang, H. (2000) 'Leadership and Culture in Chinese Education', *Asia Pacific Journal of Education,* 20(2): 58–67.

Cheng, K. M. (1998) 'Can Educational Values be Borrowed? Looking Into Cultural Differences', *Peabody Journal of Education,* 73(2): 11–30.

Collard, J. and Wang, T. (2005) 'Leadership and Intercultural Dynamics', *The Journal of School Leadership,* 15(2): 179–195.

Cushner, K. (1990) 'Cross-cultural Psychology and the Formal Classroom', in R. W. Brislin (ed.) *Applied Cross-cultural Psychology,* Newbury Park, CA: Sage.

Greenholtz, J. (2000) 'Assessing Cross-cultural Competence in Transnational Education: The Intercultural Development Inventory', *Higher Education in Europe,* 25(3): 411–416.

Gribble, K. and Ziguras, C. (2003) 'Learning to Teach Offshore: Pre-departure Training for Lecturers in Transnational Programs', *Higher Education Research and Development,* 22(2): 205–216.

Gronn, P. (2001). 'Crossing the great divides: Problems of cultural diffusion for leadership in education'. *International Journal of Leadership in Education,* 4(4): 401–414. Retrieved 18 October 2007 from: http://www.iht.com/articles/2000/10/16/rprofit.t.php

Harman, G. (2006) 'Australia as a Higher Education Exporter', *International Higher Education,* 42: 14–16.

Hofstede, G. H. (1980) *Culture's Consequences: International Differences in Work-related Values,* Beverly Hills: Sage.

—— (1991) *Cultures and Organizations: Software of the Mind,* London/ New York: McGraw-Hill.

—— (1995) 'Management Values: The Business of International Business is Culture', in T. Jackson (ed.) *Cross-cultural Management,* Oxford: Butterworth-Heinemann.

Leask, B. (2004) 'Transnational Education and Intercultural Learning: Reconstructing the Offshore Teaching Team to Enhance Internationalisation', *Proceedings of the Australian Universities Quality Forum 2004.*

Marton, F. (1981) 'Phenomenography: Describing Conceptions of the World Around 'Us', *Instructional Science,* 10:177–200.

—— (1986) 'Phenomography—A Research Approach to Investigating Different Understandings of Reality', *Journal of Thought,* 21: 28–49.

Marton, F. and Booth, S. A. (1997) *Learning and Awareness,* Mahwah: Erlbaum.

Osland, J. S. and Bird, A. (2000) 'Beyond Sophisticated Stereotyping: Cultural Sensemaking in Context', *The Academy of Management Executive,* 14(1): 65–77.

Putnis, P. and Petelin, R. (1996) *Professional Communication: Principles and Applications,* Sydney: Prentice Hall.

Ribbins, P. and Gronn, P. (2000) 'Researching Principals: Context and Culture in the Study of Leadership in Schools', *Asia Pacific Journal of Education,* 20(2): 34–45.

Tsolidis, G. (2001) 'New Cultures, New Classrooms: International Education and the Possibility of Radical Pedagogies', *Pedagogy, Culture & Society,* 9(1): 97–110.

Walker, A. and Dimmock, C. (2000) 'Insights into Educational Administration: The Need for a Cross-cultural Comparative Perspective', *Asia Pacific Journal of Education,* 20(2): 11–22.

Wang, T. (2004) 'Understanding Chinese Educational 'Leaders' Conceptions of Learning and Leadership in an International Education 'Context', unpublished PhD thesis, University of Canberra.

—— (2005) 'Exploring Chinese Educators' Learning Experiences and Transnational Pedagogies', *International Journal of Pedagogies and Learning,* 1(3): 44–59.

—— (2006) 'Leadership Practice Change: Critical Perspectives from the Chinese Educational Leaders in an Australian Offshore Program', in A. Bunker and I. Vardi (eds) *Critical Visions: Thinking, Learning and Researching in Higher Education. Proceedings of the 2006 Annual Conference of the Higher Education Research and Development Society of Australasia Inc (HERDSA),* 9–13 July 2006, The University of Western Australia, Milperra: HERDSA.

—— (2007) 'Understanding Chinese Educational 'Leaders' Conceptions in an International Education Context', *International Journal of Leadership in Education,* 10(1): 71–88.

7　Dimming Down Difference …

Sandra Egege
Flinders University

Salah Kutieleh
Flinders University

INTRODUCTION

The phenomenon of transnational education highlights the complex relationship between culture and educational practice. Any field of knowledge contains an implicit set of cultural values that it brings to the students, and all students bring an implicit set of cultural values with them to the educational setting. The issue for transnational education is the potential clash of cultural values this entails and its impact on the learning experience. In this chapter, we discuss the related issues of cultural dominance and cultural difference. Our aim is to show that differences do not always need to be problematized. We argue that the perceived differences between cultures have less impact on teaching and learning than believed and that striving to address differences by developing culturally specific teaching practices is not only fraught with difficulties but runs counter to the aims and objectives of transnational education. We demonstrate how it is possible to acknowledge cultural diversity in one's teaching without having to work within specific cultural paradigms. This is based on the premise that not all differences need to be either explicitly catered for, as in local cultures, or deliberately eliminated, as with Western teaching practices.

The demand that transnational educational courses should have consistent quality, comparable course content and access to experienced non-local academics, in line with what is available to the host institution's domestic market, raises the spectre of cultural dominance. Hallak (quoted in James, 2000: 16) states that no education is neutral because of the effects of culture. If true, there is the danger of hegemony, and the concomitant accusation of neo-colonialism or cultural imperialism. A related concern is that education-exporting countries will be pushing the same (educational and other) standards in each new market, regardless of the host country's own standards. The danger of this approach, according to Hallak (in James 2000: 16), is that education becomes disassociated from the social fabric and origins of a country. Any dissonance between the international education received and the local culture of the newly trained professional could severely limit their potential economic returns. Additionally, uniformity in delivery could lead to a form of what Liston calls homogenization (1998), a situation where all transnational providers perpetuate just one set of values, one world culture that could, potentially, undermine local differences. Cultural dominance is then manifest not by an imposition of cultural values on another culture but by the standardization of values across all cultures.

Concern about cultural dominance in the transnational setting is often one of the drivers behind proposed changes to curriculum and teaching practice. It raises questions about the relevance of course content to the local cohort, the possibility of a culture-value clash, the applicability of academics' teaching styles, and their effectiveness in a cross-cultural context. These concerns lead to a growing demand for cultural awareness of, or sensitivity towards, the student body, along with a demand for culturally appropriate, even culturally specific, teaching.

CULTURAL DOMINANCE

It is outside the scope of this chapter to fully address the issue of cultural dominance. Nevertheless, it is worth noting that the demand for consistency of content, high standards and similar teaching methodologies between the home institution and the offshore branch will result in similar values and approaches being taught across cultural boundaries, and irrespective of them. This is what is meant by ensuring quality and consistency between the mother institution and its offshoots. It is part of what the importing country demands, even expects, and is the reason students want to enrol in transnational degree programmes, a point we deal with later. Consequently, it is not clear how this uniformity of approach could be avoided, or even if it should be avoided. On the other hand, one could argue that there are moral grounds, which should lead us to prevent a blanket imposition of 'alien' cultural values and practices. However, this assumes that such an imposition is both deliberate and actually occurring, neither of which may be the case. It also gives little credit to the critical faculties of the thousands of culturally diverse students who access transnational education every day. So while the claims of cultural dominance or cultural uniformity sound plausible, they should be treated with caution.

Gribble and Ziguras (2003) question the contextual relevance of courses developed for a domestic market delivered to a culturally different audience in an international context. Again this reflects a concern that the values and standards transmitted to the students represent a narrow culturally specific focus that is alien to, and even in conflict with, the student's own cultural standards. The question is whether or not this is cause for concern. Just because people come together from a range of different cultural backgrounds with possibly different perspectives is not, in itself, a rationale for the delivery of different content. Neither is the ready accusation of cultural hegemony or cultural imperialism enough justification to change what and how one teaches. There need to be persuasive reasons to show that it is necessary.

THE CASE FOR DIFFERENCE

According to Ziguras (1999: 2), 'international...learning environments bring together in an unfamiliar environment students and educators whose experience of teaching and learning stems from very different cultural traditions.' He goes on to say that, if we are to teach appropriately in accordance with student expectations and demands, then academics 'should become familiar with their students' educational assumptions and expectations, as well as the educational practices that the student would be used to in their home country.' (Ziguras 1999: 3)

Similar issues have been expressed by Dunn and Wallace (2006) and Leask (2004). While putting forward slightly different requirements, they all agree that academics teaching offshore need to understand the culture of their audience and accommodate for student diversity in academic expectations, their lack of familiarity with Western teaching methods, and differences in their learning styles compared to local onshore students. They justify this approach by adverting to evidence of a cultural mismatch between the students' experiences and expectations, and the academic expectations and standards of the providing institution (Pyvis and Chapman 2004; Dunn and Wallace 2006). Smith and Smith (1999: 74) raise similar issues in relation to Confucian Heritage Culture (CHC) students studying on-line, given significant differences between them and local Australians in their fear of failure and their desire for a more structured learning environment. Smith and Smith claim that 'the possible development of meanings [in their written work] different from those constructed by Australian students' could lead them to get lower marks and drop out. They suggest adaptation of course structure and more detailed explication of standards as ways to accommodate these differences and, thereby, lower both the risk and fear of failure.

These issues are not new, and have been a matter of concern for some time in relation to international students. In fact, the literature on transnational education mirrors many of the early trends in the literature on international students. All the transnational academics, who took part in the various research projects mentioned above, found very little difference between the international student body at home and the local student body abroad. The detailed accounts of student perspectives conducted by Pyvis and Chapman (2004) in three of the major countries engaged in transnational education, do little to change that perspective.

If we assume that there are minimal academic or other differences between non-local international students and transnational students studying in their own countries, then the question of cultural difference takes on most significance when discussing the differences between international/transnational students and local onshore students.

For a long time, academics and researchers have identified certain differences in academic performance between local and international students, in particular Asian or CHC students. While largely anecdotal, these differences have been uniformly reported across all institutions and disciplines where Asian students interact with a Western-style education system. What are seen as negative practices—rote learning and lack of critical thinking skills, passivity and surface learning, lack of understanding of academic scholarship and plagiarism, excessive reliance on authority, and lack of independence—have become stereotypical of the Asian student (Biggs 1999). A less negative, though still problematic, group of characteristics that have been identified as associated with predominantly Asian students, include such things as a corporate/collectivist mentality, rather than an individualistic one, a reliance on structure and detailed instructions, and a reluctance to engage in public discussion or debate (Smith and Smith 1999; Krause 2006).

If these differences exist and negatively impact on the student's academic performance, then those differences need to be addressed. Rather than target the students' perceived short-comings, as was past practice, the current approach to dealing with differences is to acknowledge that there are 'equally legitimate culturally relative differences to academic study,' stemming from different cultural perceptions and understandings (Kutieleh and Egege 2004: 2). This approach assumes that no single cultural perspective is more valid than another. Cultural differences can be accommodated by adapting one's teaching to suit the different cultural styles of the relevant student body. If the student is no longer to be fitted to our standards, then we must adjust our methods to fit the student. Not surprisingly, variations of this approach are the teaching model of choice for transnational education. We believe that this approach is not only fraught with difficulties but it assumes first, that the differences are real and do matter and second, that any differences should be addressed and, if possible, negated. We disagree with both these assumptions.

DIMMING DOWN DIFFERENCE

The first problem with tailoring one's teaching towards a specific cultural group, based on perceived differences in preferences, approaches to learning, or learning styles, is that it is easy to be mistaken about those differences, as Biggs (1999) and others have demonstrated. We have been wrong before and are likely to be wrong again. The second problem is that even if we successfully identify some cultural differences in learning styles or approaches to learning, it is hard to know how to make our teaching culturally appropriate. Attempts to teach from within an alternative (cultural) system would probably fail due to mis-understandings about what is actually occurring in that system. Even if one could make the leap and become an effective educator in a culturally different context, there is the problem of which cultural practice one adopts. Asian cultures are not homogenous, anymore than European cultures are. In theory, one would have to adopt a different methodology for each language-culture as well as for language sub-cultures within the same culture. This is not only impractical but also implausible for an academic to achieve. At the same time, as Biggs notes, not only does this approach involve 'multi-structural diversity of independent technologies of teaching' but each system is also viewed as self-contained and appro-priate only within its own cultural context (1997: 9). What works in one system has no implications for another. This means that there can be no knowledge transfer between systems; it disallows teaching innovation and learning across cultures. Thus what one adapts and learns in one context would, by definition, have no applicability in another.

The second problem is the extent of cultural, ethnic and academic diversity. We very rarely confront mono-cultural groups. An important criticism in the literature has been the identification of all Asians, or even international students, with one sub-group— CHC students (Smith and Smith 1999). The term 'Asian' includes Indonesians, Filipinos and those from the Indian sub-continent as well, all cultures very differ-ent from the CHC group and each with their own academic practices. Similarly, Smith and Smith (1999) claim that the CHC group itself is culturally and academically diverse and a number of Asian countries are culturally diverse. It would be impossible and impractical to deal with each of these cultural groups individually.

At the same time, it is becoming clear that issues of difference and diversity apply just as much to the local cohort as they do to international students. In Australia, for example, the local student group comes from a diverse range of ethnic and language backgrounds; they cover all age groups, social and educational backgrounds as well as academic abili-ties. There are likely to be as many differences within the local cohort as there are between the local and international student groups. If we are going to address diversity in our teaching, there are grounds to do this across the board, not just for one particular student cohort.

However, there is little evidence to demonstrate the need to address each cultural group in a culturally specific way. In fact, we would argue that focusing on culturally specific differences tends to not only exagger-ate differences (rather than similarities) but may actually identify some cultural differences as being educationally or cognitively significant when this may not be the case. There is a growing body of research that shows that the perceived academic differences between international/ Asian students and local Western students are not as marked as first thought (Biggs 1997). Extensive research conducted by Biggs to confirm or negate the supposed differences between CHC students, in particular, and Western students, revealed that while there were some differences in Asian students' approaches to learning, the differences did not result in the kinds of deficiencies identified by academics. In fact, Biggs (1999) claimed that Asian students performed better, achieved higher marks and scored more for deep learning and critical analysis. These findings have been supported by additional, independent research by Ramburuth and McCormick (2001) and Smith and Smith (1999), who found there were no major differences overall between CHC students' and local students' approaches to learning. These studies indicate that differences arose in relation to attitude to study, not ability or approach. Another in-depth study by Krause (2006) also confirmed that, while some differences existed between first year local and international students, these were more a matter of degree than kind and centred on their levels of dissatisfaction or course expectations.

In our view, most culturally based differences can be classified as learning preferences, resulting from past practice. Based on what students are used to, they may exhibit a preference for group work and explicit instruction, a lack of understanding of the concept of plagiarism or an expectation that there is a correct answer, model or approach (Pyvis and Chapman 2004; Biggs 1997; Volet 1999). These differences are not without their impact on teaching and learning, but they are also not unique to international students or one particular group of students. Neither do they necessarily require the academic to mould their teaching practice to suit the students' preferences.

TEACHING TO DIVERSITY—CRITICAL THINKING

It would be unrealistic to claim that differences do not exist at all, or that we never need to adapt our teaching to our audience under any circumstances. However, we do need to be cautious about what it is we are requesting from our academics, how realistic it is and whether or not it needs to be done. The recommendation that one should adapt one's teaching to suit each cultural group is what Volet (1999) refers to as the 'accommodation' approach, based on a customer-oriented model. Like Biggs, she claims that it is not only practically unrealistic to cater for all styles of learning, but such an approach involves using *individual* learning styles as the criteria for deciding on appropriate methods of instruction. This is not something academics should be expected to do, nor is it pedagogically necessary. It also assumes that there can be no transmission of knowledge from one cultural setting to another, as such

Djanogly Learning Resource Centre - Issue Receipt

Customer name: Guan, Yewen

Title: Transnational education : issues and trends in offshore higher education / Grant McBurnie and Christ
ID: 1004885071
Due: 19 Oct 2016 23:59

Title: The dynamics of international student circulation in a global context / edited by Hans de Wit ... [e
ID: 1006790641
Due: 19 Oct 2016 23:59

Title: Teaching in transnational higher education : enhancing learning for offshore international students
ID: 1005302580
Due: 19 Oct 2016 23:59

Total items: 3
21/09/2016 12:34

All items must be returned before the due date and time.
The Loan period may be shortened if the item is requested.

WWW.nottingham.ac.uk/library

knowledge is relevant only within and when applied to that specific culture. This is patently not the case. We learn from different practices all the time and many things have relevance outside the place of origin. For example, problem-based learning has been very effective in both Canada and Hong Kong, two very diverse cultures (Biggs 1999).

It should be possible to adapt a teaching methodology that is applicable across cultures. This does not mean reverting to a single model of teaching which assumes that all students are the same, but developing teaching methodologies that, as Biggs (1997: 15) suggests, are 'adaptive in their structure, which allow students to negotiate their learning objectives, preferred learning styles and methods of assessment'. The rationale behind this approach assumes that people of all cultures, despite apparent differences in approach and attitude, have similar cognitive capacities, and that there will be better and worse ways to teach, in accordance with how humans process information. Volet (1999) believes too that a teaching model based on sound principles of learning should lead to learning-enhancing facilitation for all students, regardless of cultural orientation. If one has well-grounded principles of teaching, then all students should benefit, regardless of where they come from.

We have tried to implement sound principles in the way we teach critical thinking to international students. Our method acknowledges different starting points and attempts to make these explicit by comparing them to existing (Western) practice. In this way, Flinders University's cultural assumptions, attitudes and practices are presented as alternative methods of engagement, rather than just desirable modes of behaviour that students should adopt or assimilate. We have found this approach enables students to make their own judgements about what behaviours they need to incorporate in order to be able to operate successfully in a different academic culture. Different academic practices are thus presented to students as specific cultural practices that have relevance within a specific designated sphere. This enables the students to view the adoption (or not) of those practices as a coping mechanism, which ensures their ability to move freely within the culture with the least possible anxiety or sense of alienation. Our experience has shown that not only does this process give students a choice about what parts of academic practice they might adopt but also it leads to empowerment. If one's own cultural or academic perspective is explicit, it can be more readily reflected upon.

At the same time, we do make it clear to students what our academic expectations are and why, for example, critical thinking is seen as important within the university context. The point we want to emphasize is that such skills are relevant or useful in particular situations. And like learning any new skill, there are specific rules of engagement one needs to know to be successful. Presenting the material in this way helped students to understand the role critical thinking plays within the university and to understand the criteria needed to successfully implement a critical approach in their own work that reflects the academic expectations of the university. The challenge for the student is to master the technique and, thereby, benefit. In a study we conducted to evaluate the effectiveness of this approach, student comments revealed both an appreciation of its worth and a sense of empowerment at understanding the concept (Kutieleh and Egege 2004: 8):

> ...it is the way here. We need it for evaluating. (PNG, undergraduate)

> ...and knowing, knowing that is what you are expected to do, with that knowledge you are able to explore further and to actually think of some criticism. (Kenya, postgraduate)

> ...this is why I was so interested in the process because I know when I go back to my country it will be useful in my profession. (Philippines, postgraduate)

TRANSNATIONAL EDUCATION—WHAT STUDENTS WANT

It is critical to remember that, ultimately, we are talking about what students want and why they choose to study transnationally, factors that are largely absent from the debate. It is not necessarily the case that accommodating perceived cultural differences will improve the learning outcomes for the students. Most transnational and international students deliberately choose to enrol in an offshore or international institution, rather than a local university, because they think they will receive a better quality education. As a consequence, they do not expect that education to be taught in the same way as their home institution. They expect to learn new things, and they expect to be challenged. They expect difference.

Research conducted by Pyvis and Chapman (2004), confirmed by our own experiences with international students, shows that transnational/international students enrol in Western degrees because they see them as transformative. They want to change, to develop an international perspective and gain foreign expertise. A student from the Malaysian study (Pyvis and Chapman 2004: 25) captured this notion of internationalization:

> I want my personality, my character to build. Here is the start. International students, international curriculum and international teachers mean I can progress.

Academically, most students in Pyvis and Chapman's study spoke of the challenges they faced due to different educational practices or modes of teaching. They acknowledged that they were challenged and often felt insecure about whether or not they were doing what was expected. However, their comments suggest that they eventually saw such challenges as positive, as part of the transformation process. They were learning new ways of being and doing. Many of them remarked about how they had learnt to adapt and even appreciate the new way. While finding the differences 'difficult', most felt that it was good to be confronted by different styles and perspectives as this 'enhances' the study experience.

The existence of cultural differences between the students' learning styles and those of the institution does not mean they are problematic for the student or that the student would want their Western education to be less Western and closer to their local practice. Such an attitude also assumes that the students cannot adapt or learn, that the Western model doesn't work for Asian students. Given the high success rates, this is patently not the case.

CONCLUSION

We have argued that, by and large, there are minimal differences between the educational issues confronting transnational students and those confronting international students. Both also seem to respond in similar ways and to have similar expectations and motivations, insofar as one can generalize across a large and diverse group. In addition, we have argued that many of the differences identified between international/ transnational students and the local cohort are exaggerated. Even where differences can be identified, the cohorts of both are so individually and culturally diverse that any generalization across groups becomes problematic.

More importantly, however, our position throughout this chapter had been that there is an over-emphasis on cultural difference and its impact on educational outcomes. Magnifying difference in this way is not just an impediment to student satisfaction and, possibly, to their success, but also creates undue stress for those academics teaching offshore who feel under pressure to adapt their teaching to meet specific student needs, albeit unclear. This can lead to confused lecturers and students, and vague educational objectives and teaching methodologies.

We have tried to show that adapting one's teaching to make it culturally appropriate is incoherent and theoretically flawed. In the transnational setting, not only are the students from a range of cultural or ethnic backgrounds but they are also exposed to academics from more than one cultural paradigm. It might be a lecturer from Kansas, one from Sri Lanka and/or another from within their own culture, each teaching in a predominantly Western degree course. Within this context, the concept of cultural appropriateness becomes meaningless. There is also no evidence to indicate that there is a demand from the students for the kind of cultural flexibility that researchers are recommending. In fact, the evidence indicates the opposite. Students are empowered by new ways of teaching and exposure to this kind of academic difference. It is part of the international transformative experience they desire.

REFERENCES

Biggs, J. (1997) 'Teaching Across and Within Cultures: The Issue of International Students in Learning and Teaching in Higher Education: Advancing International Perspectives.' *HERDSA Conference*. Adelaide: Flinders Press.

—— (1999) 'Teaching International Students'. In *Teaching for Quality Learning at University*, Society for Research into Higher Education and Oxford University Press, New York.

Dunn, L. and Wallace, M. (2006) 'Australian Academics and Transnational Teaching: an Exploratory Study of Their Preparedness and Experiences', *Higher Education Research and Development*, 25 (4): 357–69.

Gribble, K. and Ziguras, C. (2003) 'Learning to Teach Offshore: Pre-Departure Training for Lecturers in Transnational Programs', *Higher Education Research and Development*, 22 (2): 205–16.

James, B. (2000) 'Does Profit Put Culture at Risk? UNESCO Chiefs See Profit Motive as Threat to Cultural Needs', *International Herald Tribune*, 16 October: 17–19. Online. Available at: http://www.iht.com/articles/2000/10/16/rprofit.t.php (accessed 18 October 2007).

Krause, K. (2006) 'Student Voices in Borderless Higher Education: The Australian Experience', *The Observatory on Borderless Higher Education*, London. Online. Available at: http://www.obhe.ac.uk/resources/

Kutieleh, S. and Egege, S. (2004) 'Critical Thinking and International Students: A Marriage of Necessity', *8th Pacific Rim Conference Proceedings Conference*, Brisbane: Queensland University of Technology.

Leask, B. (2004) 'Transnational Education and Intercultural Learning: Reconstructing the Offshore Teaching Team to Enhance Internationalisation', paper presented at *AUQA* Forum, Melbourne.

Liston, C. (1998) 'Effects of Transnational Tertiary Education on Students—Proposing an Assessment Model'. Online. Available at: http://www.aair.org.au/jir/1998Papers/Liston.pdf (accessed 18 October 2006)

Pyvis, D. and Chapman, A. (2004) 'Student Experiences of Offshore Higher Education: Issues for Quality', *AUQA Occasional Publications*, 3.

Ramburuth, P. and McCormick, J. (2001) 'Learning Diversity in Higher Education: A Comparative Study of Asian International and Australian Students', *Higher Education*, 42: 333–50.

Smith, P. and Smith, S. (1999) 'Differences between Chinese and Australian Students: Some Implications for Distance Educators', *Distance Education*, 20 (1): 64–80.

Volet, S. (1999) 'Learning Across Cultures: Appropriateness of Knowledge Transfer', *International Journal of Educational Research*, 31: 625–43.

Ziguras, C. 1999. 'Cultural Issues in Transnational Flexible Delivery'. Online. Available at: http://www.monash.edu.au/groups/flt/1999/NewPapers/chris_ziguras.pdf (accessed December 2006).

8 Towards a Fusion Model for the Teaching and Learning of English in a Chinese Context

Maria Bjorning-Gyde and Francis Doogan

Fusion Teaching

Martin East

School of Language Studies, Unitec New Zealand

INTRODUCTION

Benson and Voller (1997: 10) have suggested that 'communicative language teaching' (CLT) has become 'an axiom of language teaching methodology.' CLT is the dominant model for teaching English as a foreign language (EFL), at least in Western contexts, and developing learners' communicative competence has become its principal goal. Its axiomatic position and subsequent widespread global acceptance have been strengthened by international testing practices for English, such as the IELTS examination, which inevitably have had a washback effect into teaching contexts worldwide. Various theoretical frameworks of communicative competence have been expounded (Bachman 1990; Canale 1983; Canale and Swain 1980; Hymes 1971, 1972, 1982; Savignon 1983, 1997; Widdowson 1978), with later models being adaptations of, or developments to, earlier frameworks.

It appears, then, that on a global scale a perception exists that the 'best' way to teach languages is through what has become known as the 'communicative method'. In this chapter we challenge this perspective by suggesting that in some contexts the communicative model may be found lacking. Focusing on Chinese learners of English in Chinese contexts we argue that a 'fusion' of Western and Chinese approaches is likely to work more effectively. We begin by presenting some of the challenges we believe the CLT model faces. We go on to talk about the culture that Chinese learners bring to the classroom. Finally we outline how our 'fusion model' would work to enhance Chinese learners' linguistic proficiency.

COMMUNICATIVE LANGUAGE TEACHING: CONTEXT AND CHALLENGES

The axiomatic position of CLT has carried with it an assumption that an essentially Western model of language teaching and learning would inevitably fit, in an unquestioned way, into the varieties of contexts in which languages would need to be taught and examined. This raises several problems. Canagarajah (2002) notes that for some time language teachers and applied linguists outside Western contexts have been concerned about the use of Western teaching methods and pedagogical paradigms. This has led to questions about the cultural relevance and appropriateness of these methods in local contexts (Holliday 1994; Miller and Emel 1988; Mukherjee 1986; Sampson 1984) and the need to develop teaching methods based on indigenous pedagogical traditions (Hornberger 1994; Watson-Gegeo 1988). Canagarajah (2002: 134) suggests, however, that this is a 'line of dichotomous thinking (East versus West; local versus foreign) [which] is complicated by increasing cultural hybridity, human migration, and media expansion.' In other words, Canagarajah's concern is that Western teaching methods and pedagogical paradigms have apparently been viewed from the perspective of what Robertson (1994: 37) calls a dichotomous global-local problematic that straightforwardly indicates a polarity.

East (in press) also argues that the dichotomous view of 'global' versus 'local' is insufficient to explain the complex and often contradictory forces at work upon individuals, groups and societies today. There is a need to 'move beyond the oppositional thinking of global versus local' to thinking that '[the] global constitutes and is constituted by the local and thus the global and the local interpenetrate' (Mowlana 1994: 17). East suggests that a better term to describe the reality of social interaction at the start of the twenty-first century is 'glocalization'.[1] If we accept this suggestion, 'oppositional' thinking is insufficient. There is arguably a need for a 'fusion' between Western and other teaching methods and pedagogical paradigms, and the consequent development of new paradigms for language teaching methodology in specific contexts.

THE CHINESE SITUATION AS A CASE IN POINT

The situation for Chinese learners of English is a case in point. Chinese learners of English have until fairly recently formed a substantial part of the cohort of international students learning English in English-speaking countries. When confronted with the learning of English they have been expected to engage with Western methodological approaches to communicative competence, including the notions of authenticity, learner-centeredness and negotiation. And yet these Chinese learners bring with them a complete set of understandings about teaching and learning, framed by what is known as Confucian Heritage Culture (CHC), which is at points in conflict or at variance with Western notions. Jin and Cortazzi (1998: 98) suggest that this type of culture clash may have a profound impact on classroom practices because 'it is a significant factor in how teachers and students perceive language learning and how they evaluate each other's roles and classroom performance.' Although Jin and Cortazzi acknowledge that to speak of 'Western' or 'Chinese' cultures of learning is to generalize, they recognize (1998: 101–102) that 'Chinese learners share some common cultural background, including language and clear long-standing cultural perceptions of what it means to be Chinese and how to learn. In contrast, 'Western' cultures of learning share a different set of norms, perceptions and ideals.' These different approaches to language teaching and learning may be illustrated diagrammatically (Figure 8.1).

Chinese education was organized around the Confucian classics which students were required to memorize, recite and explain (Ting 1999), with the four basic concepts of learning in the Confucian tradition being memorization, understanding, reflecting and questioning

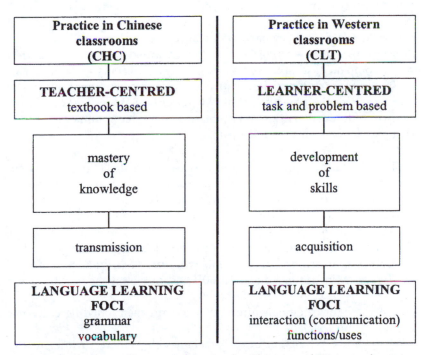

Figure 8.1 Practices of language learning in Chinese and Western classrooms (adapted from Jin and Cortazzi (1998), pp. 102–103).[2]

(Chu 1990). Memorization is a particularly key component of the model (Biggs 1996). Thus the emphasis of the Chinese cultural model of learning English may be described as 'transmission' which relies on mastery of knowledge and rote-learning of rules and meanings. The emphasis of the Western model, by contrast, may be described as 'acquisition'. This learner-centred model focuses on interactive engagement, learner autonomy and the development of communicative skills. As Jin and Cortazzi (1998: 103) explain:

> These different cultural orientations to language learning can become barriers. There may be completely different expectations about the roles of teachers and students. There may be variant interpretations about what is effective teaching. Judgments may be made of the other party which are effectively misplaced, or stereotyped views, strongly filtered by participants' culture of learning.

One response to this clash of cultures has been to allow the Western communicative model to infiltrate and influence the teaching of English in Chinese contexts. Chen (2006) argues that Western assessment tasks are increasingly being used to assess EFL proficiency in China in place of more traditional examinations which have dominated Chinese schools and universities for years, even though their introduction is leading to 'cultural conflicts'. Chen suggests that these changes are being made not only because of increasing partnership agreements between Western and Chinese universities whereby students are awarded a degree in EFL after having completed, say, two years in a Chinese university and a final two years overseas (2 + 2 model), but also because of educational reforms in China. Indeed, the *English National Curriculum Document* of China's Ministry of Education draws on the vocabulary of communicative methodology when it states the following:

> The design and implementation of the English language curriculum should be conducive to *optimizing learners' learning strategies.* Through *active learning methods* such as observation, experience and exploration, students can fully realize their potentialities and thus *develop effective learning strategies and learner autonomy.* Students should also be given opportunities to *use various information sources…*and *develop individualized learning methods and styles.*[2] (Ministry of Education 2003: 3, our emphasis)

Seen in the light of globalization, the reforms mentioned here are not necessarily unexpected.

When, however, *glocalization* is seen as the sphere of influence in which developments to language teaching methodologies are taking place, it may be argued that a better methodological framework for language learning in Chinese contexts would be one that embraces *both* a Chinese cultural model *and* a Western cultural model, since different cultures of learning are not mutually exclusive but can be reconciled or interwoven (Cortazzi and Jin, 1996). This is arguably particularly important for Chinese learners, since CHC learners have a proven record of academic success internationally (Volet 1999; Watkins and Biggs 1996) and would no doubt continue to derive benefits from the traditional methods of language learning to which they are accustomed. Jin and Cortazzi (1998: 114) propose a 'cultural synergy model' which 'suggests the need for mutual understanding of different cultures, communication styles and academic cultures'.

THE FUSION MODEL

The Fusion approach we propose provides such a model in the arena of language teaching methodology. The model may be defined as 'a synergy of selected and evolving contemporary theory and teaching techniques, predicated on the needs of Chinese teachers and learners' (Bjorning-Gyde and Doogan 2003). It is based on the belief that a combination of the CHC approach and the CLT approach leads to more efficient teaching and learning and higher levels of fluency than a single reliance on either approach. The model is intended as a way to make the communicative approach more analytical and memory focused, and model-based analysis more skills-integrated and communicatively effective. In order to select and combine approaches and techniques for the Fusion, a thorough evaluation of the perceived strengths and deficiencies in both the CHC tradition of teaching and the CLT approach was undertaken in conjunction with careful reflection on differences in social and cultural factors that affect the choice of approach and the way learners tend to interact. A summary of the model is given in Figure 8.2.

For transnational deliverers of English in China it was found that Chinese students have mixed expectations of the teacher. In the 'traditional' class environment the Chinese English teacher generally focuses on direct instruction and error correction in the form of top-down, whole-class expository lecturing. Nevertheless, as Senior and Xu (2002) illustrate, while the traditional position of the teacher is valued and respected, students in China today want their classroom atmosphere to be as lively as possible and wish to engage in activity-based learning. The transnational teacher therefore has to negotiate a persona that maintains significant teacher-centred delivery with an increasing proportion of class time spent on student-centred tasks that promote interaction and acquisition.

Cortazzi and Jin (2001) found that learner participation in a CHC context is high through the use of rapid, prepared sequences of activities

The Fusion Model is a combination of	
Practice in Chinese classrooms (CHC) and	Practice in Western classrooms (CLT)
TEACHER-CENTRED	LEARNER-CENTED
Deductive rule-based approach	Inductive 'discovery' learning
Knowledge from the teacher	Asking and answering questions
Individual work	Interactive and collaborative
Analytical, bottom-up approach	Global, top-down approach
Focus on accuracy	Focus on fluency and communicative competence
Use of models and translation	Awareness raising and 'noticing'
Repetition, memorization and understanding	Deep processing, meaningful learning
Discrete skills and items	Integration, context, whole language
Focus on product	Focus on process
Pre-viewing, preparing for class	Awareness of skills and strategies
High quantity and quality of input	Extensive skills development, autonomy

Figure 8.2 A fusion of Chinese and Western cultural language learning practices.

in which learners have been trained for appropriate classroom routines and ways of interacting. Thus, a carefully orchestrated class in which the teacher can direct efficient learning signifies a more traditional role, while expectations of the teacher as vivid and interesting can be promoted by variety in student-centred activities and a high level of interaction.

What follows is a brief and selected description of how the Fusion model is designed to work with the acquisition of grammar, vocabulary and skills.

VOCABULARY AND GRAMMAR

The Fusion promotes awareness-raising as a supplement to explicit grammar teaching. Learners are provided with ample opportunities to 'notice' the features of the target language, what gaps exist in their own interlanguage, and differences and similarities between L1 and L2. Such 'noticing' gives teachers an opportunity to extend traditional techniques such as the use of models and translation, in order for learners to analyse their own output by comparing syntax, lexis and style. This heightens learners' awareness of the target language and the culture within which it is used.

As with grammar, vocabulary learning in the traditional Chinese classroom has relied mainly on translation, analysis, memorization and review, with the additional support of vocabulary lists. This approach has significant benefits but the pressures of examinations seem to have driven a large number of teachers and learners to an emphasis on the de-contextualized rote-learning of lexis. It is important for the CHC deliverer to fully establish the context for meaning (Brown and Yule 1983) in order to make nuances, which may otherwise be lost, available to the reader. Translation and contrastive analysis will highlight differences and similarities in meaning and the cultural contexts which may create them. The use of code-switching also means that the classroom discourse resembles more closely the real world where this frequently occurs (Senior and Xu 2002). Despite the benefits, learners need to recognize that a dependence on translation for learning lexis may have quite deleterious effects on the development of fluency, as it tends to create reliance on L1 as the mediator of expression (Brown 1994).

Memorisation forces learners to attend to every detail in the text, and how words join together and function as meaning units (Ting 1999). Myles *et al* (1998) claim that learners often *internalize* rote-learned material as chunks, breaking them down for analysis later on. Given the current perception that language acquisition rests on a rich collection of formulaic expression, the benefits in memorising and analysing contextualized lexis appear to be great. In the Fusion, memorisation of text for language accuracy is an important supplementary technique to communicative language teaching, with a combination of the two providing a step towards improvement in both fluency and accuracy.

READING AND LISTENING

Pre-viewing of texts allows for personal learning according to individual needs and pace, while a great deal of class time is saved for explanation and clarification by the teacher. Too great an emphasis on pre-viewing and close analysis, however, means that learners develop a limited range of reading strategies. In the Fusion model, a balance of pre-viewing and top-down approaches is achieved through schema activation and increased awareness of reading strategies, as part of class input preceding analysis of lexis and structures.

To meet the needs of the CHC learner the Fusion model uses a phonology-based approach to listening (Bjorning-Gyde and Doogan 2004). Learners analyse phonological features such as changes in voice speed, intonation, linking and so on in part of the text. With guidance from the teacher, they imitate the recorded voice and compare their output with the original. This pre-listening stage serves as the basis of the skill of decoding spoken language. Meaning-focused listening and feedback support the use of listening strategies such as predicting and listening for gist. The transcript is then used to further increase phonological awareness, enhance sight-sound recognition, and analyse items of lexical and functional interest.

SPEAKING AND WRITING

The focus on phonology equips learners with a technique to enhance their own pronunciation as they emulate the model speaker and reflect on their own output. Techniques for further promoting accurate speech include recording, transcribing, and editing their own or their partner's speech, followed by memorization and task repetition. Richards (2002) and Willis (1996) note that in spontaneous fluency-focused communication learners have little time to reflect on the language and their production is marked by low levels of linguistic accuracy. They suggest pre-planning as a way of reconciling fluency work with the concern for acceptable levels of grammatical accuracy. Kim (2002) argues that East Asian learners are not as accustomed to problem-solving and verbalizing simultaneously and therefore benefit from the 'thinking time' that planning and delayed output provide.

Communication in CHC tends to take place in groups rather than one-to-one and commonality and agreement tend to be found quickly so as to avoid confrontation and arguments (Bond 1999). For the transnational deliverer this needs to be taken into account when planning group activities where CHC learners are expected to express feelings and opinions openly and spontaneously, complete problem-solving tasks, volunteer answers and make suggestions. In this context, the deliverer is advised to explore the Western cultural frame which supports debate and the open exchange of ideas so learners are aware of the expectation and benefits of creativity and problem solving, being able to justify and defend an opinion, and working collaboratively to reach an agreement.

For writing development the Fusion advocates contrastive analysis between essays written on the same topic in English and Chinese as a means of highlighting cultural differences in presenting and supporting an argument. The contrastive analysis is extended to syntax, and accuracy is further addressed through editing and awareness-raising activities. In the tradition of model-based learning, sample essays are analysed, memorized and reconstructed in order to provide a basis for student production. Written fluency is enhanced by regular, timed free-writing activities and the drafting stage of the writing process focusing on the communicative quality of the content.

CONCLUSION

Globalization has helped to frame a language teaching methodology—communicative language teaching—which has taken on high significance.

In this chapter we have argued that questions have been raised about the cultural relevance and appropriateness of communicative methods in local contexts. The need has been expressed to develop teaching methods based on local pedagogical traditions. We have suggested that there is a need for a 'fusion' between Western and other teaching methods and pedagogical paradigms for use in specific contexts. Our proposed Fusion method for Chinese contexts takes account of both the more teacher-centred approach central to the Confucian Heritage model and the more learner-centred approach which derives from communicative models. It is our contention that the Fusion model can be applied successfully in the areas of vocabulary and grammar acquisition, and the four key skills of reading, listening, speaking and writing. Furthermore, its use has the potential to enhance Chinese learners' communicative competence in a way that an exclusive focus on one paradigm (CHC) or the other paradigm (CLT) cannot achieve.

NOTES

1. 'Glocalization' is quite well established as a means of describing influential forces, having been used in business jargon since the 1980s (Robertson 1994).
2. It should be noted that CLT is one among several Western cultural models of language teaching, albeit the preeminent model. It does not exactly parallel the more general sociocultural framework represented by CHC.
3. It should be noted that this translation has not been approved by the Ministry of Education and can only be used for academic purposes.

REFERENCES

Bachman, L. F. (1990) *Fundamental Considerations in Language Testing*, Oxford: Oxford University Press.
—— (2000) 'Modern Language Testing at the Turn of the Century: Assuring that what we Count Counts', *Language Testing*, 17(1): 1–42.
Benson, P., and Voller, P. (eds 1997) *Autonomy and Independence in Language Learning*, London: Longman.
Biggs, J. (1996) 'Western Misperceptions of the Confucian-Heritage Learning Culture', in D. A. Watkins and J. Biggs (eds) *The Chinese Learner: Cultural, Psychological and Contextual Influences* (25–42), Hong Kong: CERC and ACER.
Bjorning-Gyde, M. and Doogan F. (2003) 'IELTS Preparation and the CHC Learner', *paper presented at the 38th RELC international seminar*, Singapore, 3–5 November.
—— (2004) 'Teaching Listening through Phonology: An Alternative Approach for Chinese Learners of English', *paper presented at the 4th international symposium on ELT in China*, Beijing, 21–25 May.
Bond, M. H. (1999) *Beyond the Chinese Face: Insights from Psychology*, Oxford: Oxford University Press.

Brown, H. D. (1994) *Teaching by Principles: An Interactive Approach to Language Pedagogy*, Englewood Cliffs, NJ: Prentice Hall Regents.

Brown, G. and Yule, G. (1983) *Discourse Analysis*, New York: Cambridge University Press.

Canagarajah, A. S. (2002) 'Globalization, Methods, and Practice in Periphery Classrooms', in D. Block and D. Cameron (eds), *Globalization and Language Teaching*: 134–150, London: Routledge.

Canale, M. (1983) 'On Some Dimensions of Language Proficiency', in J. W. J. Oller (ed.), *Issues in Language Testing Research*: 333–342, Rowley, MA: Newbury House.

Canale, M., and Swain, M. (1980) 'Theoretical Bases of Communicative Approaches to Second Language Teaching and Testing', *Applied Linguistics*, 1: 1–47.

Chen, S. (2006) 'Cultural Conflicts: Imposing Western Assessment Tasks to Replace EFL Examinations in China', *paper presented at the 31st annual congress of the Applied Linguistics Association of Australia—Language and Languages: Global and Local Tensions*, University of Queensland, Brisbane, 5–8 July.

Chu, H. (1990) 'Learning to be a Sage: Selections from the Conversations of Master Chu, Arranged Topically', trans. D.K. Gardner, Berkeley: University of California Press.

Cortazzi, M., and Jin, L. (1996) 'Cultures of Learning: Language Classrooms in China', in H. Coleman (ed.), *Society and the Language Classroom*, 169–206, Cambridge: Cambridge University Press.

—— (2001). 'Large Classes in China: 'Good' Teachers and Interaction', in D. Watkins and J. Biggs (eds) *Teaching the Chinese Learner: Psychological and Pedagogical Perspectives*, 115–34, Hong Kong: CERC.

East, M. (in press) 'Moving Towards "Us-Others" Reciprocity: Implications of Glocalization for Language Learning and Intercultural Communication', *Language and Intercultural Communication*, Clevedon: Multilingual Matters.

Holliday, A. (1994) *Appropriate Methodology and Social Context*, Cambridge: Cambridge University Press.

Hornberger, N. (1994) 'Ethnography', *TESOL Quarterly*, 28(4): 688–90.

Hymes, D. (1971) 'Competence and Performance in Linguistic Theory', in R. Huxley and E. Ingram (eds) *Language Acquisition: Models and Methods*, 3–28, London: Academic Press.

—— (1972) 'On Communicative Competence', in J. B. Pride and J. Holmes (eds) *Sociolinguistics*, 269–293, Harmondsworth: Penguin.

—— (1982) *Toward Linguistic Competence*, Philadelphia, PA: Graduate School of Education, University of Pennsylvania.

Jin, L., and Cortazzi, M. (1998) 'The Culture the Learner Brings: A Bridge or a Barrier?', in M. Byram and M. Fleming (eds) *Language Learning in Intercultural Perspective: Approaches through Drama and Ethnography*, 98–118, Cambridge: Cambridge University Press.

Kim, H. S. (2002) 'Talk Before we Think? A Cultural Analysis of the Effect of Talking on Thinking', *Journal of Personality and Social Psychology*, 83: 828–842.

Miller, T., and Emel, L. (1988) 'Modern Methodology or Cultural Imperialism?', *paper presented at the TESOL convention*, Chicago.

Ministry of Education (2003) *English National Curriculum Document for Senior High School*, Beijing: People's Education Press (Experimental).

Mowlana, H. (1994) 'Shapes of the Future: International Communication in the 21st Century', *Journal of International Communication*, 1(1): 14–32.

Mukherjee, T. S. (1986) 'ESL: An Imported New Empire?' *Journal of Moral Education*, 15(1): 43–49.

Myles, F., Hooper, J., and Mitchell, R. (1998) 'Rote or Rule? Exploring the Role of Formulaic Language in Classroom Foreign Language Learning', *Language Learning*, 48: 323–363.

Richards, J. C. (2002) 'Addressing the Grammar Gap in Task Work', in J.C. Richards and W.A. Renandya (eds) *Methodology in Language Teaching: An Anthology of Current Practice*, 153–166, Cambridge: Cambridge University Press.

Robertson, R. (1994) 'Globalization or Glocalization?', *Journal of International Communication*, 1(1):33–52.

Sampson, G. P. (1984) 'Exporting Language Teaching Methods from Canada to China', *TESL Canada Journal*, 1: 19–31.

Savignon, S. (1983) *Communicative Competence: Theory and Classroom Practice*, Reading, MA: Addison-Wesley.

—— (1997) *Communicative Competence: Theory and Classroom Practice* (2nd ed.). New York: McGraw-Hill.

Senior, R. and Xu, Z. (2002) 'East Meets West: Language Teachers from Different Contexts Discover Similar Goals', *EA Journal*, 19(1): 65–74.

Ting, Y. (1999) 'Traditional Language Learning and Chinese Students', Amnity Project Handbook. Online. Available at: http://www.amityfoundation.org/page.php?page=511 (accessed 5 November 2006).

Volet, S. (1999) 'Learning Across Cultures: Appropriateness of Knowledge Transfer', *International Journal of Educational Research*, 31(7): 625–643.

Watkins, D. A., and Biggs, J. B. (eds.) (1996) *The Chinese Learner: Cultural, Psychological and Contextual Influences*, Hong Kong: CERC and ACER.

Watson-Gegeo, K. A. (1988) 'Ethnography in ESL: Defining the Essentials', *TESOL Quarterly*, 22(4): 575–592.

Widdowson, H. G. (1978) *Teaching Language as Communication*, Oxford: Oxford University Press.

Willis, D. (1996) 'Accuracy, Fluency and Conformity', in J. Willis and D. Willis (eds) *Challenge and Change in Language Teaching*, 44–51, Oxford: Heinemann.

9 Dealing with Student Plagiarism in Transnational Teaching

Jude Carroll

Oxford Brookes University

INTRODUCTION

There is on-going discussion and debate in Western universities and the Western media on managing student plagiarism, some of it quite extreme. Nagy reviews the literature and notes that it is viewed by many as being 'of epidemic proportions' (2006: 38).

Journalists in many countries ensure that the topic of student plagiarism is regularly aired, especially if they can link articles to examples of blatant cheating by students or to the inappropriate handling of cases. Headlines for plagiarism stories often stress alarm and imply that plagiarism threatens the integrity and reliability of university awards.

Any discussion of student plagiarism in transnational teaching, therefore, sits within this wider debate and must be adapted to its specific needs and circumstances, such as:

- staff and students with widely varied experiences of teaching and learning, both before becoming involved with their off-shore study, and as it progresses;
- differing assumptions about aspects of teaching and learning (as discussed, frequently, elsewhere in this book);
- challenges in managing assessment at a distance;
- and fewer opportunities for staff to develop a shared understanding of academic standards and assessment requirements through informal interaction. Consensus is hard to achieve when they meet infrequently and/or must communicate at a distance.

EXTERNAL CHANGES IN HIGHER EDUCATION

All consideration of the growing incidence and severity of plagiarism cases, whether in academic or popular articles and commentaries, will link the issue of plagiarism, directly or indirectly, to other global developments, many particularly relevant to managing plagiarism transnationally. They include:

- The rise in opportunities for fraud. Before 2000, almost all concerns about deliberate fraud linked to plagiarism arose from activity in the US but by 2005, 'services' such as buying/commissioning essays, or 'proofreading', which guaranteed a good grade, were appearing weekly in many countries. In the UK, essay-providing businesses are said to turn over £200 million annually (Taylor and Butt 2006), and similar sites in Australia can be found with only a rudimentary search.
- Decreasing reliance on examinations for grades. In many universities, a significant proportion of students' grades are determined by coursework; a few are completely exam-free. Students often arrive in universities with qualifications gained via a similar mix. As the percentage of coursework rises, so do concerns as to whether the grades reflect authentic effort or, more correctly, students' cut-and-paste skills and/or their parents' intervention.
- An increase in student diversity. From the 1990s onward, more places became available in universities. On its own, this began to change the 'traditional' student mix, as mature, part-time students, and those with nonstandard admission qualifications, began tertiary study. In many countries, and especially the UK, Australia and New Zealand, ever larger numbers of students from other countries were recruited for higher education study and labeled 'international students' when they took up the offer. Others stayed home and signed on to transnational programs.

These changes were exacerbated in some commentators' eyes by the impact of fees and institutional financial security (real or perceived), linked to international students' fees in particular.

Staff who did not ask for these changes must adjust and adapt to them in their teaching and many do not enjoy the challenges this brings. Bretag (2007) reports on a study that collected the experiences of 14 Australian academics who all, she says, reported that students' poor English and sub-standard work were a threat to university standards. Policies and procedures to report their plagiarism were such that teachers felt unwilling or unable to use them. She entitles her article 'The Emperor's New Clothes', presumably implying that this topic is deemed undiscussable. Yet people do—certainly where plagiarism is concerned. Is plagiarism the inevitable consequence of the wrong sorts of students doing the wrong sorts of assessments and being marked by people using the wrong sorts of criteria (i.e. different ones for fee-payers)? The issue turns out to be more complex, and its solution eminently discussable and solvable.

TRANSNATIONAL STUDENTS/ PROGRAMS AND CHEATING

Partridge and West (2003), in an investigation into 'perceptions and occurrence of plagiarism amongst transnational students,' note there is no evidence to support the assumption that internationalization and international students were potentially (and in some cases, actually) a threat to academic standards and practices. This is not to say there is no problem. Some of the most high profile Australian cases of student plagiarism in recent years have involved transnational or international students. Other well-publicized scandals, both in Australia and in other countries, have involved practices in partner colleges or franchised programs. However, in many instances, stories deliberately or inadvertently stress the student's international status, and authors imply a causal connection with cheating when none exists. For example, the BBC reported publication of a wide-ranging paper on managing student plagiarism and summed up its 10,000 word message in one sentence: 'A rise in the number of students in the UK, including undergraduates from overseas, is likely to mean increased plagiarism' (BBC News, 11 September 2005). As the author of this paper, I know this was not its key message.

The first response to such comments is a referral to the growing literature on teaching international students which sets out the case against denying difference and, as student diversity increases, stresses the ineffectiveness of continuing to teach all students as if they were the ones you wished to teach, rather than the ones actually enrolled. Pedagogy appropriate to teaching international students would include explicit support and guidance on what is expected, with additional help during transition to the new learning environment, including English language support and help with developing necessary academic skills.

Adjustment to the new realities of higher education would mean using teaching methods which encouraged participation by all, a curriculum that recognized the international dimension in the learning experience, and attention paid to specific areas of difficulty such as academic writing and student plagiarism. (For more specific guidance on this aspect, see Carroll and Ryan 2005) If none of these changes is made and, instead, students are admitted with both language scores insufficient for thriving in an Anglophone university and previous educational experiences very different from the ones they will encounter, the results are predictably negative and in line with those already outlined. The converse is also true: where support and adjustment occurs, all students thrive.

Any treatment of student plagiarism in transnational teaching assumes that many other interventions dealing with the challenges of students learning in new and unfamiliar ways are also being addressed. Students at admission are not 'oven ready' and will need a range of interventions, including those that ensure they do no submit others' work as their own.

TRANSNATIONAL STUDENTS AND
INADVERTENT PLAGIARISM

Whilst the popular press, and academics themselves, seems comfortable with equating international status and cheating (though no evidence supports such a view), a parallel discourse exists in academic journals, conference proceedings and universities' teaching and learning web pages dealing with student plagiarism. From the mid-1990s most, though not all, commentators specifically refute the idea that all plagiarism is cheating, or that some students, in particular international students, are more prone to cheating than are others. (See, for example, Pennycook 1996; Carroll 2002; Angelil-Carter 2000; Shi 2004; Schmitt 2005; East 2005.) From this way of thinking about plagiarism, international students' over-representation in most institutions' penalty statistics can be explained as an artifact of detection rather than as evidence of lack of integrity. Bull et al (2001) found that three out of four markers use change of language as their primary means of spotting plagiarism. If so, then identifying cut-and-paste writing strategies will be a much easier task in an English as a Foreign Language (EFL) writer. The same explanation may explain why EFL students who purchase papers are also easier to spot.

Others explain the high percentage of international students who copy by referring to it as 'patch-writing' (Pecorari 2003). This term describes the way in which EFL writers rely on and use others' words while they are evolving their own 'voice' in English. Many see borrowing others' words as a necessary developmental step. Patch-writing shows up when electronic text-matching software is used to spot copying, since international students often import relatively long strings of words from the original, whereas 'lifts' by native speakers tend to be shorter (Shi 2004) and may account for why international students were 'a clear majority identified as plagiarists by software' Zobel & Hamilton (2002: 24) in Nagy 2006.

Some studies explain students' deliberate plagiarism as a response to the stresses of learning in a new environment, or being asked to do something that they do not understand, or might find too difficult. Lahur (2004) refers to students' 'culture shock', caused by transition to a new learning environment, even if no travel was required, and links this to pressure to plagiarize. Brennan and Durovic (2005) investigated whether students were more likely to cheat if they studied purely for a credential rather than to learn skills and knowledge. Unsurprisingly, they found that those who were studying to gain a qualification were more likely to cheat and that more than half of students on transnational programs offer this as their primary motivation. McGowan (2005) links higher rates in some students with avoidance of risk, judging it safer to copy. Certainly, international students and those investing heavily in an off-shore course will have a great deal to lose financially, and in terms of self-esteem, should they be unsuccessful, and this may prompt them to fake, rather than make, their own work.

DEFINING PLAGIARISM

Students usually are provided with information on plagiarism, and many handbooks add examples of unacceptable practices, which explain why 'doing your own work' is an important academic value. Definitions tend to be brief—'submitting someone else's work as your own'—yet questions remain. Plagiarism happens when the student hands in work (the verb 'submitting' says that), but where do requirements to 'do one's own work' conflict with co-operative learning? Is offering advice to fellow students, or checking how others have answered similar questions, acceptable (or even to be encouraged)? The phrase 'someone else's work' is probably clear to experienced academics, writing for their own discipline, but novice students wonder how ownership is conferred and where it must be shown. East (2005) notes that it is normal for orators to quote the 'I Have a Dream' speech without attribution. Politicians and even vice-chancellors rarely, if ever, acknowledge their speechwriters and many scientific notions are referred to without attribution. Explaining ownership with reference to 'common knowledge' is of little help, since students moving to a new country or discipline are not sure what 'everyone knows'. One way students manage their uncertainty is to drop in citations to avoid the accusation of plagiarism, rather than use them to show their skill as a researcher, or to showcase their reading, or their ability to select supporting evidence (though most over-cite as they develop expertise).

When students encounter the word 'work' in a plagiarism definition, many overlook that it refers to both a thing (as in the phrase 'work of art') and an action (i.e. describing the effort required to create the assessment product). To avoid charges of plagiarism, both the assessment artifact and the process that generated it must be the student's own. However, only some of the work required to make an assignment is covered by the definition. For example, the student may or may not be able to use a proofreader to improve the assignment, depending on whether the assessment criteria specify that marks reflect accurate English grammar. The student certainly should not ask a librarian to conduct her literature search, but it is hard to imagine a situation where it would be unacceptable to seek help on how to conduct the search. It usually takes time for students to be really clear about such distinctions though they often seem self-evident to experienced teachers.

It is no wonder, then, that all students require more than a handbook and/or a lecture to unravel the complexities of plagiarism. They will need practice, feedback and plentiful examples of acceptable work, as the recommendations at the end of this chapter suggest. Even if and when they master 'doing the referencing', it probably still seems a strange or arbitrary academic obsession. What's the point, a transnational student may wonder, of rewriting grammatically correct text in imperfect English? Why isn't a bibliography at the end sufficient? It certainly is in Vietnam, as Ha (2006) asserts in response to heated exchanges in the pedagogic literature about international students and plagiarism.

Satisfactory answers to these and many other 'why' questions rest on assumptions about learning which, for transnational students, may be a very different way of conceptualizing it than the one they encountered in their pre-university studies, or that their friends encounter, should they study in local, nonaffiliated programs.

WESTERN PEDAGOGY AND PLAGIARISM

In most Western universities, judgments about plagiarism are underpinned by the view that valuable learning happens when students construct their own understandings rather than remember and reproduce that of others, with the latter often being referred to as 'rote learning,' or denigrated as 'spoon feeding and regurgitation'. Understanding in Western universities is demonstrated by a student who can use a fact in a new setting, analyse a theory by taking it to bits, or explain something 'in their own words'. Not all academic systems assume that transformation must occur to demonstrate understanding. Nor do all systems equate memory with lack of understanding since repetitive learning strategies can also lead to deep understanding (Watkins and Biggs 1996). It is also true that, even in a constructivist academic culture, teachers may set tasks or problems which have only one answer (e.g. 'Describe the functions of the spleen') or where the 'right' answer is widely known and generally accepted (e.g. 'Discuss how best to manage a diverse workforce'). When this type of task is set as coursework in Western universities, students often struggle to match the requirement to 'do your own work' with the pragmatic view that copying or finding someone else's answer seems the most efficient way to proceed. Recommendations at the end of this chapter stress the need to avoid such assignments.

In many academic cultures, copying or finding others' answers may be the recognized and valued way to show one's learning. Even then, students allude to the origin of ideas but may do so indirectly rather than in a citation. According to Ha (2006: 77):

> In Vietnam, it is usual to quote Ho Chi Minh's famous statements, such as, "Nothing is more precious than independence', and we always acknowledge the source by adding 'says Uncle Ho'. We may not provide the name of the documents, the year of publication and

the publishers, but it is acceptable because his famous statements are considered common knowledge'.

In many educational settings, a student must often (though not always) match authoritative questions with teacher- or textbook-verified answers. This requires the student to hold facts, examples and theories in their memory which they will need to recall quickly and accurately to answer examination questions, a process often described as happening in the Peoples' Republic of China (see, for example, Ryan and Louie 2005) and documented in other settings such as India (Handa and Power 2005). Skills developed to meet the requirements of examinations will have some usefulness in Western university study but will almost certainly not be sufficient to ensure success.

The stress on students constructing, rather than presenting, understanding explains why students are expected to generate 'original work' although some seem to see 'original' as akin to 'novel', even implying teachers are looking for something that has never before been done (see, for example, Levin 2003). In fact, students' originality derives from the requirement that a student's own efforts/work are displayed even if the result is a repetition of what others have done. An analogy is between showing the ability to cook, on the one hand, by microwaving frozen pies and on the other, by expecting the final dish to reflect the students' shopping, chopping, combining, heating and stirring (and, for an A-grade, giving the final product that 'bit of extra something'). Where no change has occurred, students must show this to be the case by using quotation marks.

Plagiarism assumes individual ownership of ideas, a notion that is said to date from European Enlightenment and therefore, to be culturally specific (see, for example, Larkham and Manns 2002, who make this point in relation to plagiarism). Ideas about individual, named ownership of ideas is usually contrasted with academic settings where sharing, consensus and social good are valued, and where the goal of university study is not individual excellence but rather, to shape good citizens. (See Sillitoe et al 2005). Such dualistic views are problematic. Any visitor to a Chinese university will see textbooks and published papers with citations and, at least in some universities, can talk with students who are well-versed in the demands and controversies of plagiarism requirements, both in their own setting and when they travel to study.

MANAGING PLAGIARISM IN TRANSNATIONAL TEACHING

Good practice is developing in transnational settings, slowly replacing practices that have proved ineffective, such as ignoring the issue of plagiarism and/or treating it as a simple problem with a single-dimension solution. There is no instance where sorting out the problem by beefing up the handbook or introducing a text-matching tool such as Turnitin, by deterring plagiarism with penalties, or by reverting to exams has been successful. Even more dubious tactics include lowering or applying different assessment standards in on- and off-shore campuses. This is more likely to result in threats to quality, in frustrated staff and students, questionable qualifications and sometimes, high profile scandals, than it is to result in sorting out plagiarism.

Plagiarism can only be managed by combining a range of actions, all of which are harder to achieve when done at a distance, with colleagues you may not know well, and for students submitting work, perhaps without any face-to-face interaction. Those who have tried to do so, recommend the following as useful places to begin:

- Create opportunities for discussion and interaction. Staff and students will need safe contexts in which the concept of plagiarism, its complexity, and how the rules are applied in practice, can be discussed.
- Become familiar with students' previous experience and their expectations for current study. Look for real examples of how students have learned to generate work prior to enrolment. Talk with students about how they do assignments in their study and which aspects are especially challenging. Actively try to avoid stereotyping, or concluding that students' behaviour in the new setting has the same meaning as it would have in a familiar one.
- Provide clear and explicit guidance for staff and students. For students, this could take the form of a bespoke course designed to develop the skills they will need to be successful, such as how to identify reliable sources of support for an argument, how to organize and structure written work, how to take notes, read strategically, avoid or use the passive voice, and other skills.
- Teach the skills you value rather than telling them what they must avoid; adhere to appropriate standards. Negative admonitions (e.g. 'Don't quote verbatim') are of little help to a novice, whereas examples of good work (and do offer several, lest students think this constitutes a model answer) will be helpful, as will pointers on where to find more information. Ensure your feedback stresses the things that matter rather than, for example, being deflected by comment on the finer points of using the Harvard referencing system.
- Design assessment, which discourages copying. Advice on how to design such assessments is widely available. One such site is called *Acknowledgements*, and it offers a wide range of advice, including

those on assessment, at: <http://calt.monash.edu.au/staffteaching/plagiarism/acknowledgement/module6/par/intro.html>.

- Generic advice usually includes suggestions on changing the task, avoiding tasks that ask students to discuss or describe (rather than higher order verbs such as 'rank', 'choose', 'justify', or 'evaluate'), asking students to show how they went about doing the work through submitting drafts and even rough notes, and using assessments that authenticate work such as asking students to write about their coursework under observed conditions.
- Visibly monitor and detect plagiarism. This need not be too time-consuming. You might ask students for evidence prior to submission that they were active, or require evidence of process with their submission, such as drafts, or photocopies of significant sources. So-called detection software such as Turnitin is useful and can be used by students prior to submission (with your control) to ensure sources are cited. Even an advanced Google search will usually unearth the source, unless the student has tried hard to conceal it. Students need to know and see evidence that you are actively protecting academic regulations and values. If you only do this and not all the other measures described here, students may feel they are being watched and treated as cheaters. Detection should augment and strengthen other measures.
- Use penalties and feedback carefully. Ensure you distinguish in your feedback and penalty decisions between plagiarism that arises from misunderstanding and misapplication of academic conventions and that which arises from misconduct and which is unacceptable regardless of where and when it occurs.

CONCLUSION

It is not necessary to show that plagiarism in transnational teaching and learning is an especially grave concern for it to be worth addressing. All students need to understand why the instruction 'do your own work' is important and how to do so in their assignments and most struggle with both aspects (knowing what plagiarism is and how to avoid it). All teachers use phrases such as 'use your own words' or 'use Harvard referencing' but many find that colleagues using the same phrases often mean something quite different. Only through discussion, inspecting examples and investing time and effort can teachers and learners reach consensus on plagiarism. This is difficult in campus-based settings; it frequently does not happen despite the fact that most good practice advocates such an approach. In transnational and distance teaching, reaching consensus, a shared understanding and a collegial approach to managing plagiarism can be even more challenging and, at the same time, even more important.

REFERENCES

Acknowledgments. Online. Available at: http://calt.monash.edu.au/staffteach-ing/plagiarism/acknowledgement/module6/par/intro.html (accessed 30 May 2007).

Angélil-Carter, S. (2000) *Stolen language? Plagiarism in Writing.* Harlow, England: Longman.

Brennan, L. and Durovic, J. (2005) '"Plagiarism" and the Confucian Heritage Culture (CHC) Student.' In C. Eckersley, D. Both, H. Cluff, and M. Stenbeck (eds) *Educational Integrity: Values for Teaching, Learning and Research,* 2nd Asia-Pacific Educational Integrity Conference, University of Newcastle, 2–3 December 2005: 26–33.

Bretag, T. (2007) 'The Emperor's New Clothes: Yes, There is a Link between English Language Competence and Academic Standards', *People and Place*, 15 (1): 13–21.

Bull, J., Collins, C., Coughlin, E., and Sharpe, D. (2001) 'Technical Review of Plagiarism Detection Software Report". Online. Available at: http://www.turnitin.com/static/pdf/luton.pdf (accessed 18 October 2007).

Carroll, J. (2002) *A Handbook for Deterring Plagiarism in Higher Education.* Oxford: Oxford Centre for Staff and Learning Development.

Carroll, J. and Ryan, J. (2005) *Teaching International Students: Improving Learning for All.* London: Routledge.

East, J. (2005) 'Proper Acknowledgment?' *Journal of University Teaching and Learning Practice*, 2 (2): 1–11.

Ha, P L (2006) 'Plagiarism and Overseas Students: Stereotypes Again?' *ELT Journal* 60 (1): 76–78.

Handa, N. and Power, C. (2005) 'Land and Discover! A Case Study Investigating the Cultural Context of Plagiarism'. *Journal of University Teaching and Learning Practice*, 2 (3b): 64–84.

Lahur, A. (2004) 'Plagiarism among Asian Students at an Australian University Off-shore Campus: Is it a Cultural Issue?' In F. Sheehy and B. Stauble (eds) *Transforming Knowledge into Wisdom: Holistic Approaches to Teaching and Learning.* Proceedings of the 2004 Annual International Conference of the Higher Education Research and Development Society of Australasia (HERDSA), 4–7 July, Miri, Sarawak. Milperra NSW: Higher Education Research and Development Society of Australasia.

Larkham, P. J., and Manns, S. (2002) 'Plagiarism and its Treatment in Higher Education'. *Journal of Further and Higher Education* 26: 339–349.

Levin, P. (2003) 'Beat the Witch-Hunt! Peter Levin's Guide to Avoiding and Rebutting Accusations of Plagiarism, for Conscientious Students.' Online. Available at: http://www.student-friendly-guides.com/plagiarism/index.hrm (accessed 18 October 2007).

McGowan, U. (2005) 'Does Educational Integrity Mean Teaching Students NOT to 'Use Their Own 'Words'?' *International Journal for Educational Integrity* 1: 1.

Nagy, J. (2006) 'Adapting to Market Changes: Issues of Plagiarism, Cheating and Strategies for Cohort Customization'. *Studies in Learning, Evaluation, Innovation and Development* 3 (2): 37–47.

Partridge, L. and West, J. (2003) 'Plagiarism: Perceptions and Occurrence Amongst Transnational Postgraduate Students in the Graduate School of Education'. In H. Marsden, M. Hicks, and A. Bundy (eds) Educational Integrity: Plagiarism and Other Perplexities, *Proceedings of the 1st*

Australiasian Educational Integrity Conference, University of South Australia, 21–22 November: 149–154.

Pecorari, D. (2003) 'Good and Original: Plagiarism and Patch-writing in Academic Second-Language Writing'. *Journal of Second Language Writing* 12: 317–345.

Pennycook, A. (1996) 'Borrowing 'Others' Words: Text, Ownership, Memory and Plagiarism'. *TESOL Quarterly* 30: 201–230.

Ryan, J. and Louie, K. (2005) 'Dichotomy or Complexity: Problematizing Concepts of Scholarship and Learning.' In M. Mason (ed) *The Proceedings of the 34th Annual PESA Conference*, 401–411. Hong Kong: Philosophy of Education Society of Australasia.

Schmitt, D. (2005) 'Writing in the International Classroom''. In J. Carroll and J. Ryan (eds) *Teaching International Students: Improving Learning for All*, 63–75. London: Routledge.

Shi, L. (2004) 'Textual Borrowing in Second-Language Writing'. *Written Communication* 21: 171–200.

Sillitoe, J., Webb, J. and Ming Zhang, C. (2005) 'Postgraduate Research: The Benefits For Institutions, Supervisors and Students of Working Across and Between Cultures'. In J. Carroll and J. Ryan (eds) *Teaching International Students: Improving Learning for All*, 130–136, London: Routledge.

Taylor, M. and Butt, R. (2006) 'Q: How Do You Make £1.6m a Year and Drive a Ferrari? A: Sell Essays for £400''. *The Guardian*, 29 July 2006.

Watkins, J. and Biggs, J. (1996) *The Chinese Learner*. Hong Kong: Comparative Education Research Centre.

Zobel, J., and Hamilton, M. (2002) 'Managing Student Plagiarism in Large Academic Departments'. *Australian Universities Review*, 45 (2): 23–30.

10 Inside Thinking/Outside Issues

Reflective Practice in Zambia— Journey of Uncertainty

Gill Whittaker

University of Bolton

INTRODUCTION

Educators who work in transnational contexts have an opportunity to use their experience of contrasting situations to critically reflect on their assumptions about learning and teaching. Teaching in unfamiliar situations may sometimes be good for us—it compels us to reconsider what is familiar and come up with new ideas. Furthermore, we can use this opportunity to challenge ourselves and reconsider the academic rules and conventions with which we have grown comfortable. We need to embark on a journey of uncertainty.

The aim of this chapter is to question previously held assumptions about reflective practice as a vehicle for teacher development. I have used the terms *outside* and *inside* to express the dynamic tensions and complexities that may be associated with thinking critically about learning and teaching in divergent contexts. In this case, the critical exploration is situated in Zambia and concerns students who are qualified teachers undertaking a professional development degree. *Outside* also refers to the significant issues of poverty and disease that shape the lives of these Zambian students, whereas *inside* is concerned with the ways that reflective thinking may be influenced by such powerful circumstances.

The chapter begins by setting a contextual background for the discussion and continues with an exploration of reflective practice in relationship to existing ideas about power and autonomy. A critique of current assessment criteria is followed by a concluding section, which attempts to offer an alternative to reflective practice as an approach to professional development in transnational contexts.

BACKGROUND—SEARCHING BENEATH THE 'MANTLE OF OBJECTIVE SCIENCE'[1]

A demonstration of reflective practice is an explicit requirement of the professional development degree for practicing teachers offered by the

University of Bolton. All students on this course are required to complete a learning journal and present a reflective analysis of their personal and professional development throughout their degree program. This professional development degree is offered in Zambia and our students are qualified teachers from across the country who come together with University of Bolton tutors in a program that involves sequential residentials over two years. The residential, face-to-face model has been highly successful in terms of its rich interaction combined with 'two-way learning' (Smith 2006: 4) and, over the course of three cohorts of students since 1999, student evaluations have been very positive. However, the experience of teaching in Zambia has raised some personal doubts about the appropriateness and effectiveness of reflective practice as a tool for professional development in offshore teacher development.

Although my personal impressions of Zambia are subjective and unscientific, they are a necessary starting point and may be useful to others who are engaged in transnational education. In the hope that such reflexivity may move us beyond defensiveness into more purposeful learning (LaBoskey 2005), I begin with some personal views about this sub-Saharan country.

For the time that we are in Zambia we form a close-knit community with our students; formal barriers are eroded and there is opportunity to begin to understand one another at a more personal level. The residential nature of the course and the conditions in the country conspire to involve tutors closely with students. During teaching trips we have attended funerals, visited homes, and lived alongside our students. On visits to hospitals and schools in Zambia what is immediately apparent is the lack of resources: science labs without test tubes; nurses without latex gloves; a place where the chalk-board is common, but chalk is in short supply; where the functioning overhead projector is rare and computers cannot be trusted. Our external examiner reports, for example, often refer to the unreliable nature of technology in Zambia since it is subject to climatic interference, flooding in the rainy season, and stolen cables (Smith 2006). Zambian students continue to study in spite of the threat of being 'laid off' because employers are unwilling to release them from their teaching duties. Students cope with the trauma of dying relatives and friends on a regular basis, and many are badly affected by malaria and symptoms of stress. A number of our students have died from AIDS-related illness. Working in this context has a significant effect on the emotions and maintaining an objective, detached stance is virtually impossible.

A less subjective view of the situation is offered by Whiteside (2002). Drawing on statistics from the United Nations Development Program, Whiteside shows how life expectancy in Zambia has gone down from 48.6 years in 1996 to 41 in 2001. The impact of the HIV/AIDS epidemic, alongside the increase in malaria cases, has increased poverty and left few households untouched. The number of malaria cases has tripled in the past three decades to more than 4 million clinical cases. With 50,000 deaths per year, in a population of less than 11 million people, Zambia's public health system is barely coping. Almost three-quarters of Zambia's population are living in total poverty (Alexander 2006). Yet Zambia still manages to accommodate quite large numbers of refugees from some of its bordering countries, such as Mozambique, Zimbabwe and the Congo.

It is against this background of seemingly immutable problems that this discussion takes place. I wish to proceed with caution, since I am aware that much of this reflective journey runs through contestable ground.

REFLECTIVE PRACTICE AS A VEHICLE FOR EMANCIPATION AND AUTONOMY—ARE WE ON THE RIGHT TRACK?

There is an expectation that teachers' professional developments will include an engagement in reflective practice (Ghaye and Ghaye 1998; Illeris 2002; Bolton 2005). However, we are cautioned by Moon (2005) that reflective thinking and the act of reflection may have different meanings to different people and can be used for different purposes. At the University of Bolton, our approach to professional development is seated in the traditions of experiential learning; our approach emerging from a belief that *systematic reflection* on our own experiences will engage us in a search for new knowledge and that this, in turn, will help to transform our thinking about the ways in which we act and respond to situations (Rodgers 2002). Zeichner and Liston (1996: 56–58) identify four 'traditions' of reflective teaching:

- The *academic tradition*, which promotes improvements in teaching related to ones subject discipline;
- the *social efficiency tradition*, which is 'centred on how closely… practice conforms to standards provided by some aspect of research on teaching';
- the *developmentalist tradition*, which focuses on students and ways to better their understanding of the subject;
- and the *social reconstructivist tradition*, where 'the teacher's attention is focused both inwardly at his or her own practice, and outwardly at the social conditions in which these practices are situated'.

While reflective practice, in one form or another, is now familiar territory for practicing teachers in the UK, it may be true to say that, for novice teachers at least, reflections tend to move between the *academic, social efficiency and developmentalist traditions*; teachers are encouraged to develop their teaching skills and focus their reflection on performance in the classroom. However our professional development module, Research and Reflection for Professional Development (RRPD), attempts to shift thinking towards the *social reconstructivist* mode, which requires students to identify, explain and address those issues that they see as promoting or prohibiting their professional development. While maintaining an individual and personal perspective, there is an implicit expectation that such reflection will have wider benefits for the institution in which our students work.

Reflective thinking, Osterman and Kottkamp (2004: 190) say, 'ultimately enriches the organization's ability to achieve goals'. In other words, there is an assumption that the relationship between the teacher (our student) and the organization is reciprocal: teachers are given autonomy and authority to act on their reflections; organizational standards are raised; and the process is mutually emancipatory so long as the teacher has the trust and the power to enact change. However, the notion of power, its nature, and its limits in relationship to reflective thinking is contested ground (Parker 1997; Harkin 2006; Johnson 1995). While Lipman's (2003: 27) assertion is that teachers 'unquestionably have the capacity to make such changes as need to be made', there are contexts where one's sense of power to realize change is eroded; *outside* issues affect *inside* thinking. Zambia is one such context.

Within this context, the dynamic between reflection, action and professional development needs careful revision. Parker suggests that there is a 'linguistic hegemony' surrounding reflective practice which, he says 'inhibits the potential for an analysis and critique of the reflective process' (1997: 13). Nevertheless, in Western literature, at least, there appears to be general agreement that the reflective process should lead to problem solving, autonomy and emancipation (Ghaye and Ghaye 1998; Illeris 2002; Bolton 2005). In the *social reconstructivist* tradition, we expect to see tangible outcomes and the testing of new-found theories; however, as Fullan (1991: 98) asserts, we must accept the fact that some problems may be unsolvable because 'some social problems in a complex diverse society contain innumerable interacting causes that cannot be fully understood'. If *outside* problems are complex and irreparable then evidence of *inside* thinking, in the form of resolution and transformation, may not be so immediately apparent. Therefore there must be some acceptance of the unfinished, provisional nature of the reflective process and this, clearly, has implications for the way in which we approach teaching and assess professional development.

Outside issues are likely to constrain our ability to accommodate new ideas and ways of thinking. The challenge of deep reflection is to compel us to re-examine our prejudices and preconceptions; we must scrutinize existing ideas and prepare ourselves to think differently, and to do this honestly we must become aware of the way emotions—*inside* issues—shape our thinking. Goleman (1996: 8) suggests that 'two fundamentally different ways of knowing interact to construct our mental life. One, the rational mind, is the mode of comprehension we are typically conscious of: more prominent in awareness, thoughtful, able to ponder and reflect. But alongside that there is another system of knowing: impulsive and powerful, if sometimes illogical—the emotional mind', and while reflective thinking embraces subjectivity and acknowledges the affective domain (Lipman 2003), academic rationality tends to curtail and sanitize expressions of feelings. Lipman (2003: 128) suggests that emotion is regarded with scepticism in academia; it has 'undesirable epistemological status and is considered to have a 'blurring, distorting effect upon one's thinking'. Consequently in RRPD we have paid scant attention to emotions, colluding to provide a detached, de-contextualized and spuriously scientific analysis of *inside thinking*.

It seems that assumptions about the capacity for reflective thinking to bring about social reconstruction or professional development may be unrealistic when placed in the Zambian context. Also, if reflective thinking is determined by our sense of power or, indeed, *real* power to bring about change, and is also constrained by our emotional state, then these must be acknowledged and given due gravitas in the way that we expect to see evidence of reflection, and it is this issue to which we now turn.

ZAMBIA, POST-MODERNITY AND ASSESSING REFLECTIVE WRITING

Reflective thinking and critical thinking may be effective antidotes for dealing with instability and uncertainty in the classroom (Kasl and Elias 2000; Brookfield 2005), but when this becomes an academic activity for professional development in the so-called 'developing' world, it needs further consideration.

Schön (2002: 46) has suggested that professional development in teaching, which is characterized by 'complexity, uncertainty, instability, uniqueness and value-conflict' cannot be addressed by remaining on what he calls the *high, hard ground* of research-based theory and technique. However, students often find themselves in situations where they need, somehow, to prove their academic legitimacy. For those who study outside the host country, legitimacy may mean that the safest place is somewhere on the well-referenced foothills of 'higher and harder ground' even if the terrain here is unfamiliar, infertile and rather arid in terms of meaningfulness. Zambian students have tended to judiciously select issues and dove-tail arguments so that discussion can be grounded in acceptable language and supported with appropriate references to recognized (usually Western) writers and when students do manage to find a range of literature on which to base their analysis, the connections they need to make between their experiences and the literature are often tenuous and convoluted (Moswela 2006). This means that tutor and students conspire to undermine what may be the real issues in their professional development in order to satisfy so-called academic standards, although, according to Serpell (1993), this is not an alien concept to most African students, who are accustomed to the Western model of schooling. A popular coping mechanism is to detach oneself from the situation and present a rather clinical discussion, which suffers from becoming de-contextualized and de-sensitized. We collude in 'emotional amnesia', which is convenient, but erroneous.

The academic, rational imperative of assessment has de-valued emotions and has meant that students have had difficulty in writing with an authentic voice. Relying on Western texts has forced us into colluding to ignore real problems and replace them with issues suitable for academic analysis. The result has been to encourage over-simplistic and de-contextualized reflective writing (Fish and Twinn 1997; Illeris 2002; Lipman 2003). If, as Illeris contends, 'learning ... comprises a cognitive, an emotional and psychodynamic, and a social and societal dimension' (2002: 19), then our approach to engaging students in reflective writing for professional development should reflect this. In the concluding section I will begin to formulate how this can be achieved.

CONCLUSION—FROM INERT ISOLATION TO SHARED DELIBERATION

So far, I have raised concerns about the capacity for reflective thinking to result in tangible outcomes or solve problems. I have suggested that the situation in Zambia reduces teachers' power to bring about change and that we need to find a way to acknowledge and explore our feelings by relinquishing old ideas which place emotions at the lower end of the academic hierarchy. Goleman (1996: 29) suggests that '[t]he old paradigm held an ideal of reason freed of the pull of emotion. The new paradigm urges us to harmonize head and heart'. To do this, Goleman asserts, we need to begin to understand how to use emotion intelligently. Lipman (2003: 20) takes this a step further in his suggestion that education has failed because it is 'guilty of a stupendous category mistake: It confused the refined, finished products of inquiry with the raw, crude initial subject matter of inquiry and tried to get students to learn the solutions rather than investigate the problems and engage in inquiry for themselves'. On the surface, the RRPD module responds well to these criticisms, since it offers the opportunity for students to select and investigate problems and engage in inquiry, but, as I have pointed out, the selection and investigation tends to be somewhat compromised, because of our focus on the *refined, finished end product*—the analytical, well-referenced essay.

If assessment were to focus on the *process* of reflective or critical thinking then we would expect to see evidence of reflexivity combined with an engagement in enquiry that tries 'to penetrate the givens of everyday life to reveal the inequities and oppression that lurk beneath' (Brookfield 2000: 130). In other words, rather than individual reflective contemplation, students should engage critical thinking (Moon 2005). This type of critical exploration is 'inherently communicative' (Brookfield 2005: 250) and relies on 'an emergent collective wisdom that may influence ... ideas and beliefs' (Palmer 1998: 76) and, we now see a model for professional development, which has moved from individual reflection to collective, critical thinking. Huberman also promotes the idea of collegiality for professional development in what he calls an 'open collective cycle'. (See Huberman 1995). In this model, 'outsiders' act to provide supportive consultation in order to guide thinking and introduce new ideas for speculation and debate. From this perspective, my role in RRPD would shift from the existing facilitator position to one of 'supporter', working in a dynamic way to encourage meta-cognition and critical thinking, yet sitting 'towards the edge' of the group. In this respect the group becomes the source of power, they guide and challenge each others reflections through their understanding of the context and cultures that condition their thinking. In terms of cognitive milieu, the group become the experts and the teacher takes on the position of novice or apprentice to the group.

To take this analogy a step further, we could use Lave and Wenger's (1991) descriptions of apprentices' experiences in a community of practice, while bearing in mind the idea that, in this scenario, the *tutor* is the newcomer and the *students* are the 'old-timers'. In other words, the position of the tutor (in this case, myself) moves to the periphery, allowing the students—in this case, the teachers who are undertaking professional development—to determine what communal issues need to be explored. This legitimate periphery means that students must take on the responsibility for determining the nature of their research and this gives them authority and voice. The tutor may make judgments on their reflexivity and their skills in communication, but the students must decide how and on what grounds their success will be measured.

Adopting such a model for RRPD will alter the balance of power between the tutor and the student-group; for the tutor, periphery is legitimate, and the purpose and manner of the tutor's participation becomes reactive, rather than pro-active. However, as Brookfield points out, 'it is disingenuous to pretend that as educators we are the same as students. Better to acknowledge publicly our position of power, and to attempt to model a critical analysis of our own source of authority in front of them' (2000: 137). So, although the position of the tutor remains periph-eral, we must also ensure that it is truly legitimate, since both tutor and students need to be secure in the positions that they will adopt in this 'learning community'. Such a community would have some of the qualities associated with Lipman's *community of enquiry*; the quest for meaning; inclusiveness; shared cognition (see Lipman 2003: 95); and some characteristics of Rogers's *community of learners* where the pur-pose is to 'free curiosity... unleash a sense of enquiry ... open everything to questioning and exploration [and] to recognize that everything is in the process of change' (1983: 120) and may also include some features of Huberman's (1995) *open collective cycle*. Nevertheless, the signifi-cant features of this learning community would be the engagement in critical thinking (Moon 2005; Brookfield 2005; Mezirow 1978) and a demonstrable acceptance of the provisional nature of knowledge. At this stage—and no doubt further review is likely—the following points emerge:

- *Reflective thinking* is a suitable starting point for exploring profes-sional development but, as expectations of deeper reflection move towards critical thinking we would also expect that the complex nature of thinking to be reflected in more provisional and condi-tional conclusions—which may be subjected to further scrutiny.
- *Notions of power and autonomy* need to be critically explored. We know that trauma makes demands on our coping strategies, and that this, in turn, will affect our ways of thinking. A learning community can be endowed with the power to confront academic hegemony and gently challenge erroneous assumptions about pro-fessional and personal development.
- *Theories and hypotheses* about professional development need to emerge from the learning community, rather than being sim-ply 'borrowed' from Western literature. The learning community needs to be given the authority to use existing literature where and when it suits its needs, rather than simply to add weight and valid-ity to its own words. Ideas that emerge from the group are accepted as being provisional and tentative. Both tutor and group members need to work to counter the competitive and combative ethos of assessment and professional development.

Palmer's (1998: 62) words provide an apt warning:

We distort things 'because we are trained neither to voice both sides of an issue nor to listen with both ears. The problem ... is rooted in the fact that we look at the world through analytical lenses. We see everything as this or that, plus or minus, black or white; and we fragment reality into an endless series of *either-ors*. In a phrase we think the world apart'.

By *working as a community*, the individual nature of reflection is, nevertheless, respected and acknowledged. The complex and dynamic relationship between individual and group thinking must be given careful consideration. Students and tutors need to work together to reveal and acknowledge the complex connections between the *outside* and *inside*, the individual and the collective, the interior and the exterior (Wilbur 1996). The role of the tutor is to be part of that community; to move fluidly between the peripheral position of 'cultural apprentice' to the more consultative function of critical friend, but this role is never pivotal: the pace, content and purpose of enquiry all remain the responsibility of the community.

In summary, we must recognize the limited value of individualized reflection for professional development. The concerns that prompted this enquiry began with concerns for students in Zambia, where I began to suspect that the reflective exercise was inappropriate. In the past, there has been collusion between myself and my students in presenting well-referenced, objective accounts which have relied on Western writers for authenticity and validity. My belief is that this has done little to develop either individuals or communities of teachers in that country and that, in trying to present detached and so-called academic accounts, we have avoided an exploration of the emotional impact of poverty and disease on teachers' lives in that country. This account has articulated some of the issues that a transnational perspective has highlighted and has offered ideas about how professional development may look in the future both in Zambia and in the UK. These thoughts are provisional and remain open to scrutiny; certainty is always provisional. In this way, the journey may continue.

NOTES

1. Kincheloe, J. L. (1999) 'The Foundations of Democratic Educational Psychology' in J. L. Kincheloe, S. R. Steinberg, and L. E. Villaverde (eds) *Rethinking Intelligence*, New York: Routledge.

REFERENCES

Alexander, D. (2006) 'Beyond a Learning Society? It is all to be Done Again: Zambia and Zimbabwe', *International Journal of Lifelong Education*, 25, (6). Online. Available at: http:www.tandf.co.uk/journals (accessed 25 September 2006).

Bolton, G. (2005) *Reflective Practice Writing and Professional Development (2nd ed.)*, London: Sage.

Brookfield, S. (2000) 'Transformative Learning as Ideology Critique', in J. Mezirow and Associates *Learning as Transformation*, San Francisco: Jossey-Bass.

—— (2005) The Power of Critical Theory for Adult Learning and Teaching. Maidenhead: Open University Press.

Fish, D. and Twinn, S. (1997) *Quality Clinical Supervision in the Healthcare Professional*. Oxford: Butterworth-Heinemann.

Fullan, M.G. (1991) *The New Meaning of Educational Change*. London: Cassell.

Ghaye, A. and Ghaye, K. (1998) *Teaching and Learning through Critical Reflective Practice*. London: David Fulton.

Goleman, D. (1996) *Emotional Intelligence*. London: Bloomsbury.

Harkin, J. (2006) 'Fragments Stored against My Ruin: The Place of Educational Theory in the Professional Development of Teachers in Further Education', *Journal of Vocational Education and Training*, 57 (2): 165–197.

Huberman, M. (1995) 'Professional Careers and Professional Development' in T.R. Guskey and M. Huberman (eds) *Professional Development in Education*, New York: Teachers College Press.

Illeris, K. (2002) *The Three Dimensions of Learning*. Fredericksburg: Roskilde University Press.

Johnson, R. (1995) 'Two Cheers for the Reflective Practitioner', *Journal of Further and Higher Education*, Autumn, 19 (3): 74–83.

Kasl, E. and Elias, D. (2000) 'Creating New Habits of Mind in Small Groups', in J. Mezirow and Associates, *Learning as Transformation*, San Francisco: Jossey Bass.

Kincheloe, J.L. (1999) 'The Foundations of Democratic Educational Psychology', in J.L. Kincheloe, S.R. Steinberg and L.E. Villaverde (eds) *Rethinking Intelligence*, London: Routledge.

LaBoskey, V.K. (2005)'Capturing the Complexity of Critical Reflection', in C. Mitchell, S. Weber and K. O'Reilly-Scanlon (eds) *Just Who Do We Think We Are?* London: RoutledgeFalmer.

Lave, J. and Wenger, E. (1991) *Situated Learning: Legitimate, Peripheral Participation*. Cambridge: Cambridge University Press.

Lipman, M. (2003) *Thinking in Education*. Cambridge: Cambridge University Press.

Mezirow, J. (1978) 'Perspective Transformation.' *Adult Education* 28 (2): 100–109.

Moon, J. (2005) '*We Seek it Here…*' Bristol: ESCalate HEA.

Moswela, B. (2006) 'Teacher Professional Development for the New School Improvement: Botswana', *International Journal of Lifelong Education*, 25 (6). Online. Available at: http://www.tandf.co.uk/journals (accessed 12 November 2006).

Osterman, K.F. and Kottkamp, R. B. (2004) *Reflective Practice for Educators (2nd ed.)*, Thousand Oaks: Corwin Press.

Palmer, P. J. (1998) *The Courage to Teach*. San Francisco: Jossey Bass.

Parker, S. (1997) *Reflective Teaching in the Post-modern World*. Buckingham: Open University Press.

Rodgers, C. (2002) 'Defining Reflection: Another Look at John Dewey and Reflective Thinking', *Teachers College Record* 104 (4): 842–866.

Rogers, C. (1983) *Freedom to Learn*. New York: Macmillan.

Schön, D. (2002) 'From Technical Rationality to Reflection-in-action.' In R. Harrison, F. Reeve, A. Hanson, and J. Clarke (eds) *Supporting Lifelong Learning* vol. 1, London: RoutledgeFalmer.

Serpell, R. (1993) *The Significance of Schooling. Life Journeys in an African Society*, Cambridge: Cambridge University Press.

Smith, C. (2006) 'Capacity Development and Widening Participation: Is E-learning the Answer? A UK/Zambia Case Study on Alternatives.' *Paper presented at the e-Learning Africa Conference*, Addis Ababa, May 2006.

Whiteside, A. (2002) 'Poverty and HIV/AIDS in Africa', *Third World Quarterly*, 23 (2): 313–32. Online. Available at: http://taylorandfrancis.metapress.com (accessed 4 October 2006).

Wilbur, K. (1996) *A Brief History of Everything*. Dublin: Gill and Macmillan.

Zeichner, K. M. and Liston, D. P. (1996) *Reflective Teaching: An Introduction*. Mahwah, NJ: Erlbaum.

11 Training New Transnational Teachers

A Malaysian Experience

Michael R. Davidson
University of Ulster

Rachel Scudamore
University of Nottingham

Extensive international partnerships, including membership of Universitas 21, and the existence of campuses in Malaysia and China all attest to the University of Nottingham's determination to be a global player in higher education, and a significant contributor to important economies. The University seeks to develop what it calls the 'Nottingham edge' defined as 'an unrivalled combination of quality and excellence, strength and pragmatism, enabled learning, boldness and innovation, respect and tolerance'. Maintaining the integrity of its brand dictates that quality enhancement activities form a central part of its internationalisation process. Important to the teaching and learning process is the embedding of the Postgraduate Certificate in Higher Education (PGCHE), the institution's program for new academics, in campuses out of the UK. This chapter focuses on the ideological, ethical and logistical issues in establishing such grounded staff development programs in cultures not always sympathetic to the initiatives. The pedagogical distinctiveness of the Asian context, and its interface with that of its western European partner in this venture, is briefly explored.

INTRODUCTION: AN EMERGING GLOBAL PLAYER

In April 2006, the University of Nottingham received the Queen's Award for Enterprise, the UK's most prestigious corporate accolade. This recognised its worldwide inter-national recruitment and pioneering campuses in Malaysia and China. Nottingham is the first foreign university in the world to receive a license and to open a campus in China, opened February 2006. Built at a cost of £30m in the Chinese city of Ningbo, enrolments in China are approaching 1,000 students, and are anticipated to increase in two phases to 8,000 before long. Enrolment in Malaysia (opened 2005) currently stands at 1,400 and is expected to rise to 4,000 shortly. Nottingham's total international student population on the three campuses is now more than 8,700—the highest number of any UK university.

By any account the University of Nottingham is set on a bright future as it enters new international markets. But what are the issues for educational developers responsible to support such initiatives? How should the enterprises reflect sound pedagogical principles that are truly 'reciprocal', and therefore respecting, and not subtly imperialistic and plundering? This chapter argues that such ventures as determination to internationalise, by exporting institutional labels, must be underpinned by a robust theory of pedagogy. Such a theory should be capable, on the one hand, of protecting the values and ideals associated with the label being exported, and on the other hand, of respecting and enhancing the host label—'adopter'. It is in the confluence of cultures that teacher and learner bring to the context of learning in these new opportunities, that difference is clarified and similarity acknowledged. Once the differences and similarities have been exposed, both players—the learner and the teacher—face choices in how to progress the interaction. These choices will determine the extent to which learning in such contexts is either liberating or oppressing. Academic staff and educational developers bear a responsibility in clarifying the theory of pedagogy employed by those delivering the educational 'product' in the host country.

Our own roles as educational developers responsible for leading teacher training of new, and probationary academics at both the UK and Malaysian campuses, led us to consider the theoretical foundation of the program being delivered simultaneously in Kuala Lumpur and University Park, Nottingham.

POSTGRADUATE CERTIFICATE IN HIGHER EDUCATION: THEORETICAL UNDERPINNINGS

There is almost two decades of experience that has informed the Learning and Teaching program for new and probationary academics at Nottingham. The Dearing Report, and subsequent emergence of the Institute for Learning and Teaching (ILT), superseded by the present Higher Education Academy (HEA), strengthened early attempts to prepare university teachers. The initial program, the Postgraduate Certificate in Academic Practice (PGCAP) was replaced by the Postgraduate Certificate in Higher Education (PGCHE) in 2001, which indicated a review which moved the program towards an inquiry model, and which valued a critique of theories of learning and teaching more than passing on 'good practice'. The course values notions of critical-interdisciplinarity, social contructivism of knowledge and a negotiated curriculum, in which participants are asked to use their own teaching as a research context for exploring learning and teaching. Participants' learning is supported by collegial groups, or action learning sets, with input from experienced academics. Learning outcomes encourage skills development in a critical context, rather than as a suite of 'competencies' to be mastered.

The newly developed course has some resonance with the three primary generic cognitive areas of human interest differentiated by Habermas (1968)[1]. He described these as being evident in different aspects of social existence: namely work, interaction and power. Thus the course focused on three related sources of information and experience: the 'instrumental' (scientific, cause-and-effect information); the 'communicative' (mutual understanding and social knowledge); and the 'emancipatory' (increased self-awareness and transformation of experience). The links to critical theory were therefore clearly valued by the program designers.

Other and related influences include work by Rowland and Barnett. Rowland's (2000) critique of the notion 'generic', a term that could trivialise the epistemological foundations of disciplines in teaching a 'one-cap-fits-all' approach to improving teaching in the university, is important. This work clarifies the grounds on which critical inter-disciplinary conversations take place, so that players are not initiated into a new 'generic' discipline, but rather develop a critical perspective of their own discipline culture. This work values the opportunities courses such as the PGCHE provide to enquire into university teaching in cross-disciplinary contexts. He (Rowland 2000: 61) sees the stereotypical 'tribal' view of academic life as being challenged in such contexts, 'as people gain a realised awareness of the assumptions associated with teaching in their own discipline, and begin to question these and learn from others'. The context for such inquiry, or 'resources for learning' as he describes it, is not unlike Habermas' 'instrumental', 'communicative', and 'emancipatory' domains. Rowland (2000: 61) describes suitable inquiry contexts as: the 'Public Context' (knowledge from different disciplines); the 'Shared Context' (knowledge of the inquiry process); and the 'Personal Context' (knowledge from different teaching experiences). Further work by Barnett (1997) distinguishing fundamental human interests or domains delineates the objects of critical thinking, and give rise to 'critical being'. These are 'Knowledge' (critical reason), 'Self' (critical self – reflection) and 'the World' (critical action). Barnett (1997: 66) illustrates his notion of critical being through reference to the famous student at Tiananmen Square, who stood up to a line of tanks, a nuance that will take on meaning as this chapter develops.

Clearly the theoretical drift outlined above which was used to define the PGCHE at Nottingham was concerned to clarify the grounds of knowing, the importance of critique and the value and role of inter-disciplinarity, as opposed to developing a 'generic' program. The influence of these theorists, and the nature of a program underpinned by values emanating from their work, becomes important when the program is exported from the UK. There, notions of criticality and critical being are viewed in a way that may not be shared by those in the higher education teaching contexts of non-western countries, such as Malaysia. Yet these are the values and theoretical foundations of the course which was to become formative in training new and probationary academics at Nottingham in Malaysia. How could we be true to our belief in the value of critique, the social construction of knowledge and understanding and the need for dialogue about cultural context, and at the same time virtually impose a course laden with values associated with western liberal education?

In describing these theoretical assumptions and the links associated with this course, it is possible to convey an impression that its content is overly theoretical. In reality, course assessments value the production of practice-based information and inquiry research, informed by theory. It does not value either the reproduction of theoretical information for its own sake, or an understanding of theory, unless applied to practice. This is evidenced in the induction and assessment procedures for the course at University Park in the UK. These take advantage of large cohorts of incoming participants (up to 70 per annum) being invited to attend an introductory event followed by a bi-annual Learning and Teaching Conference. At the conference, existing participants present individual or group projects to live audiences of incoming participants, and at least two experienced academic assessors. This provides a dynamic and realistic environment in which to showcase ideas, debate practical issues, and assess progress on the course. This event follows a two-day introductory event for new participants, and together these events usually mean that new cohorts 'catch' both the course structure and the assessment requirements. This 'mentoring' approach serves the course very well, while underscoring the values of social constructivism, critique, and inquiry. Sustaining this model in smaller institutions outside of the UK is clearly a challenge, if indeed this approach would be appropriate in inter-national settings at all.

DEVELOPING THE PGCHE AT THE UNIVERSITY OF NOTTINGHAM, MALAYSIA

Early experiences of running the PGCHE in Malaysia are instructive in conveying the need to ground such courses in the host culture(s). The University of Nottingham in Malaysia comprises Malay, Chinese, and Indian students, academics, and support staff. There are a sizable number of both ex-patriot academics and (a smaller number of) students adding to the blend. PGCHE events in Malaysia represent the same sort of ethnic mix. It was at one of these occasions, which focused on 'The Reflective Practitioner', that the necessity of grounding such initiatives in host cultural contexts became apparent.

Before me (Davidson) were Malay, Chinese, Indian, Palestinian and ex-patriots from the UK. Our attention was on Barnett's (1997: i) ideas about critical being, illustrated appropriately (I assumed) by the lone Chinese student in Tiananmen Square, facing four tanks in 1989. Our conversation revolved around the words 'critique', 'criticism' and 'critical'. Some speakers appeared to have difficulty in distinguishing between what they considered the pejorative term 'being critical' and the technical notion 'critical being'. It became evident that there were values associated with each notion that took on a meaning quite apart from the processes of analysis, problemetisation and critique, which I had assumed we are all talking about. It occurred to me then that what we were really struggling with in our difficulty to understand one another were different academic literacies, or discourses. These difficulties appeared to be rising from the social and cultural differences among the speakers. Thus the differences were simply that: differences and not deficiencies. Part of my role as facilitator should have been to encourage recognition of these differences, not with the intention of inducing compliance, but rather to encourage acculturation to a point where the notion could be entertained, or challenged and dismissed (Harris[2] 1994: 96). I am not sure that this was accomplished on that occasion. What was clarified through these conversations was that the wholesale transmission of philosophical ideas or pedagogical research expertise and 'good practice', was obviously both inappropriate and unlikely to succeed. What was needed was the creation of spaces in which to contest the issues, values and ideas embedded not only in inter-disciplinary conversations, but also the inter-national concerns of transnational teachers.

A deferential attitude to authority also seemed to hinder the type of interaction that we were seeking to establish. I (Scudamore) found this with a participant's reluctance to negotiate his position (in relation to APEL) after an initial decision that it seemed inappropriate. It became clear later that the participant did not agree with me, but that was not expressed at the time. However, these levels of deference to those perceived as in authority do not seem to be problematic for participants' learning with peers, as much of the course requires. The project presentations were similar in style to those produced by UK-based participants, although they focused on issues of local concern. They showed a use of enquiry and critique, within their own teaching context; in this way the participants were acting as 'critical friends' (Swaffield 2002) in a shared work context. For us, this underlined the value of the enquiry approach over a dissemination of good practice where generic 'good practice' is largely identified in a context very different from that of these academics and their students. The enquiry approach is perhaps more easily transportable into new contexts as its flexibility leaves it open to new interpretations and implementations according to local perceptions of relevant teaching issues.

The case has been made for the professional development of teachers in higher education that decentre the world-views of course participants as a way of encouraging critical interdisciplinarity (Davidson 2004: 305). This means that course participants should be encouraged to look at other disciplines and to explore similarities and differences, from the familiarity of their own disciplinary spaces, and using the critical tools consistent with those disciplines to do so. They are not being asked to join a 'generic' space, and thereby to adopt a new discipline, but simply to stand back from their own disciplinary cultures, in the presence of others, as a way of reflecting, critiquing, enhancing or affirming their own practices as higher education teachers and disciplinary experts. If this was our *modus operandi* in running the PGCHE in the UK, it seemed consistent that such conversations in Malaysia should now embrace not only disciplinary boundaries but also the international boundaries and the tensions, differences and similarities these would bring to the discussion. It became apparent that using the Tiananmen Square photograph was not itself inappropriate as a way of encouraging discussion about the idea of 'critical being', but that expecting others to take on board this image as an illustration of criticality and critical being, with which they could identify, was. Perhaps what should have taken place was a call to identify images that could capture this notion from the various cultural perspectives and values representative of course participants, most likely to convey the same idea, and with similar impact. The challenge to identify such images may well have gone a long way towards establishing the relevance or otherwise of this concept for those coming from backgrounds that did not share the epistemological framework the course was presenting.

There were other ways in which attempts to facilitate appropriate learning contexts seemed initially unable to accommodate the differences bound to surface when exporting a course designed in the UK, to the Asian context. Traditionally the course had required attendance at a four-day introductory event, giving participants a weekend break between the introductory event (Thursday/Friday) and the Learning and Teaching Conference (Monday/Tuesday). Included in the first two days was a presentation skills course, including peer micro-teaching practice requiring peer feedback of videoed micro-teaching, and supervised by an experienced academic. In the early days, there was little infrastructure in Malaysia to offer technical support, and only one video camera available for four groups comprising 25 participants in total. Finding an audience for the conference sometimes induced a feeling of artificiality, although the concept of assessment in conference style was well received. The first two days before the conference also counted on the formation of course participant Learning Sets, which worked on a single group-project and encouraged set members to begin immediately on putting together a group-project proposal. Ideally, Learning Sets were encouraged to consist of six to eight members from a range of disciplines. It was often difficult to sustain the momentum of the Learning Sets, once the course facilitators had left Malaysia to return to the UK. Experience had taught that, logistically, it was difficult to get groups together once the introductory event had passed. The event encouraged a degree of 'bonding' that usually was sufficient to motivate members to continue meeting at least monthly, until the project work had been completed. In Malaysia, however, Friday is a prayer day, and several participants left after midday. This meant that other ways of introducing Learning Sets and recruiting participants for projects had to be found, and thus required the structure of the day to be altered. These experiences underscored the fact that, as facilitators, our planning emphasis for the introduction of the course in Malaysia had been mis-focussed. Our concern for content, and in assuming that the logistics of running the course would be similar on which ever side of the ocean we found ourselves, had led us to neglect the unique features of the participants and Malaysian context. A wise emphasis would have been to focus on such uniqueness, including the personal concern for religious observance, and the complementary processes that would be relevant to their learning, and development in criticality around issues of teaching and learning.

Our intention had been to be open to ideas about how the course might run differently in Malaysia to suit the local context, but this presented its own difficulties. In discussing the aims of the course, it was uncomfortable for both parties to break the expectations of the course participants. Asking them to share opinions of what we, the course team, were asking them to do on the course was in itself problematic with an evident unwillingness to criticise or to offer critique, based on a confusion of these notions. It became clear that 'imperialist' route can seem an easy option when there is little resistance, or apparent willingness to engage with course-design proposals, or where a culture of consensus rather than critique prevails.

Logistical issues relating to working across time-zones and, in preparing for delivering the course in Malaysia at a distance were time-consuming. Video-conference link-ups with the UK were problematic, with staff at University Park arriving exceptionally early in Nottingham, in order to meet course participants in Kuala Lumpur at the end of a busy day, with child-minding needs and, naturally, with one eye on the clock. Being prepared with videoed content may have resolved this to some extent. The fact that funding was linked to project work in the UK, for those who successfully applied for it while the same opportunity was not available in Malaysia, was a de-motivating factor for some participants. Finally, mundane but important issues like co-ordinating venue bookings for Malaysia from the UK, identifying suitable Learning Set Advisors to service Learning Sets on request, and other support structures taken for granted in the UK, was challenging. Ongoing course management issues such as encouraging Learning Set members to keep meeting and working on group project proposals, or supervising corrections required by the Abstract Review Committee (responsible for approving conference project presentations, and meeting in England) all indicated the need for an individual at the University of Nottingham, Malaysia to be responsible for co-ordinating the program in Kuala Lumpur. Building an appropriately supportive network to support the course, in Malaysia, would take several years to accomplish.

The course in Malaysia has now taken on a different shape from that in the UK. The learning outcomes, as expressed in the program specifications, are the same, but the mode of delivery has been adapted to suit the local context, both culturally and practically. The key has been to establish local equivalents of the course management bodies and procedures so that local issues can be central to the course. Much work has been done to make the PGCHE in Nottingham responsive to the concerns and interests of the academic schools and the participants by involving academics in course management and in reviewing project work and assessing portfolios. Establishing the course in Malaysia has included negotiating appropriate equivalents and finding ways to make sure that academics studying the course can still focus on issues that concern them in their own teaching context. There is now a local PGCHE Course team, made up of the more experienced academics, the Chair of which is a member of the PGCHE Management Board (hosted in the UK). We will be using video-conferencing, where possible, to facilitate their inclusion in meetings and discussions of course-wide developments (e.g. to the program specifications). The Malaysia campus PGCHE Course team oversee their own local parallel processes and make their own decisions on, for example, the timing and content of the introductory event and other course elements. The introductory event and conference have been kept as a combined course induction and assessment event, but much of the rest of the course is more structured in timing than is the case at Nottingham. The cultural context encourages a more rigid schedule of deadlines and progression, and the level of support for the course means that this is currently the most practical way to manage what will be a growing number of participants. Participants in Malaysia are expected to complete the full 60 credit course in three years and there is time-tabled support in place to support this. By contrast, in Nottingham, participants are asked to plan a route through the course that best suits their individual needs and their school context. The Malaysia campus Course team ensures that local teaching issues are addressed by recruiting and briefing local Learning Set Advisors, by running their own parallel Abstract Review Committee to oversee project developments, and by co-ordinating and briefing assessors for project presentations and portfolios. Samples of assessments are considered by the Nottingham PGCHE Course team and Exam Board to ensure that the variation in topics studied and in approach does not impact on the ability to meet the shared course learning outcomes as detailed in the Program Specifications for the course.

OUR LEARNINGS: CRITICALITY IN TRANSNATIONAL CONTEXTS

The University of Nottingham's PGCHE has valued the notion of critical-interdiciplinarity as a way of confirming disciplinary identity, whilst encouraging these cultures to enquire into and examine the theoretical underpinnings of their practices. It has thus sought to avoid creating a 'generic' space from which disciplinary specialist must 'migrate' to a new and strange world of higher education research discourse. The context of diversity and difference is therefore essential to the dynamic of challenge and critique the course seeks to offer its participants. A new opportunity and dimension of such diversity, in the transnational context, may not have been immediately apparent when the course was exported to Malaysia. Yet clearly it is this interface between cultures, contexts and practices which has the potential of unlocking greater understanding of how learners learn and teachers teach in the global village universities are helping to create.

REFERENCES

Barnett, R. (1997) *Higher Education: A Critical Business*. Buckingham: Society for research into Higher Education, Open University Press.

Davidson, M. (2004) 'Bones of Contention: Using Self and Story in the Quest to Professionalize Higher Education Teaching—An Inter-disciplinary Approach', *Teaching in Higher Education*, 9 (3), July 2004: 299–310.

Habermas, J. (1968) Knowledge & Human Interest (chapter 3), Cambridge: Polity Press. Online. Available at: http://www.marxists.org/reference/subject/philosophy/works/ge/habermas.htm (accessed 13 March 2007).

Harris, M. (1994) 'Individualised Instruction in Writing Centres: Attending to Cross-Cultural differences', in J. A. Mullin and R. Wallace (eds), *Intersections: Theory and Practice in the Writing Centre*. Urbana, Illinois: NCTE. PA/64/06 (2006) in 'University of Nottingham wins Queen's Award for Enterprise. Online. Available at: http://www.nottingham.ac.uk/public-affairs/pressreleases/index.phtml?menu=pressreleases&code=UNIV-64/06&create_date=21-apr-2006 (accessed 13 March 2007).

Rowland, S. (2000) *The Enquiring University Teacher*. Buckingham, UK: Society for Research into Higher Education Open University Press.

—— (2002) 'Interdisciplinarity as a Site of Contestation'. *Paper delivered at the annual conference of the British Educational Association of Educational Research*, University of Exeter, 12–14 September.

Swaffield, S. (2002) 'Contextualising the Work of the Critical Friend'. *Paper presented at the 15th Inter-national Congress for School Effectiveness and Improvement (ICSEI)*, Copenhagen, 3–6 January.

University of Nottingham. Onlline. Available at: http://www.nottingham.edu.my/about/nottingham_edge.html (accessed 18 October 2007).

12 Teaching for Learning in the Transnational Classroom

Betty Leask
University of South Australia

INTRODUCTION

The transnational classroom is a complex site of intercultural engagement, which provides both opportunities and challenges for teachers. Teekens (2003: 68) has noted the demanding nature of the role of the academic teaching in an international classroom. She suggests that a complex blend of personal qualities, cultural and disciplinary knowledge, language and teaching skills is required. The transnational teaching environment, whilst being a complex and rapidly changing environment (Hudson and Morris 2003: 74) that requires particular types of cultural knowledge and self-awareness (Galvin 2004: 234) and curriculum modification (Gribble and Ziguras 2003: 210), also provides many valuable learning opportunities for lecturers engaged in offshore teaching (Gribble and Ziguras 2003; Leask 2004a). Two of the major challenges for teachers in the transnational classroom are, firstly, identifying the range and balance of knowledge, skills and attitudes they need to develop to be successful transnational teachers and secondly, balancing their own learning with that of their students—understanding and meeting the immediate needs of their transnational students whilst simultaneously developing the knowledge, skills and attitudes that will make them more effective teachers in this environment. This chapter draws on insights provided by two separate research projects conducted in Hong Kong and Singapore in which the expectations of offshore students were explored both directly and indirectly through interviews with staff and students. What both groups had to say provides some insights for staff wishing to respond to the challenges of transnational teaching and has been translated into some practical guidance on teaching for learning in transnational classrooms.

THE RESEARCH

From 2003–2005 two research projects conducted in Australia, Hong Kong and Singapore provided insights into the expectations transnational students had of the knowledge, skills and abilities of their teachers and how these might be developed in academic staff. Literature reviews spanning the internationalisation of higher education, professional development in higher education and transnational teaching and learning were conducted. In the first small study 16 staff and students involved in a business program taught transnationally by an Australian university in partnership with a Hong Kong university were interviewed. This study found that:

- students needed assistance in relating the discipline knowledge presented by Australia-based academic staff to their local context;
- local tutors performed an important role in this;
- there was value in institutions providing formal opportunities for Australia-based transnational teaching staff and staff employed by offshore partner institutions to collaborate with and learn from each other;
- staff working in transnational classrooms needed assistance to critically evaluate their assumptions, stereotypes and prejudices related to teaching and learning and to modify the curriculum and their teaching practices in light of this;
- it is important to focus staff attention on assessment practices in the transnational environment ;
- and there was a need for more research in this area. (Leask 2004a: 394)

The second larger study was funded by Australian Education International (AEI) and administered by the Australian Vice-Chancellors' Committee (AVCC). It was one of 15 university transnational education good practice projects funded in 2005. The research undertaken in this project (commonly and hereinafter referred to as 'the AVCC Offshore Quality Project') provided insights into the specific lecturer characteristics, in addition to discipline knowledge, that were valued in the transnational classroom. In this study questionnaires were sent to more than 100 transnational students and staff and interviews were subsequently conducted with 61 participants in Australia, Hong Kong and Singapore. The literature assisted in the identification of 15 essential characteristics (apart from discipline knowledge) of transnational teachers working with undergraduate and postgraduate programs. These were then tested through the surveys and interviews conducted across a range of disciplines in different locations.

KEY CHARACTERISTICS OF
TRANSNATIONAL TEACHERS

Sixteen key characteristics of transnational teachers were identified in the two projects through the literature reviews and through the surveys and interviews. These characteristics are grouped into four *categories*—discipline knowledge; cultural knowledge; teaching skills, and policy and procedural knowledge—and three *types*: 'universal', 'hybrid', and 'unique'. 'Universal' characteristics are those associated with good teaching in any environment; 'hybrid' characteristics are those which are important in both a home[1]and a transnational classroom but are likely to require new and specific knowledge or skills on the part of the teacher in the transnational classroom; and 'unique' characteristics are those that are important in a transnational classroom but not relevant in a home classroom (Leask, Hicks et al 2005).

The characteristics have been listed according to their category and type in Table 12.1.

The scope of all of the characteristics identified by staff and students involved in the two research studies is broad. The categorization of the characteristics gives an indication of the scope of the challenges associated with transnational teaching. The categories encompass cultural, discipline, and policy knowledge and the teaching skills category incorporates a broad range of skills. Over half of the characteristics are classified as either 'hybrid' or 'unique' and thus provide specific challenges for transnational teaching staff. Only six are classified as 'universal'. All *categories* of characteristics (discipline knowledge, cultural knowledge, teaching skills and policy and procedural knowledge) have either hybrid or unique characteristics associated with them. It can be concluded from this that transnational teaching requires an augmented skill set from 'home' teaching; that the differences between home and transnational teaching are substantial and that they are spread across the entire range of skills and knowledge required of teaching staff. We cannot therefore assume that teachers who are experienced and effective in their home environment will necessarily be so immediately in the transnational classroom.

The research also provided insights into the specific skills, knowledge and abilities required for successful teaching for learning in the transnational classroom. The remainder of this chapter explores the implications of these insights for the curriculum and for the teaching practice of transnational teachers.

MAKING THE CURRICULUM TRANSNATIONAL

The curriculum for the transnational classroom needs to be both internationalized and localized. An internationalized curriculum will develop

Table 12.1 Essential Characteristics of Transnational Teachers

Characteristics by category	Type
Discipline knowledge	
• knowledge of the discipline and related professions in the local context as well as more broadly in an international context	**Hybrid**
Cultural knowledge	
• understanding of local culture(s) including the political, legal and economic environment	**Hybrid**
• understanding of how the teacher's own culture affects the way they think, feel and act	**Hybrid**
• understanding of how culture affects how we interact with others	**Hybrid**
• understanding of social, cultural and educational backgrounds of students	**Hybrid**
Teaching skills	
• the ability to evaluate feedback from students	Universal
• the ability to include local content in the program through examples and case studies	**Hybrid**
• the ability and flexibility to change the teaching approach to achieve different course objectives	Universal
• the ability to adapt learning activities in response to the needs of offshore students	*Unique*
• the ability to use different modes of delivery to assist student learning	Universal
• the ability to provide timely and appropriate feedback on student performance	Universal
• the ability to engage students from different cultural backgrounds in discussion and group work	**Hybrid**
• the ability to reflect on and learn from teaching experiences	Universal
• the ability to communicate with other staff teaching on the program	**Hybrid**
Policy and procedural knowledge	
• understanding of accrediting institution's policies and procedures	Universal
• understanding of the local provider's policies and procedures	*Unique*

and assess specific international perspectives (knowledge, skills and attitudes) through the inclusion of international content and intercultural perspectives on knowledge (Leask 2008). An internationalized curriculum taught in a transnational context must not only recognize the role that culture plays in the construction of knowledge in the discipline and provide students with opportunities to explore the ways in which their own culture and the cultures of others shape knowledge and professional practice internationally, it must do this within the local, transnational context. This is challenging for students and their teachers when the students' local context is not the teachers' local context and the students know the local context better than the teacher does. This is as relevant in the development of generic skills (Hudson and Morris 2003, p. 68) as in the application of discipline knowledge to the local cultural and professional context. Student participants in the research projects described above indicated that it was difficult for them to make the link between the Australia-based-but-internationalized curriculum and their locally based knowledge and practices. Thus they identified an understanding of local cultures and contexts including the political, legal and economic environment, as an important characteristic of the ideal teacher in the transnational classroom.

Teachers in the transnational classroom must be fully informed about the cultural foundations of the discipline-based knowledge and concepts with which they want students to engage. However, they must also understand and be able to talk knowledgably about differences in professional practice in the transnational context in which they are teaching as well as more broadly in the international context. The development of detailed localized case studies to illustrate theories and principles by local partner staff in collaboration with visiting staff is one way of facilitating this. As a starting point the provision of local examples to which students can relate can be provided by teachers in the partner institution. Locally based academic staff have much to contribute to the teaching team and should be treated as full and equal members of this community of professional practice (Leask 2004b).

Suggested strategies

- Develop your own international perspectives through engagement with international contacts in the professional area, including some in the transnational contexts in which you teach. This might include shared planning of curriculum and teaching and learning activities as well as joint research projects.
- Become informed on international issues, standards and practices in the discipline/professional field and how they are interpreted and enacted in the transnational environments in which you teach. You might, for example, source and read journal articles written by academic staff working in the transnational context.
- Seek out and incorporate into the course a range of international as well as local examples and perspectives from the transnational contexts in which you teach. For example, illustrating foundation principles and theories with local examples. Examples are often available in the local media and from local staff.

TEACHING EFFECTIVELY IN THE TRANSNATIONAL CLASSROOM

The transnational teaching environment is a very particular context that requires specific knowledge, skills and abilities. The second research study identified four themes related to teaching practice in the transnational classroom and specific knowledge, skills and abilities associated with each theme. The themes were that transnational teachers needed to be:

- experts in their field;
- skilled teachers and managers of the learning environment;
- efficient intercultural learners;
- and display particular personal attitudes and attributes (Leask et al. 2005).

These themes provide some guidance on the types of strategies transnational teachers can use to become more effective in these unique teaching and learning situations. Strategies to build the knowledge required to be valued as experts in the field in a transnational environment, to manage the transnational learning environment, to assess student progress, to facilitate their own and their students' intercultural learning and to demonstrate positive attitudes to transnational teaching. Students and colleagues are described in the following sections.

BUILDING KNOWLEDGE TO BECOME 'EXPERT IN THE FIELD'

Participants in both research studies indicated that culturally situated and informed disciplinary and professional knowledge is required if teachers are to be regarded as experts in their field in the transnational classroom. Transnational teachers who were able to present both theory and theory-in-practice and incorporate current examples from the local/transnational as well as the international context, and bring similarly focussed research into the classroom, were highly regarded. To be an expert in the field in a transnational classroom clearly requires particular kinds of disciplinary and professional knowledge. This includes an understanding of the local professional context—for example, local attitudes to counselling or engineering or nursing and professional and industry-based restrictions and regulations operating in the local environment. It also requires some understanding of cultural norms and values and the influence these have on those practising the profession in the local context.

Suggested strategies

- Incorporate recent readings in the reading list for the course.
- Get students to locate and review an article relevant to some aspect of the course content in the local newspaper.
- Read about and/or conduct research in the local context.
- Build strong links with local professional organizations and industries by organising visits and meetings while you are 'in country'.
- Attend conferences in the local region in your discipline area.
- Use these links and networks to become informed on local issues influencing professional practice in the discipline and related industries.

MANAGING THE TRANSNATIONAL LEARNING ENVIRONMENT

Participants in the AVCC Offshore Quality Project (Leask, Hicks et al. 2005) indicated the need for flexibility in teaching approach, and skilled and proficient management of the learning environment. As indicated in Table 12.1, many of the teaching skills that were valued in the transnational classroom, such as varying the pace of delivery and making adjustments to the way in which information is structured and presented at short notice depending on the students' initial responses, are those associated with good teaching in any environment and the facilitation of discussion amongst reluctant students in large groups.

A unique challenge for teachers in the transnational classroom is the capacity to make the material being taught interesting to students from a different cultural and educational background to the teacher's own whilst simultaneously catering for the needs of both the strongest and the weakest students in the group, within a very short and intensive teaching period (the teaching model being used was predominantly intensive delivery over a short period followed by support online and from locally employed tutors). Teachers were expected to be able to 'read' and understand the context and student needs, and to tailor their teaching to suit both.

Suggested strategies

- Talk to other staff who have taught in the same location and swap effective teaching and learning management strategies.
- Find out as much as you can about your students before you meet them from staff in the partner institution or other staff in your own institution who have taught the same group.

- Quickly jot down your assumptions of how you think the group will want to learn and therefore what you will do to help them.
- Make time in the curriculum early in the course for students to introduce themselves to you as learners (e.g. an online discussion forum where students introduce themselves to you and tell you how they like to learn, why they are doing the course and what they liked best about the last course they studied). Match this against your expectations. Make adjustments to your teaching as necessary.
- Allow a few minutes for students to write down questions anonymously on a piece of paper and hand to a class representative at a suitable time during the lecture. Read out and answer a selection of these.

ASSESSMENT

Assessment and the requirements around it were, not surprisingly, the focus of much student attention. The ability to explicitly and succinctly communicate roles and expectations around assessment requirements and provide high quality and effective feedback to students on their progress towards achievement of course goals were highly valued by students. This included being able to explain to students where they went wrong and what they needed to do to improve their performance. A related skill was that of maintaining academic standards and being aware of, and taking steps to detect and deter, any form of academic dishonesty.

Suggested strategies

- Get students to tell you, when they hand up a draft assignment, what they would most like comment on and give them that first, before you provide any other relevant comments.
- Always provide explicit information to students on the purpose of the activity before the assessment task is completed: what it is you're testing and the criteria you will use to judge their performance.
- Engage students in both peer- and self-assessment against clearly defined criteria to assist them to understand what is required within particular types of assessment task.
- When providing feedback always tell students what they have done well as well as exactly what they have to do to improve.
- Wherever possible, 'feedforward'—focus feedback on an early assignment on what students will need to do differently in the next assessment task.

INTERCULTURAL LEARNING IN THE
TRANSNATIONAL CLASSROOM

Intercultural learning is at the heart of the transnational classroom—it is what makes everything work. Not only do students need to learn about what is expected of them in a curriculum that was designed in another cultural place, but teaching staff need to be prepared to meet them half way and guide them through the course. Dialogue between staff and students is essential as it 'offers possibilities for building emergent understandings and new frameworks' (Wang 2004: 5) in relation to such things as the roles of teachers and learners, the purposes of learning and the nature of knowledge. Dialogue in the transnational classroom enables teachers and students to become intercultural learners—learning together as they challenge and critique their own and each other's previously tightly held assumptions about learning, teaching and knowledge.

Knight (2003) describes the intercultural as 'relating to the diversity of cultures that exist within countries, communities, and institutions'. Intercultural learning and engagement is not, however, an easy thing to achieve as 'communicating and interacting with culturally different others is psychologically intense' and has several risk factors associated with it, including risk of embarrassment and risk of failure (Paige 1993: 13). Transnational teachers who encourage and enable dialogue in the transnational classroom while being critically engaged and reflective about the interactions and communications they have with their students and with local tutors are effectively engaging in intercultural learning. They will develop their understandings of how the languages and cultures of their students influence their behaviour and their learning. They will also come to a deeper understanding of how their own linguistic and cultural background influences their teaching and the sorts of adjustment they may need to make to their teaching in order to be effective teachers in the transnational classroom. This is, however, complex and challenging because it involves students and staff moving into a 'third place' (Crozet, Liddicoat et al. 1999: 13) a meeting place between different cultures where there is recognition of the manifestation of cultural difference and where equal and meaningful reconstructive cross-cultural dialogue can occur. For the visiting academics who are the cultural outsiders in the transnational classroom it may be the first time that their own 'taken for granted culture becomes visible to them or they realize that other people hold stereotypes and prejudices about them' (Stier 2003: 80). The imperative to work towards intercultural understanding is therefore very strong. The result, however, may be the 'cross-fertilization' of 'different cultures of learning and teaching' (Kalantzis and Cope 2000: 42) and the discovery of new ways to approach teaching and stimulate learning in the transnational classroom.

Indeed, Australia-based staff interviewed in the first research project indicated that transnational teaching had, in some way or another, changed them as teachers. They saw the experience as 'transformative'. The following statement summarizes their perspectives:

> ... [I]t (offshore teaching) has completely shifted my assumptions of what people will want to hear, need to know, about these sorts of things ... I try and start with a baseline of what's appropriate here, what do you want. To actually shift it from being what I thought they needed, to what they really need ... I think it changes your whole perception of yourself as a lecturer. (Leask 2005 Research Report 3: 62)

These staff, who taught regularly as 'others' in an 'other' cultural context, had had their long-held views of teaching and learning challenged. Transnational teaching provides both the imperative and the opportunity for teachers to develop as intercultural learners. The importance of cultural knowledge and awareness in both students and teachers in the transnational classroom is much more obvious than it is in the home classroom.

Transnational teachers need to be able to adjust quickly to the local teaching and learning context, to manage the demands and challenges it presents and to connect with the students and the staff with whom they are working. Thus they need to listen to and learn from students and other local sources about the effects of their teaching in that particular context. This requires recognition that they are the 'strangers in a strange land'; that because of who they are 'culturally' and who the students are 'culturally', there is a higher likelihood of misunderstanding and miscommunication in this intercultural space than at home. Transnational teachers need to be willing and able to adjust their teaching, to do things differently in some situations, in order to assist students to achieve the outcomes of the program of study. They also need to be willing to, and be given opportunities to, connect with and learn from the local tutors while assisting the local tutors to learn more about the cultural background of the program of study.

Suggested strategies

- Require critical refection on and discussion of how personal attitudes and values are shaped and reflect cultural values.
- Encourage investigation of how cultural values are reflected in discipline-based knowledge and professional practices.
- Encourage students to communicate, explore, explain, inquire and negotiate meaning across cultures.
- Use a wide variety of teaching and learning activities which have been carefully selected and constructed for the transnational

classroom, and encourage students to engage with the cultural foundations of knowledge with each other and with you.

- Treat the teaching session as an opportunity to learn about your students and for them to learn about how to meet your expectations.
- Show the students you are enthusiastic about teaching and keen to know what they thought of the session by getting them to complete an anonymous ' minute paper' at the end of each session asking them what they liked most about the session, the clearest part of it and any things they didn't understand. Use their responses to assist in planning the content and approach of the next session or as the basis for an online Frequently Asked Questions Noticeboard or global email specifically focussed on clarifying areas students have identified as problematic in their minute papers.
- Make time to meet with local tutors and students to discuss aspects of culture, teaching and learning and what these mean in the context of the teaching program.
- Focus on both 'what is taught and learned' (that is, on both content and outcomes) and 'how it is taught and learned' (that is, on what both teachers and learners do).

CONCLUSION

Teaching for learning in the transnational classroom is both similar to and different from any other form of teaching activity. The curriculum for the transnational classroom needs to be both internationalized and localized. Transnational teachers must not only have the skills, knowledge and abilities identified with good teaching in any context, but they must have an understanding of the local transnational cultural, educational and professional environments, be effective intercultural learners and be energetic, and enthusiastic about transnational teaching. Transnational teaching provides unique challenges. The fundamental differences between home and transnational teaching relate to the intercultural space in which the teaching and learning occurs and the importance of building relationships within and beyond the classroom in this context should not be underestimated. Transnational teachers need particular skills, knowledge, and attitudes in order to be successful in this complex and demanding space.

NOTE

1. A home classroom being that for which the curriculum was originally designed and in which the teacher is at home, as distinct from the transnational classroom where the students are at home and the teacher and the curriculum is not.

REFERENCES

Crozet, C., Liddicoat, A. J., and LoBianco, A.J. (1999) 'Intercultural Competence: From Language Policy to Language Education'. *Striving for the Third Place: Intercultural Competence through Language Education.* Canberra: Language Australia.

Galvin, P. (2004) 'Success with Offshore DBAs: Experiences from Hong Kong and Thailand.' *International Journal of Organisational Behaviour* 7 (7): 431–439.

Gribble, K. and Ziguras, C. (2003) 'Learning to Teach Offshore'. *Higher Education Research and Development* 22 (2): 205–215.

Hudson, W. and Morris, S. (2003) 'University Teaching and International Education' in S. Eisenchlas and S. Trevaskes (eds) *Australian Perspectives on Internationalising Education*, 65–74, Melbourne: Language Australia.

Kalantzis, M. and Cope, B. (2000) 'Towards an Inclusive and International Higher Education', in R. King, D. Hill and B. Hemmings (eds) *University and Diversity: Changing Perspectives, Policies and Practices in Australia, 30–53*, Wagga Wagga: Keon Publications.

Knight, J. (2003) 'Updating the Definition of Internationalization'. *International Higher Education*, Boston: Centre for International Higher Education, Boston College.

Leask, B. (2004a) 'Discursive Constructions of Internationalisation at an Australian University—Implications for Professional Practice'. *School of Education.* Adelaide: University of South Australia.

—— (2004b) 'Transnational Education and Intercultural Learning: Reconstructing the Offshore Teaching Team to Enhance Internationalisation'. Paper presented at the *Australian Universities Quality Forum*, Adelaide: S.A., Australian Universities Quality Agency.

—— (2005) 'Discursive Constructions of Internationalisation at an Australian University—Implications for Professional Practice'. Unpublished PhD thesis, *School of Education.* Adelaide: University of South Australia.

—— (2008) 'Internationalisation, Globalisation and Curriculum Innovation' in Reed, A. and Hellsten, M. (eds) *Researching International Pedagogies: Sustainable Practice for Teaching and Learning in Higher Education*, Netherlands: Spinger.

Leask, B., Hicks, M., Kohler, M. and King, B. (2005) *AVCC Offshore Quality Project— A Professional Development Framework for Academic Staff Teaching Australian Programs Offshore*, 72, Adelaide: University of South Australia.

Paige, M. R. (1993) 'On the nature of intercultural experiences and intercultural education', in M. R. Paige and R. Yarmouth (eds) *Education for the Intercultural Experience*, 1–20 Yarmouth, Maine, Intercultural Press.

Stier, J. (2003) 'Internationalisation, Ethnic Diversity and the Acquisition of Intercultural Competencies', *Intercultural Education* 14 (1): 77–91.

Teekens, H. (2003) 'The Requirement to Develop Specific Skills for Teaching in an International Setting', *Journal of Studies in International Education* 7 (10): 108–119.

Wang, T. (2004) *Understanding Chinese Educational Leaders Conceptions in an International Education Context.* Melbourne: Australian Association for Research in Education International Educational Research Conference.

Part III

Perspectives on Learning

13 Student Perceptions of the Internationalisation of the Undergraduate Curriculum

Craig Zimitat
University of Tasmania

INTRODUCTION

Developments in the internationalisation of higher education have accelerated noticeably during the last three decades. Internationalisation by universities reflects institutional responses to globalization (Knight 2004) and can be considered as an economical imperative as much as it is a lofty ideal. However, not all institutions share the same view or regard internationalisation as a 'whole of institution' imperative, or a risk-free venture (Knight 2007). Today the term applies to a range of activities—the flow of staff and students across national borders in international and transnational programs, curriculum extension and renewal, mechanisms for maintaining academic standards and quality assurance, the development of regional agreements for the recognition of higher education programs, and alliances for advancement of research (Hamilton 1997). Ultimately, the underlying reasons for internationalisation of universities relate to relevance and survival.

The extent and intensity of internationalisation strategies at an institution depend on its mission, self-perception regarding its aspirations, and its position within the global higher education market. Some elite institutions (e.g., Harvard and Oxford) can stand alone in the international market; however, many institutions are forming international consortia (e.g., Universitas 21), or domestic consortia, to compete cooperatively on the international scene. Almost all US universities have offices that support and recruit international students and support study abroad programs (Green 2005a, 2005b; Green and Siaya 2005). Most of the top research universities in the US include international education as part of their mission and as a key strategic priority (Green 2005b), and have internal internationalisation committees to oversee institutional activities and monitor their efforts to internationalize the curriculum. These institutions have also made significant commitments to faculty development on- and off-campus for internationalisation (e.g., by providing support for conferences abroad, leadership for study abroad tours, or including international activities as part of tenure and promotion processes), whereas comprehensive universities and liberal arts colleges have been less likely to offer off-campus opportunities (Green and Siaya 2005; Green 2005a). On the basis of their work, it can be seen that, generally, the higher the profile of the institution, the greater likelihood that internationalisation is a key element of every dimension of its operations.

The literature on the internationalisation of higher education curricula focuses very much on outcomes or processes. At one level, it discusses institutional processes—strategies for internationalisation, such as student exchanges or studies abroad. At another level, it ensures that national/domestic students are better prepared through their learning experiences for participation in global employment contexts. Offering an internationalised curricula best prepares domestic, international and transnational students for successful participation in the global workforce (Smart *et al* 2000) and many universities identify graduate attributes to this end. Even if domestic graduates never leave their own country, on graduation they will be forced to compete in international, or multi-national, work and discovery environments. Today it is almost impossible to avoid these influences. For all students to be successful they need at least an international awareness; some will require a demonstrated ability to work in cross-cultural or international contexts, and others will require international expertise in specific matters involving other cultures and countries. However, the mechanisms by which universities achieve their preparation of students for international study and employment in the global marketplace are not well elaborated in the literature. In the literature, there is an overemphasis on isolated, bolt-on initiatives (i.e., staff and student exchanges, study tours, multicultural days) that are not scalable, integrated with other strategies, or likely to sufficiently infuse a curriculum to achieve an educational impact on all graduates.

In this paper the focus is on the various dimensions of internationalisation evident in a curriculum. The survey that is reported here was undertaken mid-way through an internationalisation of the curriculum project. This range of characteristics of an international curriculum and student orientations were used as a focus for exploring first-, second-, and third-year students' experiences and perceptions of different dimensions of internationalisation of their curriculum and as a mechanism for benchmarking for further development in this area, as well as identifying good practice.

METHODS

Details of students' experiences of their course and their opinions on internationalisation of the curriculum were collected using a survey conducted within the regular cycle of university evaluations and surveys.

The survey was conducted using www.SurveyMaker.com.au, a website that generates online surveys with a range of automated email and reporting features. The questionnaire was voluntary and administered in closed, confidential mode, hence all students had to explicitly provide consent to participate in the study upon access to the survey. The surveys were approved by the university's Research Ethics Committee. Students who were invited to complete this survey included all first-year students enrolled at the institution (n = 6,600), together with those second- (n = 1,560) and third-year (n = 1,780) students who had completed previous first-year surveys at university.

Curriculum internationalisation was measured using a series of 14 questions assessing curriculum content, teaching methods, perceptions of teachers and campus environment, a self-assessment of personal skill development, and the extent to which their degree program had prepared them for working in an international environment. The questions were presented with accompanying response categories on a five-point Likert scale ranging from Strongly Disagree, Disagree, Uncertain and Agree, to Strongly Agree. Survey data were combined with data from the university administration and coded before analysis.

RESULTS

Cases with less than 90 per cent complete data were removed from the dataset, leaving a total of 838 complete third-year, 1,029 complete second-year and 920 complete first-year data sets for analysis. This represented 2,787 responses from a total survey population of 9,940 (28 per cent). The respondent group consisted of 66 per cent females, 65 per cent under 25 years of age, 73 per cent Australian-born students, 14 per cent fee-paying international students, and 18 per cent were from non-English speaking backgrounds. Students were enrolled in one of four broad academic groups at the institution: Business (N = 812), Arts, Education and Law (n= 996), Science and Engineering (n = 495), or Health (n = 467). The proportion of students from each campus was consistent with campus enrolments and there was roughly equal representation from the three broad academic groups.

Overall student perceptions and experiences

The responses from all students regarding their perceptions of various dimensions of internationalisation in their university experiences are illustrated in Table 13.1. Overall, just half of students believed that their studies at university were preparing them to work effectively in overseas countries/international contexts. Whilst half of students agreed that the content in their courses was illustrated with examples drawn from

Table 13.1 Students' Perceptions of International Dimensions in Their Curriculum and Campus Environment. (n = 2787). Five point scale collapsed to three points. % Percentage of respondents.

	Disagreement %	Neutral %	Agreement %
Curriculum, Teaching and Learning			
The content in my courses is often illustrated with examples from, or applied to a range of cultural and international situations.	21	30	49
The content of my courses is presented from a range of different cultural and international perspectives.	39	36	25
I would prefer to study more about international issues than focus on Australian issues. (Reversed)	30	33	37
Assessment tasks in my courses are framed in international scenarios or require me to apply course materials or concepts to different cultural or international situations.	26	26	48
In my courses, we have been given a good introduction on how to work effectively in cross-cultural groups.	27	32	41
Group work in my courses provides a real opportunity to learn about different cultures and gain different perspectives about my area of study.	32	34	34
The teachers in my courses appear to have a deep understanding of how my discipline or profession operates in different cultures and countries around the world.	32	26	42
In my courses this year I have become aware of how culture, religion and values have influenced, or shaped my area of study.	28	26	46
I am aware of, or have had, the opportunity to include courses on language studies, country or culture studies or study overseas as part of my degree program.	20	25	55
Campus			
Socializing with students from other cultures/countries is part of my daily campus life.	15	30	55

	Disagreement %	Neutral %	Agreement %
The social environment on campus enables me to gain an understanding of different cultural and international perspectives of the world.	13	30	57
Personal Orientations			
I believe that my future depends on understanding international perspectives of my discipline.	19	29	52
I take every opportunity available to broaden my understandings and respect of different cultures, religions and other countries.	26	34	40
Overall Perception			
I believe that my studies at University are giving me the necessary content knowledge, skills and perspectives to work effectively in overseas countries /international contexts.	19	29	52

Note: Disagreement = Disagree + Strongly Disagree; Agreement = Strongly Agree + Agree.

different cultures or countries, only a quarter of students agreed that the subject matter was presented from a range of perspectives. Just over one third of all students perceived that assessment was framed in, or required them to apply their learning to, different cultural or international situations.

Working effectively in cross-cultural groups was appropriately introduced to less than half of students. A slightly greater proportion of students perceived group work as a good vehicle for developing cross-cultural perspectives. Just over 40 per cent of all students believed both that they did not have an adequate introduction to group work and that it was an ineffective approach to hearing different perspectives on, or learning about, other cultures. There was a moderate correlation ($r = 0.367$, $p < 0.01$) between preparation for group work and positive outcomes from group work. Nearly half of all students agreed that their teachers had a deep understanding of how the discipline or profession operated in various countries around the world; whilst nearly a third did not share this perception. Student awareness of opportunities for country or language studies, or study abroad was variable, with roughly one half of students either unaware or unsure of the possibilities.

More than half of students agreed that the social environment on campus enabled them to interact with international students or students from other cultural groups to develop deeper cross-cultural understandings. There was a strong correlation between regular socializing with a diversity of students and development of international perspectives ($r = 0.47, p < 0.01$). On a personal level, many students (57 per cent) indicated a belief that their future depended upon an understanding of different international perspectives of their own discipline and that they took opportunities to develop their understanding of different perspectives. The correlation between beliefs about the importance of international perspectives and taking opportunities to develop those perspectives was also strong ($r = 0.442, p < 0.01$).

Student perceptions and experiences by year in course

There were significant differences in perceptions and experiences of internationalisation based upon year of study. First-year students were less likely than later-year students to perceive a range of perspectives illustrated or referred to in course material, or to view their teachers as understanding the international dimensions of their profession, although they reported a significantly greater amount of assessment requiring application of learning to new contexts and a stronger desire to learn about international issues. First years were more likely than later-year students to report socializing with a diverse group of students on campus and to perceive the on-campus environment as one that facilitated that process. First-year students reported a significantly greater awareness of how culture, religion and values shape disciplinary knowledge than later-year students. In terms of overall outcome, first-year students were significantly less likely than second-year students, who in turn were significantly less likely than third-year students, to believe that their university studies were adequately preparing them to operate on the global scene.

Student perceptions and experiences by academic group

There were significant differences in perceptions of internationalisation amongst students from the four different academic groups. Overall, Business students reported significantly more positive views and Science and Engineering students reported the least positive views of internationalisation of the curriculum and campus environment. Business students also reported significantly more positive perceptions that their studies at university were preparing them for work in international contexts than students in any other group In terms of personal orientations to internationalisation, Health, and Science and Engineering students, compared with Arts, Education and Law, and Business students, were significantly less inclined to take opportunities to interact with individuals from diverse backgrounds and did not see an understanding of the international dimensions of their discipline as important to their future. These personal orientations were consistent with social interactions with international students on campus. The Health, and Science and Engineering students also held significantly less positive perceptions of the usefulness of the social life on campus in fostering cross-cultural interaction and reported lower levels of interaction with students from other countries or cultures.

Internationalisation of the curriculum was generally seen most positively by Business students, compared with Arts, Education and Law students, Health students and Science and Engineering students. There were significant differences amongst students from all four Academic Groups in terms of teachers' use of examples or applications of concepts to different international or cultural groups in the curriculum. Business and Law students had a significantly more positive sense than Arts and Education, or Health and Sciences students that the content in their courses was presented from a range of perspectives. These significant differences were reflected in students' views on assessment in their courses and on the extent to which they had become aware of how their discipline (or profession) has been shaped by culture, religion, and other countries. In terms of the international content in courses, Health, and Science and Engineering students indicated a preference for focusing on more Australian material in their course that was generally consistent with their personal international orientation. The introduction to group work and use of group work as a vehicle for developing cross-cultural understanding was seen most positively by Business and Arts, Education and Law students, compared with those from Health, or Science and Engineering. Students from all four Academic Groups at the institution expressed similar views on their teachers' understanding of how the profession or discipline operates internationally.

Perceptions of domestic and international students

Overall, compared with domestic students, international students reported more positive perceptions of social climate and personal orientations to internationalisation than domestic students, and they reported significantly less positive perceptions of the adequacy of preparation for group work and of their teachers' understanding of how the profession operates on an international level. They reported greater awareness of how culture, religion, and values shape knowledge in their discipline area than domestic students. On campus, international students reported a more positive view of the social environment on campus, and significantly greater social interaction with other international students, than domestic students. Overall, international students were more positive than domestic students in their perceptions of how university was preparing them for employment on an international level.

DISCUSSION

There were three significant findings arising from this study. First, nearly half of all students recognized international dimensions of their curriculum and university experiences. Second, there were significant differences in perceptions, orientations and experiences between years, between different academic groups, and between domestic and international students. Third, there were correlations between beliefs about internationalisation and related behaviours.

Internationalisation of the curriculum

International elements within the curriculum were generally identified by less than half of students surveyed. The least positive responses related to group work, whilst the most positive responses related to social interactions on campus and general overall perception of the contributions of study for preparation to work in a global community. It may be the case that courses surveyed did contain some international dimension; however, it may not have been explicitly referred to by teachers, or drawn upon in the course as a focus for learning (i.e., considered optional). Student confusion about whether international examples or perspectives were core or peripheral to the subject matter may have contributed to the significant proportion that indicated that they neither agreed nor disagreed with the statements. There was no majority view regarding a need for an increased focus on international issues in courses, and this no doubt reflects the diversity of courses in which students in these surveys were enrolled. Only one fifth of students indicated that their studies at university were not advancing their knowledge and skills necessary for working abroad or in international contexts.

It needs to be considered that this survey is a snapshot across the institution revealing a general pattern of internationalisation across courses and years of the undergraduate curriculum. Whilst the data suggest that only half of courses have international dimensions, and a high proportion of students across all years do not perceive any international dimension in their curriculum, it does not comment on the extent to which internationalisation is developed horizontally, or vertically, within any one specific degree program. A broader survey and audit of course outlines within programs will be necessary to address these issues. Some of the differences between students on the basis of year of study and domestic/international status need to be examined to determine factors underpinning their viewpoints and experiences, and whether the questions in the survey adequately capture all international dimensions of curricula.

Differences between years

First-year students' responses to questions were generally less positive than those of either second- or third-year students. This may reflect the general nature of first-year courses, though first-year courses arguably should lay the foundations for developing relevant skills and global perspectives of their discipline and profession. The differences in international orientations between first-year and later students, if confirmed in subsequent research, may provide supporting evidence for tailoring of advertising and marketing of exchange and study abroad programs. It would also be useful to see how students' perceptions change during their academic career.

Differences between academic groups

There were significant differences in terms of curriculum content, and preparation and effectiveness of group work amongst students from the four Academic Groups. Business (first) and Arts, Education and Law were seen as the two groups offering the most international curriculum. Students in these groups reported greater social interactions across cultures and stronger international orientations and aspirations, perhaps reflecting the large numbers of international students in these programs. They also reported the most positive perception about the preparation that university study was giving them for working in a global environment. Whilst some degree programs and courses may be considered inherently international (e.g. International Business, Public Health, Environmental Science), and may require little change, in other courses international perspectives may be present, but require more explicit reference and development within the curriculum. This may be the case in the pure and applied sciences (Cronin *et al* 1999; Becher 1989) where the degrees are often internationally recognized (or accredited). Whilst there is some support for the argument that 'science is international' by its very nature, clearly students do not seem aware of, nor share these perceptions. Of course, internationalizing curricula is not just about content, it also requires changes in pedagogy to encourage students to develop critical skills to understand forces shaping their discipline and challenge accepted viewpoints. There is considerable room for improvement in these discipline areas, at least in making explicit the international dimensions of their courses. However, a logical starting point is the development of a philosophy or framework for internationalisation of their curricula.

Differences between domestic and international students

There were significant differences between domestic and international students on almost all dimensions of internationalisation, except their recognition of group work as a positive strategy for developing cross-cultural skills and awareness. Overall, there appears to be a relative failure of domestic students to gain the most out of the diverse student population in class, and on campus, compared with international students. The foundations of this may be obvious, but need to be confirmed—international students enrol in transnational programs to gain skills for success in a global employment market, whereas domestic students are less focused on international goals.

Group work

Group work, whether used formally or informally, has always been an important vehicle for learning. Today, group work is often used as a strategy for managing large classes, as well as developing team work skills necessary for employment. About half of all students agreed that they had a good introduction on how to work effectively in cross-cultural groups, with less than one-fifth disagreeing with the statement. First-year students responded significantly less positively than others to the question about preparation for effective group work. This might reflect the large class sizes typical of first year in Australia (200–700 students) and the difficulty in building such activities into curricula. International students also responded significantly more positively to this question than domestic students, which may reflect their personal goals to interact with domestic, native English-speaking peers, their previous membership of collectivist societies, or, perhaps, targeted support for them in particular courses.

Preparing students for cross-cultural group work was positively correlated with the development of cross-cultural perspectives. Thus, as the explicit preparation for successful group work, cross-cultural communication skill development exercises should be considered when planning for better group work outcomes. Significantly, nearly one third of students believed their group work experiences were ineffective in developing these understandings. Simply putting students in cross-cultural groups is insufficient for developing necessary team work or intercultural skills (Nesdale and Todd 1993), and the absence of guidance or strategies to resolve conflict may do more harm than good. There is some suggestion that, although students are willing to work in cross-cultural groups, they find the time for establishing common ground too time-consuming, and many students would not choose to work in cross-cultural groups again, given the choice (Cronin *et al* 1999).

Socializing on campus

There were significant differences in students' perceptions of the social climate on campus, based upon academic group, and domestic/international status. Of greatest significance here is the relative failure of domestic students to gain the most from the diverse student population in class, and on campus. International students often express dissatisfaction with the level of interaction with local students (Australian Education International 2002), though one suspects there is perhaps equal dissatisfaction from local students regarding their desired level of interaction with international students (Daly and Brown 2004). These reciprocal perceptions no doubt relate, in part, to equally poor understandings of each other's culture and appropriate ways to communicate (Mak *et al* 1999). Many international students lack confidence in starting and maintaining social conversations, whilst domestic students may have too many other commitments (Krause *et al* 2005) to adequately commit sufficient effort and time to such interactions. There is room for improvement in facilitating social interactions amongst students from diverse backgrounds, as nearly 20 per cent of students responded negatively to the socialization questions and nearly 30 per cent of students offered neutral responses. Developing students' cross-cultural communication skills in group work situations will help improve these social interactions, as would the use of buddy-mentor programs. Inter-cultural communication workshops (such as the Excel program—Mak *et al* 1999) have the potential to improve the inter-cultural competencies of all participants and enhance social interaction across the board. Too often these programs are seen by domestic students as optional or marginal to campus life, whereas they have as much to gain as other participants in improving the social climate on campus.

CONCLUSIONS

Internationalisation of the curriculum is a response to globalization and is seen as a priority by universities that wish to make and maintain their reputation in the world. This study is the first at university level in Australia to explore students' perceptions of the international dimensions of their curriculum and campus experiences. There is scope for further work to develop the instrument, understand the basis for reported perceptions, and then to respond through curricular reform. Internationalisation philosophy and strategy ought to be articulated and situated within the overall institutional strategic plan, and explicitly addressed in curriculum development and monitoring processes. This research represents the beginning of a monitoring process and shows that international students are gaining the most from their university studies in terms of preparation and competition within the global workforce. More work needs to be done to ensure that internationalisation works for the benefit of all students. The good news is that many students are interested in gaining international perspectives of their disciplines, they do experience international dimensions in their studies, and they believe that the courses they are studying at university are preparing them for successful participation in a global workforce, and a globalized society.

ACKNOWLEDGMENT

I would like to acknowledge the contribution of our students to this work, as well as the constructive feedback received and input from colleagues MB and RGC.

Development of www.SurveyMaker.com.au was funded by a Griffith University Quality Grant, and the Griffith Institute for Higher Education.

REFERENCES

Australian Education International (2002) 'How international students view their Australian experience: A survey of international students who completed a course of study in 1999.' Canberra: DEST.

Becher, T. (1989) 'Academic tribes and territories. Intellectual enquiry and the cultures of disciplines.' Bury St Edmonds: Society for Research into Higher Education.

Cronin, C., Foster, M., and Lister, E. (1999) 'SET for the future: Working towards inclusive science, engineering and technology curricula in higher education.' *Studies in Higher Education*, 24: 165–181.

Daly, A. and Brown, J. C. (2004) 'New Zealand students' international competencies and co- and cross-ethnic interactions.' *4th Annual Hawaii International Conference on Business*. Hawaii.

De Wit, H. E. (1995) 'Strategies for internationalization of Higher Education: a comparative study of Australia, Canada, Europe and the United States of America.' In De Wit, H. E. (ed.) *Strategies for internationalization of Higher Education*, Amsterdam: EAIE.

Green, M. F. (2005a) *Measuring internationalization at Comprehensive Universities*. Washington, DC: American Council on Education.

Green, M. F. (2005b) *Measuring internationalization at Research Universities*. Washington, DC: American Council on Education.

Green, M. F. and Siaya, L. (2005) 'Measuring internationalization at Liberal Arts Colleges.' Washington, DC: Centre for Institutional and International Initiatives, American Council of Education.

Hamilton, S. (1997) 'Policy implications for Australian universities in the economic development enhancement role.' *Paper given at American-Australian Conference on Strengthening Post-Secondary Education's Contribution to Economic Development*, Sydney.

Knight, J. (2004) 'Internationalization of higher education practices and priorities.' 2003 IAU Survey Report. Paris: International Association of Universities.

Knight, J. (2007) 'Internationalization brings benefits and risks: Survey results.' *International Higher Education*, 46: 8–9.

Krause, K., Hartley, R., James, R. and McInnis, C. (2005) *The first year experience in Australian universities: Findings from a decade of national studies.* Melbourne: Centre for the Study of Higher Education, University of Melbourne.

Mak, A., Westwood, P. J., Barker, M. and Ishiyama, F. I. (1999) 'Developing sociocultural competencies for success among international students. The Excel program.' *Journal of International Education,* 9: 33–38.

Nesdale, D. and Todd, P. (1993) 'Internationalising Australian universities: The intercultural contact issue.' *Journal of Tertiary Education Administration,* 15: 189–201.

Smart, D., Volet, S. and Ang, G. (2000) *Fostering social cohesion in universities: Bridging the cultural divide.* Canberra: Department of Education Training and Youth Affairs.

14 International Outcomes through Groupwork in Transnational Higher Education

Maureen Bell

University of Wollongong

Lois Smith and Lejla Vrazalic

University of Wollongong, Dubai

Over here it's nice because everyone is different.

UAE student from Africa

Dubai is a city of skyscrapers, some fantastically shaped as waves or sails rising through the haze from the desert floor. Artificial waterways bring the ocean into the desert forming marinas, lakes and canals for acres of new waterfront properties. Offshore islands appear in shapes of palm trees and crescent moons. Giant desalination plants supply inland lakes for housing developments set amidst manicured green lawns and cascading fountains. Walking across the university campus past the neat sandstone buildings, it is only the sandstorm that reminds one of the remarkable fact that in 1970 the United Arab Emirates did not yet exist. Here were the sheikhdoms on the Gulfs of Arabia and Oman, a harsh and arid environment of Bedouin groups and fishing villages.

The United Arab Emirates (UAE) is a federation of 7 emirates formed in 1971. The population is approximately 4 million, however only 20.1 per cent are UAE citizens (Interact 2006). Other residents are from a range of countries such as Lebanon, Palestine, Egypt, Oman, Pakistan, India, Iran, and the Philippines; and Western European nations. By 1999 the United Nations Human Development Index had placed the UAE as the fourth most developed of the Arab states (UAE 2006). The UAE is fast becoming the tourism and economic/business hub of the Gulf region.

In Dubai it is possible to step from the 45°C heat of the desert onto a chairlift servicing a gigantic internal ski slope. In this refrigerated wonderland, snow only falls overnight when the temperature reaches down to −8°C, and each day is a cool −2°C under a dome of pale blue, artificial sky. With an environment crafted by science and technology in the context of globalization, Dubai is fertile ground for the growth of transnational higher education enterprises.

HIGHER EDUCATION IN THE UAE

With over half of the UAE's citizens under 18 years of age, the UAE government, through the Ministry of Higher Education and Scientific Research, is keen to implement the vision of the late president H. H. Sheikh Zayed Bin Sultan Al Nahyan: 'The wealth of any nation is its intellectuals and the progress of peoples and nations is judged by the level and extent of education they reach' (H. H. Sheikh Al-Nahyan 2005). The two existing national universities and twelve federal higher colleges of technology provide free and universal education to Emiratis (UAE nationals).

Some of the broad objectives of the UAE government are: to build local business, IT, infrastructure, economy and expertise; develop the UAE as an IT/business hub for the Middle-East, initially through bringing in foreign expertise (Nicks-McCaleb 2005); provide for the needs of the private sector; and build international workforce standards (Coffman 2003). The UAE therefore hosts a range of private sector higher education institutions. For the 79.1 per cent majority expatriate population higher education provision in the UAE is mostly through transnational institutions, of which there are currently almost 50 in the UAE, with 23 of them accredited by the Ministry of Higher Education and Scientific Research (MOHE 2006).

Transnational Education (TNE) providers require accreditation for credibility and government support and the UAE national government wields considerable power in regulating the forces of the transnational higher education economy through a rigorous accreditation process. The UAE Ministry's Commission for Academic Accreditation has very exacting Standards for Licensure and Accreditation (CAA 2005), with which accredited UAE institutions must comply. These include the requirements to vest full control of curricula in the UAE and to provide a range of general education subjects such as Psychology and Islamic Culture Studies that are compulsory within the undergraduate program.

A TRANSNATIONAL INSTITUTION IN THE UAE

The university in the UAE that is the focus of this chapter was conceived in the early 1990s by an Australian university as part of their diversification strategy. By 2006 more than 2,000 students were enrolled in 12 different undergraduate and postgraduate programs at the UAE-based university. The student population comprises more than 75 different nationalities with the majority from India and Iran. Emiratis are the second largest group at the postgraduate level however at the undergraduate level they comprise less than 10 per cent. Students also come from

Pakistan, Lebanon, Russia, Syria, Kenya, South Africa, and the UK. Australian students comprise 2 per cent of the total student population. Academics, recruited both internationally and in the UAE using merit and equity-based recruitment policies and procedures equivalent to the Australian university, come from a variety of countries and regions.

At this stage only degrees in business and information technology are offered. These degrees are in high demand worldwide, support UAE government objectives, and have the potential to generate substantial revenue. This situation exemplifies the growth in market-oriented programs and the decline in liberal arts, social sciences and pure science disciplines in TNE (UNESCO 2004).

The UAE-based university is accredited as an independent private university in the UAE; however, equivalence of curriculum content, assessment outcomes and academic standards is crucial for both the Australian university and the UAE-based university. Equivalence is achieved through a systematic quality assurance process, staff development and training, and planned and regular communication between academic and executive staff using both communication technologies and site visits.

All of the staff we interviewed stressed the importance of equivalent academic vision and standards and agreed that there is now a culture of modern pedagogical practice at the UAE-based university. According to the Australian executive and academic staff, the significant factors in developing this culture have been quality assurance mechanisms, the use of information and communication technologies, and the Foundations of University Teaching course (compulsory for academic staff at both universities). Over time, curriculum decisions such as the design of assessment tasks and other pedagogical responsibilities have been devolved, affording a level of academic independence to the UAE-based lecturers such that academics and executive staff report feeling a sense of authority, credibility and a mutually equitable partnership.

The achievement of balance between equivalence and autonomy, and between the requirements of the UAE and the Australian university, has been recognized by external audit (through the Australian Universities Quality Agency). This has been achieved through adjusting content and teaching and learning strategies to the local context, and by employing and empowering local lecturers and tutors; strategies noted as effective for offshore courses by Pyvis and Chapman (2004) and McBurnie and Ziguras (2006).

The vision of an international education that develops the liberal values of enquiry in an environment where critical thinking is both encouraged and nurtured is expressed in the strategic plans and prospectuses of both universities. The characteristics that the university expects of graduates are referred to as graduate attributes and these include an 'appreciation and valuing of cultural and intellectual diversity and the ability to function in a multicultural or global environment'. In addition, a 'capacity for, and understanding of, teamwork' is sought for graduates and at both universities this attribute is developed largely through utilising groupwork—structured and unstructured, long- and short-term—as a key teaching and learning method.

The practice of engaging students with their international peers in the mutual construction of international knowledge 'deserves recognition as a central pillar of an internationalizing methodology' (Whalley 1997: 1). The TNE environment in the UAE suggests opportunities for intercultural engagement of students and academics from many cultures and nations within the formal learning experiences, including groupwork. It is the student achievement of international perspectives and intercultural skills, and the peer learning pedagogy that supports their development, that this chapter explores.

THE STUDENT EXPERIENCE

Our study explores the intercultural groupwork experiences of students from three third-year subjects within the business degree program at the UAE-based university. We carried out group and individual interviews with students, academics and executive staff at both universities from which we developed a questionnaire to survey student responses to various aspects of their educational experience at the university. Students rated a series of statements from 1 (strongly agree) through to 6 (strongly disagree) and were also asked to respond to open-ended questions. A total of 115 students completed the survey. A little over half were males with almost a third of the students from India, followed by Iran and Pakistan. Only a few students were from western or Arab countries. One third of students were born in Dubai; however, as expected, the number of UAE national respondents was low at less than 1 per cent.

THE ADVANTAGES OF A MULTICULTURAL
EDUCATIONAL ENVIRONMENT

The survey results show that almost all students agreed to some extent (ranging from strongly to mildly) with a set of propositions related to the university's engendering of the graduate attribute an 'appreciation and valuing of cultural and intellectual diversity and the ability to function in a multicultural or global environment'. Of the 115 students surveyed, 91 per cent agreed to some extent that the curriculum offered an international focus. The international focus was developed through the use of international examples to explain theory (90 per cent agreed); the teaching of appreciation of world cultures (88 per cent agreed); and the teaching of the importance of intercultural understanding (78 per cent agreed). As a result of the educational experience at the university, 86 per cent of students reported they were more accepting of cultural differences than they used to be and 89 per cent agreed that their degree program had prepared them for a multicultural work environment.

Of course the UAE environment beyond the university is an important factor in the development of these students' attitudes, with 97 per cent agreeing to some extent that they enjoyed living in the multicultural environment of the country. Nevertheless, the possibilities for intercultural engagement within the university are clear, with 88 per cent of students reporting daily interaction with students from other cultures. Pyvis and Chapman (2004) have found that offshore students highly value the experience of mixing with people from other cultural groups. In this study, the advantages of studying in the multinational TNE environment were clear and were described by one of the students in interview:

> I love the mix because it makes it interesting ... you get the best of everything. (Student 3)

And from the survey, as one student put it:

> It is great to come in contact with students and staff from different countries and cultures. It teaches us more about them and their cultures.

Despite this, some students considered the environment to be less multicultural than they would like. Several indicated they were keen to interact with faculty from more diverse backgrounds. For example, one student wrote:

> It is nice to have a multicultural environment. Therefore more multicultural staff needs to be employed.

Some students also referred to perceived segregation within the diversity:

> The students at UOWD are culturally diverse but they are not a cultural mix or melting pot because students socialize only with people of the same culture. We need something to stir the mix.

For these students, what seems to be missing is the broader sense of a university supporting the development of students 'in a holistic sense, incorporating not just intellectual growth but social, emotional and cultural development as well' (Tam 2001: 51). The Australian university's own review has indicated this as an issue for future development and the students interviewed commented on the need for broader support for extra-curricular activities. This was also mentioned by some students in the survey, for example:

> Good education but not very social—no university life.

This situation may be common to the early development of offshore higher education (Pyvis and Chapman 2004) in that the development of the university as a learning environment that integrates the broader social contexts, roles and demands of students' everyday lives may be an evolving process.

THE COMPLEXITIES OF INTERCULTURAL GROUPWORK

Carefully nurtured and supported groupwork activities may develop meaningful interaction and cooperation between students of differing cultures (Biggs 1999; Chalmers and Volet 1997; Curro and McTaggart 2003; Leask 2001; Patrick 1997; Schapper and Mayson 2004; Volet and Ang 1998). The UAE environment offers an opportunity for the development of international perspectives and intercultural skills through having students work together in intercultural groups. Using group assignments as a means of assessing student learning is common practice in most subjects. For most group assignments students are expected to work together outside class. The Australian university's Code of Practice-Teaching and Assessment states that teachers are responsible for establishing 'specific guidelines for groupwork' and are expected 'to manage the planning, development and implementation of processes and procedures for learning'. In practice this ranges from very little involvement by teachers to regular meetings between group members and the teacher. However, in many cases teachers require student groups to document minutes of group meetings and submit some form of peer assessment and self-contribution to the group assignment.

The academics we interviewed all used groupwork in their classes. One teacher interviewed described how she sets up groupwork:

> So a lot of the group activities are based on ... how you work with each other ... sometimes we fix the group, sometimes we allow them to choose or sometimes we put a precondition to the groups—like you must have a mix of so and so and so people (Teacher 1).

Eighty-two per cent of the students surveyed considered that over their degree program small groups had worked well and 61 per cent of students agreed that teachers selected group members to mix nationalities.

The mixing of cultures offers the opportunity to develop international skills. Asked about their appreciation of other peoples' cultural values one of the students interviewed replied:

> The way we learnt it, is really in group study because our lecturers never helped us as such. And just working with others is like—that's how we learnt how ... (Student 4).

Nevertheless there were some who would like more interaction, for example, the student who wrote in response to the survey:

> Lecturers should give us students more opportunities to interact with other students.

When teachers asked them to choose their own groups, the survey indicated that 29 per cent chose, at least to some extent, group members according to nationality. The students we interviewed had commented quite extensively on the relationship between certain nationalities and group member selection. An extract from an interview with a student who studied at both universities highlights the complexities of inter-cultural contact both within and outside the teaching space. From this student's perspective, her education in Dubai enabled her to mix with a wide variety of students, including students from Asian countries:

> ...I had Pakistani as friend, I had South African friend, I had like Indian friend, and Chinese ... because I was the only [nationality deleted] in the class, so it was a really mixed class, so we always had this interaction going on in Dubai, because we all knew each other (Student 6).

Yet in her Australian classes, Asian students were in the majority and she felt excluded from their groups:

> In [Australia] the problem that I got, and I always get it ... when you are with Asians ... and they're not that much, like you know open ... to try to get to their groups, it's like an impossible thing that you're going to do ... Some of the classes I've got, it's 90 per cent Asians, and you're left with no one, and then you have to find a friend in the class, and then you try to make you know, friendship with them, but then the problem that it gets that, they've got their own groups, and like they're always talking Chinese and all of that ... so you never can come into their groups ... I think it's better like when they put us in the group then than we choosing (Student 6).

When multicultural groups were formed there were still difficulties:

ke in the groups that I had ... it was really a Chinese and Tai-
e person and one from, I think Sri Lankan I think, and then
t's really hard to sit down and try to be nice, talk together,
because, you know, the first thing is, you can't understand (Student
6).

Two students in another interview group who were from two different
African countries described a similar experience:

There are a few groups who work with people from their own cultures (Student 5).

Like the Arabs work with the Arabs (Student 4).

And the Indians with the Indians (Student 5).

But for us ... really (Student 4).

We just – (Student 5).

It's different – (Student 4.)

We just pick anybody (Student 5).

A few open-ended comments on the survey also mention this grouping
of nationalities, for example:

Usually students from similar nationalities form groups, not too
cool.

While classwork groups in the subjects surveyed were reported as effective, 50 per cent of the students agreed to some extent with the proposi-
tion that students from different nationalities did not mix together. This
may be related to language as much as culture:

People like to, you know, be with people who speak their language
because they do understand them better (Student 2).

Preparedness to accept the views of students from various cultures may
affect the level of critical debate around controversial issues within
student groups. In the survey 85 per cent of the students agreed that
their degree program had encouraged them to question what is usually
accepted and 87 per cent agreed that they were now able to analyse
problems and come up with solutions as a result of their education. The
majority of students surveyed (57 per cent) thought disagreeing with
someone was acceptable at the university. However, 43 per cent indicated that at least to some extent it was not a good idea to disagree with
others, as seen in this interview extract:

Actually we can't always have our own opinions (Student 5).

And if somebody has one we can't really say no, we don't accept that, don't like that opinion—so I guess we just try to like expand a bit that opinion and give our ideas and stuff (Student 4).

Working and studying in a culturally mixed environment may foster international attributes; however, it is also possible that students may involve themselves in differing levels of critical debate according to how they perceive the characteristics of people from other cultures.

If I am dealing with an American I will not be that enthusiastic of taking it on and fighting with them. If I am wrong I will just back off ... I mean even if [an American is] wrong you accept it. And if you are not wrong you do not accept—you keep on fighting. But in our culture even if you are wrong you still do not accept that you are wrong (Student 1).

Cultural stereotyping occurs amongst students and staff in the higher education environment (Chalmers and Volet 1997; Devos 2003) and can lead to miscommunication and discomfort. Consider this interview interaction in which the same student describes a negative view of a particular group while another student values the engagement.

I only feel uncomfortable when I work with Arabs because they are very arrogant (Student 1).

Being from another culture they can give me different ideas and I am doing marketing. I need ideas from every culture to do my assignments (Student 3).

Clearly, studying in a highly diverse and multicultural environment such as the UAE and being exposed to TNE practices does not necessarily break down stereotypes, and in some cases may exacerbate them.

IN CONCLUSION

From our study of this transnational higher education environment, intercultural understanding has been promoted and achieved through groupwork within the classrooms of the students interviewed and surveyed. From the student perspective, the development of graduates' international skills and understandings is actively supported through curriculum content and pedagogy. That this is of great value to graduates is exemplified by student responses when asked if the cultural mix of the environment had been helpful.

Yes—because it teaches us to socialize with different cultures (Student 5).

Yeah and when you go into practical life you know how to handle people and when you visit other countries it's like—like say for example India and Pakistan—everyone is like very hostile towards other cultures (Student 4).

This university, with its multicultural staff and student body located at the hub of the burgeoning business and IT interests of the Middle East, would seem to be perfectly positioned to provide the international education envisaged by the International Association of Universities, that is, 'an education system where internationalization promotes cultural diversity and fosters intercultural understanding, respect and tolerance among peoples' (IAU 1998: 1). Yet the complex issues that affect intercultural engagement through groupwork—minority/majority cultural groupings, language differences, critical discussion and stereotypical views of 'the other'—raise questions as to the extent to which, and the means by which, international skills and understandings are intentionally conveyed to students both experientially and theoretically.

The teachers and coordinators we spoke to in this study were hopeful that international outcomes would develop from groupwork within the multicultural setting rather than from carefully designed groupwork processes to nurture, support and discuss international perspectives with the specific intent of developing intercultural dialogue and understanding. This is hardly surprising given the complexity of intercultural engagement as a pedagogical strategy, as revealed in this study. We recommend a more overt approach to developing international attributes through mixed culture groupwork. In particular academics could discuss the meaning of internationalization with students, explore stereotypical thinking, and have them reflect on the development of international skills and attitudes achieved through their inter-cultural learning experiences.

Our study suggests the way forward is not simple. Academics need support in designing and developing learning environments that intentionally engender the kind of global intelligence that enables graduates to empathetically view the world from the perspective of the 'the other', and that builds graduates' commitment to international cooperation beyond the needs of global business ventures. However, despite the limited range of existing degree programs, the transnational environment that has been developed at this UAE-based university offers a strong foundation for the ongoing development of a pedagogy that supports the graduation of students with the capacity to appreciate and value cultural and intellectual diversity and function effectively in the global environment.

REFERENCES

Biggs, J. (1999) *Teaching for Quality Learning at University.* Buckingham: Open University Press.

CAA. (2005) *Standards for Licensure and Accreditation.* Online. Available at: http://www.caa.ae/caa/images/STANDARDS2005.doc> (accessed 18 October 2006).

Chalmers, D., and Volet, S. (1997) 'Common Misconceptions about Students from South-East Asia Studying in Australia.' *Higher Education Research and Development,* 16 (1): 87–98.

Coffman, J. (2003) *Higher Education in the Gulf: Privatisation and Americanisation.* Online. Available at: http://www.bc.edu/bc_org/avp/soe/cihe/newsletter/News33/text009.htm (accessed 10 August 2006).

Curro, G., and McTaggart, R. (2003) 'Supporting the Pedagogy of Internationalisation.' *Paper presented at the 17th IDP Australian Education Conference,* Melbourne, Australia.

Devos, A. (2003) 'Academic Standards, Internationalisation, and the Discursive Construction of 'The International Student''. *Higher Education Research and Development Society of Australasia,* 22 (2): 155–66.

H. H. Sheikh Al-Nahyan N. M. (2005) Ministry of Higher Education and Scientific Research. Online. Available at: http://www.uae.gov.ae/mohe/ (accessed 5 August 2006).

IAU (1998) *'Towards a Century of Cooperation: Internationalization of Higher Education.* Online. Available at HTTP: http://www.unesco.org/iau/internationalization/i_statement.html (accessed 4 July 2007).

Interact (2006) *UAE At a Glance.* Ministry of Culture of the UAE. Online. Available at:http://www.uaeinteract.com/uaeint_misc/glance/ataglance.pdf (accessed 12 December 2006).

Leask, B. (2001) 'Bridging the Gap: Internationalising University Curricula'. *Journal of Studies in International Education,* 5 (2), 100–115.

McBurnie, G., and Ziguras, C. (2006) *Transnational Education: Issues and Trends in Offshore Higher Education.* Abingdon, Oxon: Routledge.

MOHE (Ministry of Higher Education and Scientific Research 2006) *The Commission for Academic Accreditation.* Online. Available at: http://aei.dest.gov.au/AEI/CEP/UAE/EducationSystem/HigherEd/InstitutionalStruc/default.htm (accessed 18th October 2007).

Nicks-McCaleb, L. (2005) 'The Impact of State Funded Higher Education on Neighbourhood and Community in the United Arab Emirates'. *International Education Journal,* 6 (4): 501–511.

Patrick, K. (1997) *Internationalising the University: Implications for Teaching and Learning at RMIT.* Melbourne: RMIT.

Pyvis, D., and Chapman, A. (2004) *Student Experiences of Offshore Higher Education: Issues for Quality* (Government report No. 3). Melbourne: Australian Universities Quality Agency.

Schapper, J. M., and Mayson, S. E. (2004) 'Internationalization of Curricula: An Alternative to the Taylorization of Academic Work'. *Journal of Higher Education Policy and Management,* 26 (2): 189–205.

Tam, M. (2001) 'Measuring Quality and Performance in Higher Education'. *Quality in Higher Education,* 7 (1): 47–54.

UAE (2006) *Employment and Social Security.* Online. Available at: http://www.government.ae/gov/en/biz/employment/employment.jsp (accessed 5 September 2006).

UNESCO (2004). *Higher Education in a Globalized Society*. Online. Available at: http://unesdoc.unesco.org/images/0013/001362/136247e.pdf (accessed 5 September 2006).

Volet, E. E., and Ang, G. (1998) 'Culturally Mixed Groups on International Campuses: An Opportunity for Inter-cultural Learning'. *Higher Education Research and Development*, 17 (1): 5–24.

Whalley, T. (1997) *Best Practice Guidelines for Internationalizing the Curriculum*. Online. Available at: http://www.jcu.edu.au/office/tld/teachingsupport/documents/Whalley-Best-Practice.pdf (accessed 6 November 2006).

15 Local Time, Global Space and Glocal Identities in Transnational Education

Catherine Doherty

Queensland University of Technology

The 'self' is conceptualized as more fragmented and incomplete, composed of multiple 'selves' or identities in relation to the different social worlds we inhabit, something with a history, 'produced', in process. The 'subject' is differently placed or positioned by different discourses and practices.

Hall 1996: 226

INTRODUCTION

Transnational online education is a set of practices that offer new resources, discourses and pathways for individuals to pursue their aspirations. It promises educational networks imagined beyond national boundaries and local protocols. It is this transnational imaginary that is reshaping how people interact in 'globally defined fields of possibility' (Appadurai 1990: 5). 'Borderless' online pedagogy and the imagined lifeworlds it opens are nurtured through strategic partnerships between institutions to mutual benefit to source and sell educational products. This chapter delves beyond the visionary promise into lived though virtual realities, to probe the delicate cultural politics that are enacted online, and to demonstrate how the 'local' can still assert itself for better and for worse in the transnational imaginary. It offers an ethnographic account of selected interactions within a semester-long unit in a Masters of Business Administration (MBA). The unit was offered online by an Australian university to a student cohort including both 'domestic' enrolments and students enrolled through a Malaysian college.

This reconstruction focuses on episodes in which 'hermeneutic problems' (Bauman 1990) erupted around a delay for the students in Malaysia to receive their marked assignments. Their explicit sense of exclusion is contrasted with an Australian student's grievances about her 'local' provider going 'global' and being too inclusive. Using interview data and online postings, these events are unpacked to reveal the different 'range of foci' (Featherstone 1995: 10) in the identities expressed, with competing senses of ownership of the global/local opportunities and their respective disciplinary regimes. Such contradictory troubles demonstrate that students felt both insufficiently and overly differentiated by transnational pedagogy and that the 'selves' they were able to construct in this setting's relations rubbed uncomfortably against their aspirational selves.

The chapter is presented in seven parts. First, transnational education is framed within larger questions of transnational identities and cultural globalization. The study's parameters are then outlined and the data selection justified. The events are then reconstructed—firstly the grievances of the students from Malaysia, then the 'local' student's complaint. Their contrasting stances on being 'local' in transnational interactions are then interpreted with reference to the intrusion of local time, spaces and contradictory identity orientations in such globalizing relations. The final section draws implications for practice that might better handle such cultural potentials in transnational online education.

THEORISING THE TRANSNATIONAL THROUGH THE LOCAL

'Transnational imaginaries' (Ong 1997: 171) propel individual investments beyond the nation. In this study's site of virtual mobility and educational investments, the students were able to access cultural resources by virtual means to progress their transnational imaginaries. For Ong, the concept of transnationalism captures more than the idea of global flows (Appadurai 1996) and acknowledges 'the tensions between movements and social orders' (Ong 1999: 6) through which their routes pass. Her concept of 'graduated sovereignty' denotes a series of 'zones that are subjected to different kinds of governmentality and that vary in terms of the mix of disciplinary and civilizing regimes' (Ong 1999: 7). In other words, Ong's transnational 'flexible' citizens cannot move effortlessly through or above the local, but must engage with any local regime on its own terms to achieve their strategic end. This friction-in-movement may require a temporary and opportunistic acquiescence to the local's 'disciplining structures' (Ong 1991: 14). Thus transnational space is not a benign, neutral, deterritorialized space, but rather a landscape of local filters and interim orders, shaping who transnationals can be as they negotiate their aspirational routes.

In a similar way, the concept of glocalization highlights 'the ways in which localities are 'produced' on a globe-wide basis' (Robertson 1994: 33). Robertson (1994: 38) disputes the simplistic polarization of 'global/universal' and 'local/particular', and criticizes typical problems of global *versus* local interests, arguing that it is the 'simultaneity and inter-penetration' of these two frames that distinguishes globalization from previous international relations. Localities in this view are not 'things in themselves' (Robertson 1994: 38) but relational categories, 'a product of boundary-making' (Robertson 2001: 466). For this paper, the notion of 'glocal' identities reflects the 'simultaneity and inter-penetration' of locally sourced identity positions and more globally oriented identity processes. It is understood not as an either/or binary, but as a both/and nexus.

In the virtual realm of online education, the matter of which 'local' regime applies becomes less self-evident, and more problematic, with increased potential for problems or resistances:

> [T]he sense of heaps, congeries and aggregates of cultural particularities juxtaposed together on the same field, the same bounded space, in which the fact that they are different and do not fit together, or want to fit together, becomes noticeable and a source of practical problems. (Featherstone 1995: 123–124)

In online 'sites' there is a surplus of possible cultural scripts and operative 'locals'. To impose any 'local' rules is to presume ownership and draw a boundary between the local 'us' and the Other 'them' amongst virtual participants. In this case study of an online unit offered between international partners, a sense of 'local' is considered both enabling and constraining by different parties, depending on who invoked such a boundary where on whose behalf.

THE STUDY AND ITS PARAMETERS

This research draws on a virtual ethnography (Hine 2000) of the case study unit, involving close observations and data collection over the 19 weeks of online interaction to explore how cultural identities were performed and how cultural difference was produced online. Of the 79 completing students, 29 were enrolled through the Malaysian partner. These students were not necessarily Malaysian citizens; some were from the People's Republic of China while temporarily residing in Malaysia. Thus the term 'Malaysia' rather than 'Malaysian' is used for this cohort. Following Hine (2000) and Carspecken (1996), the online interaction was analysed firstly as interaction with attention to what became typical and what was disruptive, and secondly as text using sociolinguistic analyses. The ethnography also drew on course materials, repeated semi-structured interviews with staff, and email interviews with a self-selected sample of students.

This chapter focuses on a series of events whereby 'cultural differencing' emerged as an unplanned pedagogical problem. These events played out in Zone F—a discussion thread that was designed to allow students to raise procedural concerns (as opposed to questions about curricular content). This Zone quickly became a very active space for student grievances, to the point that a culture of complaint became the unit's typical online interaction. Relevant postings are reproduced verbatim below, and are identified by Zone and then chronological order—thus 'F158' denotes the 158th posting in Zone F.

SELECTING THE DATA: TEXTUAL EXCLUSION

Text in this Zone was analysed further to identify exchanges where members of the student body expressed a schism along cultural lines. Following Wodak (2002) on the textual construction of 'them' and 'us', a number of searches were conducted to identify how the pronouns 'we', 'us', and 'our' were used in Zone F. The personal pronoun, 'we', and its derivatives can carry two senses (Halliday and Matthiessen 2004: 325): 'speaker plus listener'; and 'speaker plus other(s)' but not including 'you', the interlocutor. The former is termed the 'inclusive we'; the latter, the 'exclusive we'. Using a search tool in the qualitative research software package, NVivo, to identify instances of 'we/our/us' in their textual contexts, it became evident that the vast majority of 'we/us/our' invoked by students in this space used the exclusive 'we' which designated the complete student body in dialogue with 'you', the lecturer, who was not included amongst 'us'. For example: '... can you show us how we are supposed to reference ...'

As a marked departure from this typical pattern of 'we', meaning all the students, three postings were distinguished by their use of the exclusive 'we' to refer only to the Malaysia cohort, as distinct from the domestic cohort. They were made by different Malaysia students over six days in the midst of domestic students' complaints about the paucity of constructive feedback on their first marked assignments:

> When will we Malaysians know of our assessments? Is a local examiner involved in the markings? (F158)

> (Title: When for Malaysians?) When will the Malaysian students know our results? (F166)

> I was wondering whether you might have an idea as to when we Malaysian students will be able to obtain our results to the first assignment (Assessment 2). (F171)

These three postings, flagged by their marked linguistic choices, indicated that some of these students felt unfairly distinguished from other students by virtue of belonging to the Malaysia cohort, that is, by being both 'localized' and 'Othered'.

RECONSTRUCTING WHAT HAPPENED

The lecturer replied to these queries on the sixth day:

> I am sorry to report that there has been a delay with the results for the Malaysian students. Examiners have to first send the marked papers to me for moderation (...) I am expecting them in the next few days. (F173)

In this way, it became public knowledge that the assignments were in the proverbial mail, their physical matter crossing oceans, mountains and plains between the partner institutions' localities. Ironically, a complaint about the passage of 'real' time rendered salient the distributed nature of the relations in 'real' space, which had thus far been masked or considered irrelevant in the 'timeless time' and 'space of flows' (Castells 1996: 376) of the online environment.

This reply also produced the first knowledge Malaysia students had that their assignments were to be locally marked, as per the contractual agreement between the partner institutions. In an interview, the educational designer supporting the lecturer in this unit offered further insight into the trouble arising. She suggested that these three postings were indicative of more widespread frustrations from the Malaysia students, not only over the delays, but also over the use of local markers:

Designer:　… and there's been quite a lot of flack coming by email to us from the Malaysian students.
Researcher: All right, so this is coming behind the scenes?
Designer:　They feel hardly done by, but the funny part about it is, when we are doing the moderation of these assessments, the Malaysian students are being marked more severely by the Malaysian markers than we would have liked.

This flare of trouble thus produced an issue of respective localities and their spatial distribution which then served to produce a systematic distinction between two groups of students, one of which became the 'normal' by default. Having established that the Malaysia cohort had felt 'differenced' by this series of events and contractual arrangements, I now explore the tension between local and global frames of reference that produced this schism between the categories of 'local' and 'Malaysia' students and their markers.

GLOCAL SPACE AND GLOCAL
IDENTITIES BEING CONFINED

The delay of the assignments might be seen purely as a 'real' space/time problematic, unnecessary perhaps in an online mode of pedagogy. In contrast, the Malaysia students' reported sense of injury over the use of 'local' assessors, whose employment caused the delay, cannot be seen in the same light. This could be interpreted as a matter of feeling confined to their local context by the contractual arrangements when they intended and felt entitled to participate in the promised transnational relations, or more possibly, in a notionally authentic 'Western' qualification. In other words, they had a larger horizon in mind, and were more transnational in their identity orientations. Where they may have been prepared to submit to the Australian universities 'local' rules, they were less satisfied by being confined to their own 'local' setting's regime of markers.

This 'localized' identity produced for the Malaysia students did not arise from any solidarity achieved between category insiders (though this may have emerged retrospectively as a result of their shared sense of injury), but rather the localized identity was imputed, or constructed for them, by virtue of the intervening administrative layers embedded in the corporate contracts. They had cultivated a larger, 'glocalized' sense of their 'local' context, and were not aware that a boundary had effectively been erected around them.

In this sense, Featherstone's (1995: 10) expression, 'range of foci' helps to overcome any false 'local'/ 'global' binary and to capture the 'simultaneity and inter-penetration' (Robertson 1994: 38) of their being both in Malaysia and participating in an Australian higher education experience. 'Range of foci' also describes how contingent and adjustable 'local boundaries' can be:

> It is the capacity to shift the frame, and move between varying range of foci, the capacity to handle a range of symbolic material out of which various identities can be formed and reformed in different situations, which is relevant in the contemporary global situation. (Featherstone 1995: 10)

This tangle of interactive trouble, revealed only when the brave new world of 'fully online' education got caught in snail mail, could be reconstrued as a matter stemming from parties looking through different ends of a telescope—the Malaysia students seeing themselves as part of a larger picture, a wide range of focus with a global horizon, while the host university saw them framed within their local provider's 'range of focus'. The incongruence between projected identity maps

and 'local' boundaries demonstrated here accords with similar disjunc-
tures, reported by Rizvi (2000), Kenway and Bullen (2003), and Bullen and Kenway (2003), between how the higher education institution
understands/represents the international student, and how international
students understand/represent themselves. The common point in these
studies is how the 'local' identity that the institution respectfully offers
the international student ultimately constrained who these students
could be in such transnational space.

LOCAL SPACE AND LOCAL IDENTITY
BEING INFRINGED UPON

The lecturer had welcomed the Malaysia students inclusion in the online
interaction as a sign of the university's 'coming of age as an international provider', thus rhetorically scoping the university's 'local' field as
larger than, and disembedded from, its physical location. Where were
the domestic students constructing their 'local' boundaries in this virtual geography?

As a comparative foil to the lecturer's 'international' rhetoric and the
Malaysia students' expression of broader horizons, one domestic student expressed a strong opinion that the 'local' context, belonging to
an exclusive Australian 'us', should have been limited to some national
if not smaller local scale. In her email interview after the unit's completion, this student described herself as:

> [B]orn in Zimbabwe, but have lived in Australia since I was 3. My
> parents are South African, but I definitely identify with being Aus-
> tralian (whatever that is!)'.

In her account, she was wary of Other participants and their potentially
competing interests when it came to globalizing her local university:

> The international students or even interstate students could per-
> ceive that we have an advantage by being able to drop in and talk
> to our lecturers. Plus in my last course the international students
> got live lectures which we didn't for the same course, I know lots
> of our students didn't agree with that. I believe our uni should be
> more vigilant about the help that the international students are
> receiving.

She reported becoming aware of the presence of international students in
the unit interactions 'by their names and conversation over the [course-
ware]', and felt that they added to the learning: 'I think it was great,

they added their cultural dimension to the conversation ...'. However, in regard to the assessable tasks involving small group discussion, she expressed a sense of impatience, injustice and resentment over having to deal with the non-standard English of the international students:

> I love the international contribution, however I think many of them are not on the same playing field. Part of our assessment was to post our own case studies, and some of the language used by some international students was atrocious. We discussed these at our study group to try to help each other out to understand what they were trying to say. I thought it was quite unfair to us, and could not see how those students were allowed to do this course with such poor English. However there where others whose English was acceptable and their contributions were very wise and definitely contributed to my learning.

This account firstly used an exclusive 'our' to denote all students, then shifted so that 'we' and 'us' are the local, domestic students, and the excluded 'they' are the Malaysia Others. She also reported deciding to purposefully not adapt her language to facilitate their participation:

> I don't think I ended up adjusting my language really, but I thought very hard about it before I wrote something. I remember writing a complicated word and wondering whether they would understand it, and decided to use it any way, because if I didn't, I wasn't helping them to advance their English skills.

This student thus expressed a strong sense of ownership of English in contrast to the deficient 'non-native' Malaysia students who were considered learners. Her critique highlights how tightly this student constructed and upheld her 'local' boundary and the locally anchored orientation of her identity's 'range of focus'.

Her critique of the Malaysia students' inflected language resonated in another way with the original problem of having 'local' markers for the Malaysia cohort. By the lecturer's account, his moderation of the Malaysia assignments revealed that the Malaysia markers had in fact been quite harsh in their assessments of the students' work, in particular, regarding their English expression:

Lecturer: Some of the markers were very hard, and actually much harsher in the tone of their comment than I would ever have been, in fact one of them ... The term was just too strong in the saying you know, 'your English language is awful!' and I've changed it ... so I said that, something like 'There's room for improvement in your English expression'. It's just a softer way of saying that the person's not quite right ...

Researcher: How much does it impinge on your judgements you're making in terms of assessment? Would you see the language problems in the assessment criteria, or would you look through the language competency to what they were saying?

Lecturer: I think I always look through the language to see whether they've got the ideas, some ideas straight ...

By this account, control of word-perfect Standard English was upheld and wielded by the Malaysia markers as a necessary condition for success in this site of internationalized education, though the lecturer suggested he was prepared to be more tolerant and inclusive of different Englishes.

The dissonance between the stances taken by various parties in this site demonstrate the variety of scripts constructing self and Other and the variable strength of boundaries between those categories, in terms of how much differences are considered to matter. Such 'difficulties of handling multiplicity and cultural disorder' (Featherstone 1995: 84) emerge in the tensions between globalization and localization, and the frictions in transnational routes. This empirical window into one participant's subjective realm allows us to understand how some of the undercurrents and stresses in transnational education are lived. This student wanted a 'local' university, not a global provider, and felt that her needs and rights were being impinged upon or compromised by any accommodation of international students. She could see the advantages to herself in their inclusion, but for her, equity should be interpreted as demonstrable and transparent equality, not through circumstantial adjustments. Thus accommodations accorded to the cultural Other were construed as displacement, erosion or unwelcome de-centring of her 'local' experience.

This student's construction of an embattled 'local' context was not necessarily representative of all the domestically enrolled students. However, the account has been included here as a comparative foil to the complaints of the Malaysia students to illustrate how the presence of contested 'local'/'global' boundaries, transnational and national identity orientations, and their differing 'range of foci' produced tensions in the online interaction.

In another way, the two protests share an aspect in the students' strategies to resist or undermine their positioning by the unit's disciplinary regime. The Malaysia students protested both online and behind the scenes, but ultimately had to succumb to the contractual arrangements in place. The domestic student refused to adapt her language choices, but still had to engage in the mixed group discussions.

CONCLUSION: CHALLENGING DEFAULT SETTINGS

This chapter reported how a politics of difference emerged as a peda-gogical problem in the conduct of a transnational online unit, and how trouble emanated from differing horizons for 'glocal' identities and produced unwelcome distinctions between groups of students. Such problems could be viewed as troubles with 'default settings', with an intentional metaphorical play on computing terminology. By 'default settings', I mean the invisible decisions encoded into the pedagogical set-ting and design. Given the 'increased context' (Featherstone 1995: 102) and cultural surpluses of transnational education, unexamined defaults encoded in software, assessment tasks, or in the identities attributed to self and others, amount to presumptuous assumptions that can court trouble. The domestic student had presumed that participants in the online unit should speak Standard English. The Malaysia tutors had pre-sumed that the lecturer would demand Standard English. The Malaysia students had presumed that they would be treated the same as other stu-dents in the assessment regime. When each of these precepts produced interactive trouble, there was someone to blame, identifiable because of their difference.

Featherstone (1995) argues it becomes 'more difficult to retain last-ing and oversimplified images of others' (p. 103) which suggests that such issues will not be solved by merely resetting or updating default assumptions. As Meyer and Geschiere (1999: 14) point out: 'identity has another side: it also has to relate to people's fascination with globaliza-tion's open-endedness and the new horizons which it opens up.' Of all globalizing practices, transnational education, with its promise of access to new high status cultural resources, should be open to the notion of speculative identities, 'new symbolic modes of affiliation and belonging' (Featherstone 1995: 110) and complex cultural potentials.

This analysis also sheds light on the more general enterprise of online transnational education and its opportunistic discourse. The 'business of borderless education' (Ryan and Stedman 2002; Cunningham *et al* 2000) is eager for new markets, and equally eager to slough off constraining considerations of problematic difference that curtailed previous models for the export of education. The contractual detail forged between the two institutional partners in the case study was shown to have produced its own pedagogical tensions between competing 'zones of graduated sovereignty' (Ong 1999) and these in turn produced grievances over too much or not enough cultural differencing. This analysis has shown that cultural politics can flourish in unforeseen, subtle and protean ways when knowledge is sold in the global market. This does not discredit the high value that all participants placed on aspects of the transnational curriculum. It does however suggest that cultural difference will come to matter pedagogically in online transnational education, and imaginary boundaries will be actively constructed, dismantled and re-constructed when any local institution goes global.

REFERENCES

Appadurai, A. (1990) 'Disjuncture and difference in the global cultural economy', *Public Culture* 2: 1–24.
Appadurai, A. (1996) *Modernity at Large: Cultural Dimensions of Globalization*. Minneapolis: University of Minnesota Press.
Bauman, Z. (1990) 'Modernity and ambivalence', in M. Featherstone (ed.) *Global Culture: Nationalism, Globalization and Modernity*, London: Sage.
Bullen, E., and Kenway, J. (2003) 'Real or imagined women? Staff representations of international women postgraduate students', *Discourse: Studies in the Cultural Politics of Education*, 24: 36–50.
Carspecken, P. F. (1996) *Critical Ethnography in Educational Research: A Theoretical and Practical Guide*, New York: Routledge.
Castells, M. (1996) *The Rise of the Network Society*, Oxford: Blackwell.
Cunningham, S., Ryan, Y., Stedman, L., Tapsall, S., Bagdon, K., Flew, T., et al. (2000) *The Business of Borderless Education*, Canberra: Department of Education, Training and Youth Affairs.
Featherstone, M. (1995) *Undoing Culture: Globalization, Postmodernism and Identity*, London: Sage.
Hall, S. (1996) 'The meaning of New Times', in D. Morley and Kuan-Hsing Chen (eds.) *Stuart Hall: Critical Dialogues in Cultural Studies*, London and New York: Routledge.
Halliday, M., and Matthiessen, C. (2004) *An Introduction to Functional Grammar*, (3rd edn), London: Arnold.
Hine, C. (2000) *Virtual Ethnography*, London: Sage.
Kenway, J., and Bullen, E. (2003) 'Self-representations of international women postgraduate students in the global university 'contact zone'', *Gender and Education*, 15: 5–20.
Meyer, B., and Geschiere, P. (1999) 'Globalization and identity: dialectics of flow and closure. Introduction', in B. Meyer and P. Geschiere (eds.) *Globalization and Identity: Dialectics of Flow and Closure*, Oxford: Blackwell.
Ong, A. (1991) 'The gender and labor politics of postmodernity.',*Annual Review of Anthropology* 20: 279–309.
Ong, A. (1997) 'Chinese modernities: narratives of nation and of capitalism', in A. Ong and D. Nonini (eds.) *Ungrounded Empires: The Cultural Politics of Modern Chinese Transnationalism*, New York: Routledge.
Ong, A. (1999) *Flexible Citizenship: The Cultural Logics of Transnationality*, Durham and London: Duke University Press.
Rizvi, F. (2000) 'International education and the production of global imagination', in N. Burbules and C. Torres (eds.) *Globalization and Education: Critical Perspectives,* London: Routledge.
Robertson, R. (1994) 'Globalization or glocalization?', *Journal of International Communication*, 1: 33–52.
Robertson, R. (2001) 'Globalization theory 2000+: major problematics', in G. Ritzer and B. Smart (eds.) *Handbook of Social Theory*, London: Sage.
Ryan, Y., and Stedman, L. (2002) *The Business of Borderless Education: 2001 Update*, Canberra: Department of Education, Science and Training.
Wodak, R. (2002) 'The discourse-historical approach', in R. Wodak and M. Meyer (eds.) *Methods of Critical Discourse Analysis,* London: Sage.

16 The Professional Doctorate in Transnational Education
Narrative Inquiry into Student Experience

Anne Chapman
The University of Western Australia

INTRODUCTION

This chapter emanates from the findings of research into student experiences of transnational education in Hong Kong. A qualitative case study investigated the experiences of professional doctorate candidates enrolled in a coursework and thesis program delivered in Hong Kong by an Australian university. Narrative research methods were used to explore the perspectives of students throughout the final year of their course. This chapter features the voice of one student, whose narrative provides insights into the dynamics and complexities of doctoral studies for transnational learners. The discussion is built around three key issues: expectations of the program; membership of a learning community; and the relation between learning style and research supervision.

THE PROFESSIONAL DOCTORATE

Professional doctorates are a means through which universities are becoming directly involved in research training for industry and the professions. The professional doctorate is 'a program of research and advanced study, which enables the candidate to make a significant contribution to knowledge and practice in their professional context [and in which]...the candidate may also contribute more generally to scholarship within a discipline of study' (Evans *et al* 1998: 1). It is a development of the 'taught doctorate', an award that includes a significant component that is both taught and formally assessed. The key feature of the professional doctorate is that the field of study is a professional discipline rather than academic enquiry and scholarship (UK Council for Graduate Education 2002).

Scott *et al* (2004) link the emergence of the professional doctorate to: the changing roles of the university and society in the production and use of knowledge; pressures for diversification and more professionally relevant programs; massification of higher education; demand from some professions and workplace requirements for high level skills and knowledge; the wider acceptance of the concepts of 'evidence-based' practice and the 'reflective practitioner' by professionals; and the development of work-based learning. According to Green *et al* (2001), professional doctorates are also a response to criticisms of the traditional PhD, in terms of its narrow focus, the limited set of skills acquired by PhD candidates, and its isolation in general from the work place.

The number of professional doctorate programs in Australia has increased since their introduction just over a decade ago (McWilliam *et al* 2002). Between 1996 and 2000 their offerings more than doubled from, 48 to 105, and student enrolments increased by more than 150 per cent, to 2,500 (Maxwell and Shanahan 2001). There has been a parallel growth in interest in and commitment to professional doctorates in Britain, the USA and Canada (McWilliam *et al* 2002). No data are available on the number of transnational professional doctorates presently on offer. However, given the recent acceleration of international student enrolments in higher education in Australia, with the strongest growth being in transnational programs particularly at the postgraduate level, it seems likely that transnational offerings of the professional doctorate will continue to expand.

THE RESEARCH CONTEXT

The focus of this chapter is a professional doctorate offered in Hong Kong by an Australian university with the involvement of a government funded local university partner. The program is a Doctor of Education (EdD) course operated and delivered by the Australian university at the campus of the university partner.

The course involves a combination of coursework and thesis offered over a part-time enrolment period of four years, with the coursework component delivered offshore by the Australian university staff in four intensive 25-hour units during the first year. Following successful completion of the units, a principal supervisor and a second supervisor each visit the student twice per year. The principal supervisor's first visit involves working on the development of a research proposal, which is to be presented orally and in writing to an academic committee within three months of the commencement of the supervision. The proposal must be approved by the committee before the research phase can commence.

THE RESEARCH PROJECT

The findings reported in this chapter form part of larger study that was undertaken with the aim of exploring the impact of the internationalization of higher education on student identity. A qualitative case study was made of the experiences of 21 students enrolled in the Hong Kong EdD program outlined above, to explore the impact of three main factors on the formation of student identity: reasons for choosing to enroll in the particular program; the social practices of the educational program; and the integration of family, work and study.

Narrative research methods were used to track six of those students through the final year of their doctoral thesis studies. This approach was considered useful because it 'captures both the individual and the context' (Moen 2006: 4). Narratives provided the means for these students to construct reflective accounts of their experiences of the doctoral program. Informal interviews were conducted frequently and regularly in person, by telephone and email. These 'episodic' interviews recurrently asked interviewees to present narratives of situation. They sought to foreground the voices of the students and their sense of 'lived experience'. Participants were asked to reflect, over time and in-depth, on their educational goals, expectations, learning experiences, learning orientations and strategies, and their relationships with their supervisors. The stories provide their perspectives on how they adapted, reacted and responded to the experience of being a transnational doctoral student. Excerpts from the narrative of one student provide the basis of the discussion to follow.

ALAN'S STORY

Alan, a mature-aged student, is married with two young children. He is a Chinese citizen and a Hong Kong national, for whom English is a second language. Alan's employment and educational background are in the general fields of electrical engineering and information technology education. Like most of his student peers, Alan is well-educated and well-qualified, and has experienced a variety of teaching and learning models in both English and Chinese. His educational qualifications include a Bachelor of Engineering degree and a Masters degree from a North American university. He also has a postgraduate teaching diploma from the Hong Kong university that is the local partner institution for his current Australian course. His doctoral study is his first experience of transnational education.

Expectations of the program

Alan reflects on his initial expectations of the course:

> Working in the education dimension as a lecturer, I found that a more in-depth knowledge in this dimension would be helpful for myself to

further make progress and contributions to my work. Studying an EdD program would allow me to understand more about education and, in particular, it allows me to work on research that is of my particular interest and field that relates to my work. I believe that through the process, especially with professional guidance from the professors, I would be able to benefit a lot.

Alan chose his doctoral program primarily as a means to professional development in his work as an educator. His longstanding goal has been to translate his doctoral research into practice. The professional development approach he describes draws together the student, the supervisor, and the knowledge and skills developed through his research project. This approach reflects a collaborative style similar to 'inhouse' inservice teacher education programs conducted amongst peers, an approach valued in many professional development programs in Australia (Bobis 2000). A consistent theme in these and other recent approaches to professional development is a commitment to a participatory, or democratic, form of professionalism through whole 'community' collaboration, teacher cooperation, and an informed knowledge base. Democratic discourses in education have a concern for giving voice to teachers, learners and other key stakeholders in educational practices through the processes of participation, collaboration and cooperation. Democratic discourses seek to demystify the professional work of teachers and foster the development of communities of practice where 'emphasis is placed upon participation in a community of practitioners, rather than merely the acquisition of a set of skills, or practices deemed to satisfy bureaucratic requirements (Sachs 1997: 272).

Encouraging its students to 'take up research questions that are germane to their current or projected career interests', the doctoral course in which Alan is enrolled can be viewed as operating to some degree within the discourse of democratic professionalism. The aim is for students to develop understanding and ownership of their research by focusing on relevant real life issues and problems. This perspective goes some way towards fostering a model of professional development that provides theoretical and practical resources and support for educationists to take control of their own professionalism.

This professional education doctorate starts with a year of intensive coursework activity with a 'community of practitioners' keen to enhance their professional practice. At the initial coursework stage of the doctoral program, students develop a strong sense of community through the perceived need to 'fit in well with the kind of program', as Alan puts it. They engage with other professional education students in small group discussions and workshop activities to address contemporary issues and problems in the Hong Kong education sector. These issues and problems derive from the students' own research questions, which are later developed into their doctoral research proposals.

However, the discursive practices of participation, collaboration and cooperation in the coursework units give way to the more 'solitary' activities of the supervision phase. A recurring theme in Alan's narrative is the attrition of the student 'community of practice', in favour of one-to-one communication between student and supervisor, conducted mostly by email, and with very few meetings each year. The shift from whole group learning to individual instruction is a major issue. It is at this point that the vision of this offshore professional doctorate as a form of democratic professionalism is compromised.

Learning community

With regard to learning community:

> If I could change any aspect of the course, I would probably want that the course can set a fixed gathering time (e.g. once a year or once every six months) for all students to attend, with a supervisor as the host. This should be in the form of a casual gathering for students to share their research experiences and update their research progress. The supervisor should act as a facilitator and provide constructive comments. I think this can benefit all students in terms of gaining more research insights. Right now, each student is pretty much working on his/her own. Even if you are in touch with a few other students, you won't be able to do this with everyone.

Research has found that membership of the academic community has been rated below professional learning and development by the 'non-typical' local and international student cohorts of professional doctorate programs (McWilliam *et al* 2002). However, for Australian students in transnational postgraduate programs in Hong Kong, the notion of the academic community is problematic (Chapman and Pyvis 2006). It was found that student identity is constructed through membership of a multi-layered 'learning community' including, for example, the international community, the classroom community and the professional community. There is a clear preference for collaborative approaches to learning in the classes, apart from discussing one's own research project, but individualistic approaches outside the classes. At the same time, students seek to maintain an intellectual independence with regard to their assignment work.

Alan's keen desire to maintain membership of the community of practice is somewhat at odds with this notion of intellectual independence. His perspectives are with the hindsight of nearly three years of supervision, mostly at a distance. He now sees great value in the learning community of his peers, and believes that 'scheduled, casual gatherings organized by the university can help build a better sense of belonging, as well as enrich the research knowledge of all students'. Most of the supervisors of Alan's cohort were supervising three or four students. Their schedules typically involved the doctoral students 'running into' each other either on the way to, or from, a meeting. Some supervisors, or students, arranged informal get-togethers over lunch or dinner, but these were generally ad hoc arrangements and students were often too busy with work commitments to attend. The common view of supervisors for this cohort was that students *desired* group meetings and close relationships with their peers, but work commitments typically took precedence over these activities.

Alan suggests that the onus is on the university to preserve the learning community. He states that 'casual' meetings should be part of the course, and facilitated by the supervisors. This is in line with the view of Clark and Clark (2000: 60), who maintain that the 'real strength of intensive teaching is that students get to know each other well' and that educators should utilize a number of introduction exercises to develop relationships of trust conducive to an effective learning experience. Transnational education sets up new learning communities and new social practices for learners and for teachers. What is significant, from Alan's narrative, is that the relationships between supervisors and students afford the *opportunity* to maintain and foster the community of practice as they engage in this particular kind of situated learning. The clear message is that *someone* needs to take responsibility in this regard.

Learning and supervision

Alan explains his feelings about the course:

> The major differences between this learning experience and my previous ones include the part-time study mode, no need to attend courses except for the first year of study, and a higher flexibility in selecting research topic and scheduling research timeline. I communicate with professors mainly via emails.

Alan recognizes that a number of 'trade-offs' are inherent in taking a transnational course. These are magnified in the context of thesis supervision. A major reason for choosing this mode of study was its convenience. In this case, the coursework units are compressed courses, taught over one week, during evenings and on weekends. Getting the classes 'out of the way' in one week is a means to managing work, study and family commitments. In their case studies of Australian courses delivered in Hong Kong, Evans and Tregenza (2002) found that family commitments and long working hours make study difficult. In compressed offshore courses more broadly, reading tends to be the task that suffers most due to lack of time (Chapman and Pyvis 2006). This is so for Alan who, even during the research and thesis phase, describes his main difficulty as the 'physical aspect', which includes 'allocating time to complete the planned tasks and to keep myself up-to-speed'.

> It is not easy to fit a study of this level into an already tight work schedule. In fact, the most difficult part I found was at the stage where I have to do interviews for my research, because it is very difficult to arrange interviews with interviewees that can fit into the time schedules of all parties. To overcome the difficulties, I have to set up a progress timeline in advance and check it regularly to ensure that a major lag in schedule does not happen. In case it does happen, I have to find ways to make up the time or to make alternate plans.

As a result, Alan believes that this course requires a different kind of learning style to that of his previous studies:

> I think the learning style needs to be more self-proactive and trial-and-error, where I have to try many different things, find problems during the process, and eventually seek for guidance before I can proceed further. I said this is more self-proactive because if I don't try and look for problems myself, I just cannot achieve anything by just sitting there and hoping to be fed with information. Therefore, the learning style certainly needs to be adjusted when compared to the time studying the bachelor or master degree. I think this is a positive change.

Alan's learning style has changed over time in line with his perspectives on learning. The overall shift is towards a more self-regulated style. Alan has developed an awareness of his academic strengths and weaknesses. He is now alert to the 'need' to become more proactive and take risks in trying 'different things'. He has reflected on the limitations of waiting for direction and instruction from his supervisor. His motivation waned at times, in which cases he relied on his supervisor for inspiration and 'prompting'. Now in the final semester of the course, he sees the benefits of taking control of his learning. This involves developing new learning skills, such as 'scheduling my own timeline for learning and research work' and 'openly discussing any issues I may have encountered during my research work with my supervisor'. It is not surprising that a doctoral student becomes more independent and develops self-regulated learning strategies over the duration of their course. It is likely, however, that self-regulated learning develops by *necessity* in the transnational environment. Of interest here is the influence of the offshore model of delivery on this process, and the role of the supervisor in providing support.

Alan describes his experience of research supervision as 'being mentored rather than being taught'. He takes the view that he has a responsibility to develop a good working relationship with his (principal) supervisor. He states that the 'second' supervisor has more of a 'background' role, and is not directly involved in the research project. Alan does not like to 'bother' his supervisor. He thinks it inappropriate to contact her with what he refers to as 'minor issues', even though 'she encourages frequent email communication and is always able to respond quickly. She is also able to provide constructive and guiding feedback'. Alan likes the model of several visits per year and regular email communication between visits. He can schedule his work and family commitments around both supervisors' visits to Hong Kong and is motivated to 'work hard on drafts' in time for these meetings. Alan likes to be 'directed' by his supervisor to complete tasks by set dates, but also appreciates the freedom to be able organize his own timeline. He states: 'I do not think that there is any obvious difference in the cultures of learning between myself and my supervisors'.

Reflecting on his overall experiences, Alan describes the best aspects of the course:

> I can achieve my goal (research of interest) with quite a large degree of flexibility (including timeline, topic, approach, etc.), and I can learn ways of conducting research through the communications with my supervisor. For a colleague who is thinking about doing this course, I would recommend him to ensure that he can fit the study well into his work schedule. I would also recommend him to plan his research schedule on a realistic basis, and be free to talk upfront to the supervisors during any stage of the research for any problems encountered.

CONCLUSION

The narrative account discussed in this chapter suggests that the experience of being a professional doctorate candidate in the transnational context is not straightforward. As a means to professional development as an educator, the Doctor of Education cited here provides an opportunity for a democratic approach to professional development, through membership of a strong learning community. Democratic discourses involve participation, collaboration and cooperation in a learning community. Coursework units typically provide access to this community. However, when students enter the research and thesis writing phase of the doctoral program, their sense of community may give way to one of isolation, as they engage in mostly solitary learning activities, and this is compounded by the physical distance between supervisor and student. There is an imperative for students to adapt and respond to the 'loss of community' by becoming more self-directed learners. The challenge to sustain and foster the learning community throughout all stages of a program should be taken up by providers of transnational courses. Alan's story is a provocation to do so.

REFERENCES

Bobis, J. (2000) *Count Me In Too Report: A Case Study of Implementation.* Sydney: NSW Department of Education and Training.

Chapman, A. and Pyvis, D. (2006) 'Quality, Identity and Practice in Offshore University Programmes: Issues in the internationalization of Australian higher education,' *Teaching in Higher Education*, 11(2): 233–245.

Clark, E. and Clark, P. (2000) 'Taking the Educational Show on the Road: The promises and pitfalls of intensive reading in off-shore post graduate coursework,' *International Education* 4(1): 1–13.

Evans, T., Fisher, A. and Gritchting, W. (1998) 'Guidelines: Professional doctorates,' Unpublished paper prepared for the Council of Deans and Directors of Graduate Studies, Brisbane, Australia.

Evans, T. and Tregenza, K. (2002) 'Academics' Experiences of Teaching Australian 'Non-local' Courses in Hong Kong,' Paper presented at the *Australian Association for Research in Education Conference*, Brisbane.

Green, B., Maxwell, T. W. and Shanahan, P. (eds., 2001) *Doctoral Education and Professional Practice: The Next Generation?* Armidale: Kardoorair Press.

Maxwell , T. W. and Shanahan, P. J. (2001) 'Professional Doctoral Education in Australia and New Zealand: Reviewing the scene.' In B. Green, T. W. Maxwell and P. Shanahan (eds.) *Doctoral Education and Professional Practice: The Next Generation?* Armidale: Kardoorair Press.

McWilliam, E., Taylor, P. G., Thomson, P., Green, B., Maxwell, T., Wildy, H. and Simons, D. (2002) *Research Training in Doctoral Programs: What Can be Learned From Professional Doctorates?* Canberra: Commonwealth Department of Education Science and Training.

Moen, T. (2006) 'Reflections on the Narrative Research Approach', *International Journal of Qualitative Methods*, 5(4): 1–11.

Sachs, J. (1997) 'Reclaiming the Agenda of Teacher Professionalism: The Australian experience', *Journal of Education for Teaching*, 23(3): 263–275.

Scott, D., Brown, A. J., Lunt, I. and Thorne, L. (2004) *Professional Doctorates: Integrating Academic and Professional Knowledge*, Buckingham: Open University Press.

UK Council for Graduate Education (2002) *Professional Doctorates*, Lichfield: UK Council for Graduate Education.

17 Experiences of Transnational Learning

Perspectives from Some Undergraduates in the People's Republic of China and Singapore

Michelle Wallace and Lee Dunn
Southern Cross University

INTRODUCTION

While transnational higher education has been a focus of study for almost a decade, much of the research has focussed on issues of quality assurance, culture and learning from the provider or 'supply' perspective. For some time one of the missing links in the literature was the student perspective. The in-house student feedback undertaken by universities in a number of countries as part of their quality processes tends to be reported publicly in a form that does not reveal nuanced information about transnational students' learning experiences. However, there is now a developing body of scholarship that attends to transnational students' perspectives and this chapter contributes to that through examination of the experiences of students in programs in the People's Republic of China (PRC) and Singapore.

BACKGROUND

Themes that have emerged from recent studies with transnational students include the reasons for undertaking a foreign degree and identity formation as a student of a foreign degree program (Chapman and Pyvis 2006a, b, 2007), curriculum and pedagogy, how students prefer to learn and the learning 'mix' of activities (Chapman and Pyvis 2005; Dunn and Wallace 2003; Evans and Tragenza 2003; Pannan and Gribble 2005), perceptions of the authority and credibility of the 'local' academic in relation to the 'foreign' academic (Bennington and Xu 2001; Evans and Tragenza 2003; Mileswska, 2006; Wallace and Dunn 2005) and time management and study/life balance (Chapman and Pyvis 2006a; Crossman 2005; Evans and Tragenza 2003; Dunn and Wallace 2003).

What strikes us in these studies is that a greater proportion seem to have focussed on the experiences of post-graduate students and (and we include our own previous research here) have seemingly regarded transnational students as somewhat homogenous. Here we focus on undergraduate students' experiences and examine some of the experiences of women and men, earner/learner and full-time students. In doing this explorative research on the diversity of transnational students we acknowledge that we have raised many further questions hitherto unexplored.

METHODOLOGY

A questionnaire was administered to students in two transnational business programs of an Australian university, one in Singapore and one in the PRC. Both programs are taught in one of the typical transnational modes—an Australian lecturer delivers one intensive block of teaching and this is supplemented with local academics teaching the remainder of the program. Study guides and other materials are also provided to the students. The Australian lecturer is the unit assessor; he or she designs the curriculum and assessment and either marks all of the assessment or moderates assessments marked by the local academic.

The questionnaire focussed on three distinct areas. The first was undergraduate students' reasons for undertaking their particular foreign degrees; the second explored the amount of time these students could devote to their studies and the perceived barriers to devoting more energy to study. Finally, the questionnaire investigated the students' current and preferred mix of learning activities. The questionnaire was administered online and at workshops.

STUDENT PROFILE

Twenty-six students were from a program in the PRC (seventeen women and nine men) and thirty-seven were from a program in Singapore (twenty-two women and fifteen men).

Fifteen students in the PRC program were between eighteen and twenty years of age (thirteen women and two men) and thirteen were from the twenty-one to thirty years age group (six women and seven men). No students in the PRC program were over thirty years of age. Only one in the Singapore program was in the eighteen to twenty age group (a woman), with thirty-two in the 21–30 years age group (twenty one-women and eleven men). Only four students from the Singapore program were aged over thirty and these were all men. There were five married women and four married men and all were from Singapore. The married men were in the thirty-plus age group and the women in the twenty-one to thirty age group.

Almost all of the students in the PRC program were full-time students and were not in paid employment. In the Singapore program, five women and ten men were in employment with the majority in full-time work. Thus, overall, 21 per cent of the Singaporean students were working but none of the PRC students were working, which provided some interesting contrasts. We would have been delighted to have more earner/learners from Singapore in our survey but their relatively low response rate may be indicative of their very busy lifestyles.

FINDINGS

Why study a transnational degree?

Forty percent of students gave the main reason for studying their particular degree as accessing an international qualification: 'My job requires international business knowledge which I believe this degree would help me with'. Of these respondents, 68 per cent were female and 32 per cent were male: 56 per cent were from the Singapore program and 44 per cent were from the PRC program.

The second reason (21 per cent of respondents) was that the chosen degree offered credit transfer for previous study. The third reason was that their country did not offer that type of degree (16 per cent) and males outnumbered females two to one in this response. Thirteen per cent cited that they could not get admittance into a similar degree in their own country. Here the proportion of males was slightly higher than females.

It can be noted that Waters (2005), albeit in relation to international rather than transnational students, has argued that such students desire a western degree because of the international prestige of the awarding institution and 'western' discipline skills and knowledge that contribute to identity formation. However, she draws a longer bow in arguing that this type of education is also valued for the tacit knowledge, and cultural and social capital of the overseas learning experience where 'fluency in the English language as well as less obvious qualities, such as confidence, sociability and cosmopolitanism' increase the social capital of the individual and their family in order to attain citizenship of one or more other countries (Waters 2005: 363). Doherty and Singh (2005: 7), again in relation to identities of international students in Australia, support this view of a foreign education as an 'investment in Western cultural capital and English language competence'. We (Dunn and Wallace 2003) also found that earner/learner students in Singapore wanted to earn a foreign degree in their own country for its prestige and relative convenience and because it offered western ways of knowing and specific skills that they deemed important to their occupational advancement.

However, in our current study we have found that proportionately more females and somewhat more students overall from the Singaporean program appear to have 'bought into' the concept of the worth of an international qualification and the need for credentials. Credit transfer also seems more important to female students while lack of the qualification in their home country and inability to gain admission to the types of degree in their own country seem of relatively more relevance to males, especially from the PRC.

FACTORS THAT LIMIT EFFECTIVE STUDY

While there is a robust literature on how students, studying in their own countries, balance their studies with other work/life commitments (for example Darab 2004; Hayden and Long 2006; Ogonor and Nwadiani 2006), there is less information of the interface between learning and work/family in relation to transnational students. Evans and Tragenza (2002) also found that the post-graduate Hong Kong students in their study had significant work life balance issues due to long-waged work hours and family commitments. Crossman's (2005) study of nine transnational, post-graduate, Thai learners found that the workplace environments of the students had an effect on their learning, that study time was managed around work and sometimes occurred in snatches during work time. Chapman and Pyvis (2005) found that their students tended to try to compartmentalise their work and studies but that more routine study activities were undertaken at work, including those that required computer access.

In our current study, Singaporean students, especially the males, cited the demands of their paid work as the main factors limiting their effective study. These men reported spending 33 per cent of their time on work and 22 per cent of their time on study while Singaporean women spent 21 per cent of their time at work and 32 per cent of their time on study. In comparison, PRC men reported spending 8 per cent of time on work and 33 per cent on study, the women spending 7 per cent of time on work and 38 per cent of their time on study. As all of these PRC students studied full time and only a handful had part-time jobs, this is not surprising. What is arresting is that 'lack of encouragement' was reported as the most critical barrier to more effective study for PRC students with the males citing this as twice as important a factor as the females.

Time management may be an issue for the fifteen Singaporean students, who are full-time earners and this is borne out by comments such as, 'I have a 9 a.m. to 6 p.m. job in Singapore then have to go to my lessons starting at 6:45 p.m. It's quite tiring and I don't know how long I have to do my part-time study'.

The next most significant barrier for Singaporean students was family commitments. As one woman stated: 'In my case I have kids so in class the lessons are being taught at high speed. Finishing up (with) the lessons for the day is hard'.

Despite some Singaporean women discussing parenting roles as a barrier, there were no significant gender differences from students in either program in relation to the demands of household domestic duties (which they reported as taking up between 4 per cent and 5 per cent of time for men and women in both programs). This may be indicative of family support or paid household help, which is much more prevalent in some Asian countries than in the west.

PREFERENCES FOR TYPES OF LEARNING ACTIVITIES

While acknowledging curriculum and other issues discussed in relation to transnational learning and teaching (see for example Leask [2003, 2004] on pedagogy; Evans and Tragenza (2003) on English language proficiency; and Ziguras (2001) on globalizing and de-traditionalizing tendencies of transnational education), our focus in the questionnaire was on delivery. It has been shown (again more usually with post-graduate students) that students have a preference for more face-to-face interaction with foreign academics from the university awarding the degree (Bennington and Xu 2001; Chapman and Pyvis 2005; Shanahan and McParlane 2005; Dunn and Wallace, 2003; Wallace and Dunn 2005).

Mileswska's (2006) recent study of three transnational, undergraduate, IT related programs in Hong Kong has revealed some further data. She found that students perceived the most important attributes to assist their learning were the development of strategies and formats that would enable communication between students and academics and students and students. Students expressed the most satisfaction with activities such as frequent face-to-face contact with their foreign academics, who displayed advanced instructional skills and understanding of the students' interests, contexts and needs. A high level of transactional presence, whereby technologies were used to support the perceptions of psychological presence (Shin 2003), was also highly valued. Mileswska (2006) concluded that increasing the teaching involvement of the Australian academics so that they taught 50 per cent of the course content and increasing student access to Australian academics through interactive technologies would assist student learning.

We (Dunn and Wallace 2003) have also found that students had some concerns about the credibility and authority of the local academics, as they did not set the curriculum or assessments. Other unpublished data from our 2003 research indicates that the Singaporean students wanted more and shorter workshops so they could digest material, more opportunities to talk with their lecturers on a one-to-one basis, and lecturer help in interpreting texts. They found self-directed learning with print-based study guides very onerous. Again, these factors point to the wish for more interactive, real- and virtual-time association with their foreign lecturer.

In our study, which is the subject of this chapter, students were asked to estimate the percentage of their total learning time currently devoted to a range of learning activities and then suggest the percentage of time they would ideally like to spend on these and other learning activities. Overall, the students expressed a decided preference for more learning time in face-to-face lectures/tutorials with their Australian lecturer and slightly less time with their local tutor. On all other activities—formal online classes with the local tutor, online interaction with fellow students, reading, researching in the library or online—there was no significant difference between current practice and what the students would wish for. There was some slight difference in relation to preparing for exams and assignments with students wishing to spend slightly less time on this activity. Thus far our data confirms previous findings.

However, a gender analysis reveals some interesting differences in relation to PRC students. The women want more time with their Australian lecturer (almost double the time they currently have) while the men want slightly less time with the Australian lecturer. In relation to face-to-face tutorials with the local tutor, PRC women want about the same amount of time but men want less by half. While PRC women want about the same amount of formal online classes with their local tutor, the males want less by half. However, these males want almost double the online interaction with fellow students; the women want about the same. The women want slightly less time spent on reading while the men want significantly more time spent on researching in the library or online. This appears to show a clear preference by males in the PRC program for less face-to-face and structured learning experiences and more 'high-tech', independent learning and is a new finding.

Some of the PRC men's perspective may be related to possible current restricted access to the Internet in PRC but forms an interesting, albeit speculative, picture when allied to the men's reports of 'lack of encouragement'. It appears that the women appreciate and want more of the traditional modes of education, wishing for more face-to-face interaction while the men do not find this an 'encouraging' teaching method and are more interested in newer technologies, which demand a different type of learner subjectivity: autonomous and self-directed. The sample of PRC men here is insufficient to draw broad conclusions but this aspect of their learning, and possibly social interactions, requires further research.

In relation to the Singaporean students, both males and females express a clear preference for almost three-times the time currently spent on attending face-to-face tutorials with their Australian lecturer. The women want less time with their Singaporean tutor while the men want slightly more. Singaporean males want less time spent on online classes with their local lecturers and tutors, while females want slightly less online interaction outside formal classes while the males want somewhat more. Both want slightly less time on meetings with fellow students, reading study materials and preparing for assignments and exams. There appears to be a clear preference among Singaporean program students for structured learning experiences and increased face-to-face learning with their foreign lecturers.

Other than the male PRC students, the overwhelming result was that the students wanted more time with their Australian lecturers. There were a number of reasons cited for this. Firstly, students wanted to understand more what the Australian lecturer's standards were. As one student put it: 'It would be better to have lecturers from XYZ university come over and lecture more so we would know what they expect from us'. Secondly, there were issues around English language. On the one hand, students wanted more of the lecturer's time as English was difficult for them: 'I hope the (Australian) teacher will stay a long time because language is so difficult for us to study in this program and we have so many questions to ask the teacher'. On the other hand, students wanted more exposure to what they called 'native English tutors' in order to improve their English language skills. One student suggested that transnational students communicate with English-speaking students online and even gain work experience in a company where staff must use English. English proficiency is clearly seen both as a means to understand the course content and as an avenue to the cultural and social capital that would enhance employment opportunities in a globalised labour market.

Students also asked for greater communication between their Australian lecturers and local tutors: 'I hope that our local lecturer can communicate more with the Australian lecturer because sometimes they did not communicate and hence it caused students a lot of confusion'; and, 'I hope local and Australian lecturers have discussed more and guided us more and shared their ideas together'. This confirms Pannan's and Gribble's (2005) findings, that communication needs to be increased and fostered among those staff at all levels of a transnational educational partnership.

However, some students reported that their local tutors helped them understand the 'ways' of the Australian lecturer, including interpreting assessment requirements. These students also accorded local tutors less 'expert' status than the Australian lecturers possibly because the Australian academics have the power over the curriculum and assessment protocols.

CONCLUSION

This study has been explorative in nature. However, some lessons have been learned. Clearly, western notions of gender differences regarding work and family commitments and women's 'double shift' do not seem as applicable as the social setting and labour market appear to support middle-class women in achieving some balance as Brooks (2006) has noted in her study of women in Hong Kong and Singapore. It is the earner/learner males from Singapore who exhibit the most role stress around work and study, perhaps because they are a little older and are in more demanding jobs. The working women do not seem to be more taxed by work and family commitments, presenting a somewhat different picture to that of female earner learners in western societies. Given that this study canvassed the perspectives of a small number of earner/learners and seems to provide contrary information to studies such as those by, for instance, Evans and Tragenza (2003) and Chapman and Pyvis (2005) further investigation would be warranted into the situation for undergraduate earner/learners in transnational programs. A diary approach (Nonis *et al* 2006) would lend itself to a more fine-grained analysis.

While strong preference for traditional, discursive approaches to learning appear to come from the majority of students, with Singaporean students most desiring additional face-to-face time with their foreign lecturers, PRC males appear to value more independent learning opportunities utilizing technologies. This finding may be an aberration or may reflect a non-learning related variable such as attraction to new technology. However, the learning preferences between male and female students and students in transnational programs in different countries warrants further research, particularly as the same programs from any one institution may be taught in a number of host countries in similar delivery modes. One size may not fit all and differentiation may be needed to cater to different learning preferences

The issues around students' perceived differences in authority and credibility between the foreign and local academics remains a vexed one. Clearly, greater communication between foreign and local academics, including partnerships in the development of curriculum and assessment and the professional development of both foreign and local academics in relation to transnational pedagogy, would be highly desirable. Further research on best practice models for developing more equal learning and teaching partnerships in contracts would be helpful.

Arguably, the most complex issues in the model of transnational education evidenced in these Singapore and PRC programs are those around the acquisition of cultural capital and possibilities for cultural dissonance. On the one hand, even though the students do not leave their own country, they may find that the pedagogy and curriculum are highly at odds with their prior learning experiences and the educational traditions of their own culture. Added to this may be difficulties with English language and the academic English language of certain disciplines. Culture/cognitive shock or cognitive dissonance can ensue (Ryan and Hellmundt 2003; Chapman and Pyvis, 2005) thus making the learning experience problematic. This can be mollified by skilled local academics in interpreting the cultural givens behind a specific curriculum content or pedagogy. The local academics may well be the boundary riders holding the cultural borders together but may also be perceived as less authoritative because they do not control the curriculum and assessment.

On the other hand, it is clear that students, who relocate to another country to undertake a western degree, are part of the accumulation of not only economic but cultural and social capital. However, one wonders whether students, who undertake foreign degrees as transnational students in their own countries, participate as fully in the accumulation of the social and cultural capital they desire. It would seem that their relatively limited exposure to native English speaking academics from the foreign university, greater contact with local tutors, who may interpret the foreign academics' pedagogy and curriculum, often in the local language and a curriculum that has been adapted to their cultural milieu could have the effect of watering down such elements as English fluency, sociability and western cultural capital. That students overall ask for more contact with the foreign lecturer seems to imply that they want not only the authority of the western academic but want to see inside the western way of thinking in an unmediated way. They want to 'buy into' the cultural and social capital but it is less available to them because of the mode of course delivery. Further research, comparing the identity formation and cultural capital accumulation of international students who travel abroad and transnational students who remain in their own cultures, would be helpful.

We advocate that transnational students not be regarded as a homogenous group and suggest that differences, some of which we have alluded to here, be taken into account when designing and delivering transnational programs.

REFERENCES

Bennington, L. and Xu, L. L. (2001) 'Relative Benefits of Offshore MBA Study: An Australia-China twinning model', *Journal of Higher Education Policy and Management*, 23 (2): 219–230.

Brooks, A. (2006) *Gendered Work in Asian Cities: The new economy and changing labour markets*, Burlington, VT: Ashgate.

Chapman, A. and Pyvis, D. (2005) 'Culture Shock and the International Student ÒOff-shoreÓ'. *Journal of Research in International Education*, 4: 23–42.

—— (2006a) 'Quality, Identity and Practice in Off-shore University Programmes: Issues in the internationalization of Australian higher education', *Teaching in Higher Education*, 11 (2): 233–245.

—— (2006b) 'Dilemmas in the Formation of Student Identity in Off-shore Higher Education: A case study in Hong Kong', *Educational Review*, 58 (3): 291–302.

—— (2007) 'Why University Students Choose an International Education: A case study in Malaysia', *International Journal of Educational Development*, 27: 235–246.

Crossman, J. (2005) 'Work and Learning: The implications for Thai transnational learners', *International Education Journal*, 6 (1): 18–29.

Darab, S. (2004) 'Time and Study: Open foundation female students' integration of study with family, work and social obligations', *Australian Journal of Adult Learning*, 44 (3): 327–352.

Doherty, Catherine A. and Singh, Parlo (2005) International student subjectivities: biographical investments for liquid times. In Proceedings AARE Education Research Conference,'Creative Dissent: Constructive Solutions', University of Western Sydney, Parramatta Campus, Australia. Online. Available at: http://eprints.qut.edu.au/archive/00002868/ (accessed 2nd November 2007).

Dunn, L and Wallace, M. (2003) 'Learning at Home, Teaching Off-shore: Experiences of students and academics in an Australian degree taught in Singapore', *Proceedings of the IDP Conference*, Melbourne. October.

Evans, T. D. and Tragenza, K. (2002) 'Academics' Experiences of Teaching Australian ÒNon-localÓ Courses in Hong Kong', *paper presented at the Australian Association for Research in Education Conference, 'Crossing borders: new frontiers for educational research'*, Brisbane, 1–5 December.

—— (2003) 'Students' Experiences of Studying Australian Courses in Hong Kong', in Weiyan Zhang (ed.) *Global Perspectives: Philosophy and Practice in Distance Education*, Beijing: China Central Radio and Television University Press, 322–335.

Hayden, M. and Long, M. (2006). 'A Profile of Part-time Undergraduates in Australian Universities', *Higher Education Research and Development*, 25 (1): 37–52.

Leask, B. (2003) 'Beyond the Numbers—Levels and layers of internationalization to utilise and support growth and diversity', *17th IDP Australian International Education Conference proceedings*. Online. Available at: http://www.idp.com/17aiec/selectedpapers/Least%20%20Preparing%20students%20for%20life%2022-10-03.pdf (accessed 27 June 2005).

—— (2004) 'Transnational Education and Intercultural Learning: Reconstructing the off-shore teaching team to enhance internationalization,' *Proceedings of the Australian Universities Quality Forum 2004*. Online. Available at: http://www.auqa.edu.au/auqf/2004/proceedings/AUQF2004_Proceedings.pdf (accessed 27 June 2005).

Mileswska, I. (2006) 'A Multidimensional Model for Transnational Computing Education Programs,' unpublished PhD thesis, Victoria University, Australia.

Nonis, S., Philhours, M. and Hudson, G. (2006) 'Where Does the Time Go? A Diary Approach to Business and Marketing Students' Time Use', *Journal of Marketing Education*, 21: 121–134.

Ogonor, B. O. and Nwadiani, M. (2006) 'An Analysis of Non-Instructional Time Management of Undergraduates in Southern Nigeria', *College Student Journal*, 40 (1): 204–217.

Pannan, L. and Gribble, K. (2005) 'A Complexity of Influences on Teaching in Transnational Environments: Can we simplify and support it?', *paper presented at the Open and Distance Learning Association of Australia (ODLAA) conference*. Online.

Available at: http://www.odlaa.org/events/2005conf/ref/ODLAA2005Pannan-Gribble.pdf (accessed 18 October 2007).

Ryan, J. and Hellmundt, S. (2003) 'Excellence through Diversity: Internationalization of curriculum and pedagogy', paper presented at the 17th IDP Australian International Education Conference, October.

Shanahan, P. and McParlane, J. (2005). 'Serendipity or Strategy? An Investigation into Entrepreneurial Transnational Higher Education and Risk Management', *On the Horizon*, 13 (4): 220–228.

Shin, N. (2203) 'Transactional Presence as a Critical Predictor of Success in Distance Learning', *Distance Education*, 24 (1): 69–87.

Wallace, M. and Dunn, L. (2005) 'Cultural Teaching and Teaching Culture: Lessons from students and academics in some transnational degree programs', *The International Journal of Knowledge, Culture and Change Management*, 1: 1–18.

Waters, J. (2005) 'Transnational Family Strategies and Education in the Contemporary Chinese Diaspora', *Global Networks*, 5 (4): 359–377.

Ziguras, C. (2001) 'Educational Technology in Transnational Higher Education in South East Asia: The cultural politics in flexible learning', *Educational Technology and Society*, 4 (4): 8–18.

Part IV
Implications for Institutions

18 Quality Assurance for Transnational Education

International, National and Institutional Approaches

Grant McBurnie

RMIT University

INTRODUCTION

Due to geographical (and perhaps organizational) distance from the provider institution, transnational education (TNE) programs are inherently more prone than their domestic counterparts to disconnection and negligence. The offshore enterprise appears to be far less stable than the home operation: there are several well-publicized instances of transnational programs haemorrhaging funds (McBurnie 2006). In cases where fees are charged, there is always the possibility of friction between academic and commercial priorities, and the potential for corruption in the form of low entry requirements, soft marking and rubbery academic standards. From a pedagogical perspective, there are particular demands involved in delivering a foreign course to international students based in their home country. All of these factors underline the need for sound and effective quality assurance. Where quality is poor, several parties are affected. At the very least: the students who receive substandard education; the host-country that receives suboptimal human resource development, with damaging implications for nation-building; the provider institution—and by extension the provider country—that suffers a damaged reputation and financial loss.

Students, exporting and importing countries, foreign provider institutions, and their local partners, and international organizations that address cross-border education— all have an interest in fostering the quality of transnational education. In reality, there is significant overlap between these categories: many countries are both importers and exporters (though most are predominantly one or the other); regional players are also members of global forums (such as UNESCO—the United Nations Educational, Scientific and Cultural Organization); and national regulators and institutionally based academics serve on regional and international forums on higher education.

This chapter looks at the national and international construction of principles for transnational quality assurance (QA) and considers how these can be applied at the institutional level. Balancing principle and practice requires us to lift our sights from the daily minutiae, in order to consider the broader issues involved in transnational education (including why we are doing it at all), and then conversely look at ways of integrating these principles into the practical operational require-ments of TNE. I focus in turn on international approaches (global and regional), national approaches (importer and exporter) and institutional approaches, considering: Who are the key actors? What are the policy drivers (considerations, goals, etc.)? What are the outcomes (documents and methodologies)?

INTERNATIONAL APPROACHES

Rationales for international cooperation on quality assurance include promoting consumer protection, and facilitating smooth pathways for student and academic mobility through the international recognition and portability of qualifications. Reasons for regional cooperation include: strengthening the region as a competitor in terms of being an exporter; conversely, strengthening the region in terms of dealing effectively with imports (eg, it is in the interests of the Asia Pacific to work together to get the best for their students and not all invent the regulatory wheel from scratch). There is also concern on the part of many educationists to ensure that trade agreements (such as GATS—the General Agreement on Trade in Services—and various bilateral and regional Free Trade Agreements) do not supplant or over-rule agreements that have been developed in the context of international cooperation for the enhance-ment of educational values, rather than commercial priorities.

GLOBAL

The key global organizations addressing this issue are UNESCO and the OECD (Organization for Economic Cooperation and Development).

UNESCO comprises 191 member states and on its web site describes itself as functioning as a 'laboratory of ideas and a standard-setter to forge universal agreements on emerging ethical issues.' A leading arena for the discussion of quality issues is the UNESCO Global Forum on International Quality Assurance, Accreditation and the Recognition of Qualifications in Higher Education, which aims, *inter alia*, 'to promote education as a public good' and 'to promote quality assurance beyond national borders.' There is a concern to ensure that international educa-tion is not perceived and regulated solely in terms of trade priorities. In this light, the intergovernmental organization notes that more than 100 of its member states have signed a range of legally binding UNESCO conventions concerning education. These can be used constructively to influence, interpret, and modify the outcomes of GATS in relation to education (Uvalic-Trumbic 2002: 8–10). The UNESCO position paper on *Higher Education in a Globalized Society* sets out the organization's concerns about the effect of trade-oriented cross-border education on the capacity of states to regulate quality and ensure consumer protection, and its aim to use its 'standard-setting, capacity building and clearinghouse functions to assist Member States in the formulation of appropriate policies and strategies to meet the challenges posed to higher education by globalization' (UNESCO 2003: 3).

The OECD—comprising 30 developed countries and relationships with a further seventy countries—describes itself as 'a unique forum where the governments of 30 market democracies work together to address the economic, social and governance challenges of globalization as well as to exploit its opportunities' (OECD 2005: n.p.). It has run from 2002–2004 a series of important international conferences on trade in education services, also addressing concerns about consumer protection and quality assurance. Recently the two organizations have collaborated in the creation of 'Guidelines for Quality Provision in Cross-Border Higher Education' (OECD 2005). Recommendations, principles and suggested actions are addressed to six sets of stakeholders: governments; higher education institutions/providers, including academic staff; student bodies; quality assurance and accreditation bodies; academic recognition bodies; and professional bodies.

Rather than simply setting out principles as abstractions, the guidelines are notable for urging that each set of stakeholders take responsibility for ensuring good practice within its sphere. These include activities to promote consumer protection; transparency of information about courses and qualifications; ensuring that institutions and national systems address quality issues in crossborder education— including appropriate measures for approval, monitoring and review; promoting international networking among peers; and, of course, promoting the use of the *Code of Good Practice in the Provision of Transnational Education*. The *Code* sets out 11 principles relating to matters including: quality and standards; admission requirements; promotional information; staff members; conduct of agents; financial arrangements; and recognition of qualifications (UNESCO/Council of Europe 2001).

REGIONAL

There are numerous regional networks specifically focusing on quality assurance for higher education. Two regional examples are focused on below: Asia and Europe, covering a mixture of developed and developing countries, and countries in transition. East Asia provides an example of a loosely integrated approach in its early stages, and Europe illustrates a region striving for close integration in education and other fields.

As part of the larger project of European integration, 40 European states are engaged in the building of the 'European Area of Higher Education' by 2010. In the context of seeking means of convergence, delivery arrangements that do not fit the traditional mould—such as TNE—come under close scrutiny. Dos Santos notes that 'many of the instruments to be developed ... to deal with the "promotion of mobility by overcoming obstacles to the effective exercise of free movement" may be of relevance for the regulation of transnational education and vice versa' (dos Santos 2000: 1).

In early 2005, the European Association for Quality Assurance in Higher Education, with the support of the European Commission, published *Standards and Guidelines for Quality Assurance in the European Higher Education Area*, addressing QA within Higher Education institutions, external QA, and external QA agencies. The document includes recommendations for the future direction of QA in the region, and declares that:

> The proposals offer increased transparency, security and information about higher education for students and society more generally. They equally offer higher education institutions recognition and credibility and opportunities to demonstrate their dedication to high quality in an increasingly competitive and sceptical environment. For the quality assurance agencies the proposals enhance their own quality and credibility and connect them more productively to their wider European professional fraternity. (EAQAHE 2005: 34).

The details of implementation must be further worked out. In the concrete European context of a regionally agreed goal, and an imminent deadline, it is likely that the most practicable solutions will prevail.

The Asian region is a major importer and exporter of transnational education. From an educationist viewpoint, a key development is the establishment in early 2003 of the Asia Pacific Quality Network (APQN) as a sub-network of the International Network of Quality Assurance Agencies in Higher Education (INQAAHE). Project committees were assigned to work on six priority areas:

1. Compilation of Quality Indicators.
2. Information Gathering and Dissemination on QA Agencies in the Region.
3. Compilation of Information on National Qualifications Frameworks.
4. Facilitation of Regional Training and Development Workshops.
5. Quality Assurance of Distance Education.

6. Staff Exchange and Secondment among QA Agencies (Peace Lenn 2004: 20–21).

Published output to date includes the *UNESCO–APQN toolkit: Regulating the quality of cross-border education* (2006). Covering both receiving and sending country perspectives, this document discusses problems that can arise with cross-border education, discusses the functions and operation of regulatory frameworks and looks at various examples of frameworks from receiving and providing countries.

NATIONAL APPROACHES

Importers

The key concerns for the host country come under the umbrella of consumer protection: ensuring that students are not defrauded or fobbed off with substandard educational provision. In some cases, the governments are also concerned with questions of how the role of foreign providers fits with the nation building priorities of the country. In the case of Malaysia and Vietnam, for example, this extends to requiring specified subjects to be taught as a compulsory component of the curriculum.

The chief mechanism for the importing country is to establish regulations for the entry and operation of the foreign provider. This can include setting conditions for market entry (generally a registration or licensing requirement that sets out the criteria that must be met in order for a provider to operate in the host country); a periodic reporting requirement for the provider to update information on developments; a mechanism for reviewing/assessing the provider's conduct; and a mechanism for receiving and responding to public complaints. McBurnie and Ziguras (2007: ch. 6) suggest that the type of regulation depends upon whether the country is in a 'demand absorption' phase or an 'enrichment' phase; as capacity is built, host governments will increasingly ratchet up quality requirements as a means of regulating the market, squeezing out lower-standard providers and ensuring that transnational education contributes more effectively to the high end of the spectrum. At the end of the day, quality requirements will be the preferred lever for dealing with cross-border education.

An excellent example of an information transparency approach is the Non-Local Higher and Professional Education (Regulation) Ordinance, operating in Hong Kong since 1997 (documentation on the Ordinance is provided at: http://www.emb.gov.hk/ncr). In order to operate on Hong Kong soil, foreign providers must obtain government registration (or exemption from registration if partnered with a recognized local public provider). The foreign provider must furnish a suite of information on the course, and an annual report on developments and any changes to the course. The information is publicly available to interested persons. Required information includes such matters as course details; the division of responsibilities between local and foreign partner in terms of administrative roles (advertising and marketing, provision of facilities, receipt of fees, collection and return of assignments, administration of examinations, gathering of student feedback, and so on) and academic roles (course design and adaptation of learning materials, selection and appointment of local teaching staff, student selection and admission, setting and marking of assessable tasks); details of resources and services provided in Hong Kong (course materials, library access, IT facilities, language and study support, pastoral care); and details of fees and refund arrangements, qualifications and experience of teaching staff, and quality assurance procedures.

It is notable that, whether or not a provider operates in Hong Kong, the Ordinance documentation can be used by an institution as a template for describing in detail the resourcing and delivery of any transnational course. One might wonder whether every institution operating transnationally could answer in detail all of these questions for all of its courses.

It must be stressed that transparency of information is not by itself a guarantee of quality, but it is an important component.

Exporters

Exporters' concerns about the quality of TNE are enmeshed in trade, trade policy and trade agreements. Key examples of export country guidelines include those produced by the UK Quality Assurance Agency (QAA 2004), the Australian Vice Chancellors' Committee (AVCC 2005) and the USA's New England Association of Schools and Colleges (NEASC 2003). At stake are national reputation and international relations, as well as revenue. Failures (at least, *conspicuous* failures) damage not only the individual institution but also the 'national brand'. Like healthcare—another service intimately entwined with the wellbeing and future of the person—poor-quality education has implications and an emotional resonance beyond that of most faulty industrial products (unless your car brakes fail or your gas barbecue explodes).

In this context, education industry body IDP Education Australia emphasized the value of a national quality approach in terms of protecting the country's reputation in an international marketplace:

Essentially, if Australian transnational education service providers are to maintain and grow this important economic, cultural, and social resource in a highly and increasingly competitive market, a foundation requirement is product excellence and wide appreciation of that excellence by consumers.

Equally, a quality failure by even a small minority of providers could, and almost certainly would, have a negative impact across the sector and on the reputation of Australia, and potentially other Australian products and services, in at least the transnational arena immediately affected by such failure. (IDP 2005: 2)

The Australian government has recently developed a Transnational Quality Strategy (TQS) aimed at 'ensuring the quality of Australian education and training delivered offshore' (DEST 2006). With national codes and any type of self-regulation, there is, of course, the issue of credibility. (A variation on the old saying 'Ask my brother if I'm a liar,' is, 'Ask me if I'm a liar'.) The answer is, perhaps, independent, international external review, publicising the reports, and provision of optimal detail. The latter would require explication of principles, methodology, findings—showing warts and all—as well as instances of good practice and, where appropriate, enough detail to be of use to other institutions such governments and professional bodies as well as students and whatever other stakeholders are involved, in pursuing their own work.

Treated with critical caution, these national approaches provide a useful contribution to the construction of a rigorous approach to the quality assurance of transnational education.

INSTITUTIONAL APPROACHES

Three elements are essential to an effective institutional approach to the quality assurance of transnational education. First, a stated set of principles that define good practice. (At a basic level, for example, that students should have access to appropriate computer resources.) As discussed above, there is plenty of material for institutions to draw from. Next, a set of measures/benchmarks that give flesh to the principles. (To continue the example: there should be a specific ratio of students to computers, and that the latter should meet stated hardware and software specifications.) Naturally, some qualities are not so readily quantifiable and call for critical qualitative judgment. Last, it is necessary to have a sound methodology for reviewing programs, determining whether principles and measures are being met, and for taking action to remedy shortcomings and build upon strengths. This will normally involve periodic reviews by a panel that may consist of external members as well as university staff.

In turn, there are five key areas to be addressed:

1. Publicity, marketing and promotion: The principle is that the institution should provide accurate, truthful, and transparent information about its transnational course offerings. Students should not be misled about such matters as the resources that will be available to them, or the recognition accorded to the course in terms of professional recognition, employment or entry to further study. (Of course, the aim of marketing materials is to attract clients by presenting the service in the best possible light. Fraud and factual misinformation aside, whether the program is as wonderful as the glossy brochure suggests is a matter of opinion.) From an informational viewpoint, the Hong Kong approach is a beacon of clarity and transparency. However, as noted above, information in itself does not guarantee quality. Caveat emptor!

2. Student administration: The general principle is that admission requirements and assessment standards for the transnational program should be the same as those in the counterpart course in the home institution. (Comparability is not always straightforward. It is notable that multi-campus institutions in the home jurisdiction often have a range of entry requirements for similar courses, varying according to the geographical convenience, facilities and reputation of the campus.) Due to concerns about the relative influence of commercial and academic considerations, fee-charging courses are, justly or unjustly, more readily open to allegations of soft-marking and other forms of corruption.

   It is necessary to ensure that the recording of marks, the filing of student documentation, and the production of results transcripts are handled centrally by the credentialing institution. This ensures the integrity, accessibility and longevity of data (on the assumption that, even if the TNE operation closes, the home institution will nonetheless live on) as well as reducing the dangers of mishandling and possible fraud.

3. Curriculum and pedagogy: The general principle is that the curriculum for TNE should be the same as the home campus course, with appropriate adaptation to suit local circumstances. Behind this simple statement lies a world of oft-vexed debate about what is 'appropriate'. At one end of the ideological spectrum, critics decry TNE as cultural imperialism, whereby (usually) western values, concepts and approaches are imposed on (usually) less-developed countries, undermining and stifling local values, practices, and creativity. On the other hand, many students insist that they want the full-strength dose of foreign education that they are paying for—not a watered down version for local consumption. Some are indeed very blunt in their views, making it clear that they don't want to pay the price for what they (perhaps unfairly) see as the fashionable political correctness of guilt-ridden western academ-

ics, or ambitious local identities looking for a nationalistic cause to champion.

A sensible position is probably somewhere in between. The solution—easier said than done—is to ensure that all curricula are infused with an international perspective. At the very least, appropriate adaptation should include local examples, explain foreign terms and provide context for foreign examples.

4. Teaching and learning resources: The general principle is that the credentialing institution is responsible for ensuring adequate staff numbers and appropriate qualifications and experience of staff, and suitable provision of classroom space, computer facilities, library holdings, and so on. These can be measured against home institution standards, or against specifications that set minimum thresholds below which the course cannot be effectively conducted.

5. Finance, governance and management: This principle addresses the importance of such matters as carrying out due diligence on potential partners; the need for carefully drawn and detailed contractual arrangements; rigorous business planning and financial forecasting (enthusiasm for a new activity frequently leads to an overestimation of enrolments and an underestimation of costs); and ensuring that the offshore program is run as an integral part of the institution's academic activities with clear lines of responsibility and control.

There are numerous useful resources for helping institutions in putting principle into practice (and indeed distilling into pithy principles the lessons of years of practice). The Australian Universities Quality Agency (AUQA) publication *Quality Audit and Assurance for Transnational Education* (2006) discusses matters from the perspectives of both the auditor and the audited, and provides critical reflections on the findings of several years of reviews of offshore programs. The published audit reports of AUQA and QAA, and institutional research commissioned under the Transnational Quality Strategy provide important resources, as does the growing literature in academic journals and reports by the UK-based Observatory on Borderless Higher Education.

CONCLUSION

During the 1980s and much of the 1990s, the rapid development of transnational provision outpaced the nascent discussion of quality assurance for cross border education. There is now a raft of QA resources, ranging from the philosophical, to the hard-nosed practical. These are produced by national and international stakeholders, with various motivations, including enhancing international mobility, consumer protection, ensuring an appropriate balance between academic and trade priorities, and protecting national and institutional reputation. Some of these may be regarded as platitudinous and self-serving; some are carefully crafted statements of general principle (that seek to reach a form of words that is a workable compromise between contesting pro- and anti-trade viewpoints, and sometimes opposed national interests); and some are (critical or disingenuous) accounts of institutional practice. Much of it is sound advice, and thoughtful delineation of issues involved, and categories of action that need attention. QA is an evolving field that repays repeated visits to the information resources discussed in this chapter. It is likely that growing competition in transnational education will mean that quality requirements will be used by governments as a primary lever for regulating the flow of programs and institutions across borders.

REFERENCES

AUQA (2006) *Quality Audit and Assurance for Transnational Higher Education*. Melbourne: Australian Universities Quality Agency.

AVCC (2005) *Provision of Education to International Students: Code of Practice and Guidelines for Australian Universities*, Canberra: Australian Vice-Chancellors' Committee. Online. Available at: http://www.avcc. edu.au/documents/publications/CodeOfPracticeAndGuidelines2005.pdf (accessed 3 November 2005).

DEST (2006) 'Quality of Offshore Education and Training'. Australian Government: Department of Education, Science and Training. Online. Available at: http://aei.dest.gov.au/AEI/GovernmentActivities/QAAustralianEducationAndTrainingSystem/Default.htm (accessed 30 July 2006).

dos Santos, S. M. (2000) 'Introduction to the Theme of Transnational Education'. *Keynote Address to the Conference of the Directors General for Higher Education and the Heads of the Rectors' Conferences of the European Union*, Aveiro, Portugal, 3 April. Online. Available at: http://www. crue.org/eurec/transed.htm (accessed 18 October 2007).

EAQAHE (2005) 'Standards and Guidelines for Quality Assurance in the European Higher Education Area'. Helsinki: European Association for Quality Assurance in Higher Education. Online. Available HTTP: http://www. enqa.net/files/BergenReport210205.pdf (accessed 4 April 2006).

IDP Education Australia (2005) 'Submission to the Discussion Paper: A National Quality Strategy for Australian Transnational Education and Training'. 3 June. Online. Available at: http://aei.dest.gov.au/AEI/GovernmentActivities/QAAustralianEducationAndTrainingSystem/QualStrat_Submssns/IDP_pdf.pdf (accessed 30 July 2006).

McBurnie, G. (2006) '"Leveraged Footprints", "Dark Clouds" and "Bleeding Millions": Perspectives on Australian Universities' Offshore Campuses'. *Perspectives in Education*, 24 (4): December.

McBurnie, G. and Ziguras, C. (2007) *Transnational Education: Issues and Trends in Offshore Higher Education*. London: Routledge.

NEASC (2003) 'Principles of Good Practice in Overseas International Education Programs for Non-U.S. Nationals'. Bedford, MA: New England Association of Schools and Colleges Commission on Institutions of Higher Education. Online. Available at: http://www.neasc.org/cihe/overseas_programs. PDF (accessed 3 November 2005).

OECD (2005) *Guidelines for Quality Provision in Cross-border Higher Education.* Paris: Organisation for Economic Cooperation and Development.

Peace Lenn, M. (2004) *Quality Assurance and Accreditation in Higher Education in East Asia and the Pacific.* Washington, D.C.: World Bank.

QAA (2004) 'Code of Practice for the Assurance of Academic Quality and Standards in Higher Education. Section 2: Collaborative Provision and Flexible and Distributed Learning (Including E-learning)'. Gloucester, UK: Quality Assurance Agency for Higher education. Available at: http://www.qaa. ac.uk/academicinfrastructure/codeOfPractice/section2/collab2004.pdf (accessed 3 November 2005).

UNESCO (2003) *Higher Education in a Globalized Society,* Paris: UNESCO. UNESCO and Council of Europe (2001) *Code of Good Practice in the Provision of Transnational Education,* Bucharest: UNESCO-CEPES. Online. Available at: http://www.cepes.ro/hed/recogn/groups/transnat/ code.htm (accessed 6 November 2005).

UNESCO-APQN (2006) *UNESCO-APQN Toolkit: Regulating the Quality of Cross-border Education.* Paris: UNESCO.

Uvalic-Trumbic, S. (ed., 2002) *Globalization and the Market in Higher Education,* Paris: UNESCO.

19 Risky Business
Effective Planning and Management of Transnational Teaching

Shelda Debowski
University of Western Australia

Australia has established an active role in educating students from around the world within its own borders or transnationally. As a long-standing provider of education to Asia and some other areas of the world, it has gained a strong foothold as a local educational provider within the region (e.g. Huang 2003). Transnational education offers many advantages for students: they can remain at home with family and friends, contain educational costs, maintain part-time or full-time work and gain a reputable degree from a highly regarded international university (Sheldon 2006). Universities have also seen this method as offering a number of benefits—they increase the successful attraction of students (visa entry to Australia is not an issue), and in many cases, the cost of maintaining the campus may be perceived to be significantly lower.

However, the assured market in Asia is no longer so certain. Many Asian countries are becoming more self-sufficient in building their own educational sectors and retaining their talented young students at home (Sheldon 2006). Other countries have suffered downturns, which have greatly affected their capacity to fund a foreign education. Competition has become much tougher. As students are provided with increasing access to locally based education from foreign providers, Australian university offerings are being more strongly critiqued. Mok (2003) notes that many universities are responding to the market pressures through increased consideration of quality assurance, performance management and other governance strategies to ensure they remain competitive. However, these initiatives reveal considerable challenges that must be addressed to successfully operate in a competitive transnational setting.

This chapter will briefly examine five areas of corporate risk, which should be considered in planning and managing a transnational strategy. It will explore the challenges associated with reputation management; controlling teaching quality; the student experience; staffing issues; and the need to conduct rigorous risk assessments when establishing and maintaining a campus offshore. This integrated approach emphasizes the need for many different stakeholders to be engaged in the management of offshore ventures.

REPUTATIONAL ISSUES

Australia has demonstrated its capacity to be an educational leader in Asia, particularly given its proximity, long-term relationships and close familiarity with the Asian context. However, the market has become more challenging. The general credibility of the institution, its reputation for loyal and fair treatment of its students; its long-term relationship with the local community, and the capacity to provide a long-standing affiliation for the students, are all carefully considered by potential students. The league tables from Jiao Tong, the Times Higher Education Supplement, and other sources (Academic Ranking of World Universities 2006; Australian Education Network 2006; Williams and Van Dyk 2006) are closely monitored. And of course, with a plethora of institutions clamouring for enrolments, each nation's reputation for quality education also plays an important part in choosing a university.

With these considerations in mind, the variability of quality in Australian transnational education provision, as evidenced by reports from the Australian University Quality Agency (AUQA), has been most concerning. There are many examples of offshore initiatives—some successful, many not. In some cases they have operated as sound ventures for many years. In others, they have been short, intense presences followed by a fizzled demise. In recent years there appear to have been some major and very public program or campus closures as universities undertook a cost/benefit analysis and realized that their offshore ventures were not viable. Of course, this ebb and flow of an institution's commitment to the local community does not pass unnoticed, and increases the level of scrutiny from those wishing to enrol with an overseas provider. Closures damage the reputation of the university and may also flow across to other institutions from the same nation. Certainly, other programs from the same university will find it hard to enter the same market after a previous course has been rescinded.

POOR TEACHING QUALITY

A major risk for many universities working in transnational settings is the quality of teaching which is provided to students.

Teaching is a complex process, which requires careful consideration of the student needs, the learning context, and the desired outcomes. In an Australian university setting the teaching program operates as a dynamic adaptive curriculum where the teacher responds to cues from students and the emerging socio-political context in which the learning takes place. The teacher is commonly from the same local community and is culturally aligned with many students. The students are privileged in that they are working within a pedagogic framework that replicates their previous learning experiences. They have teachers with similar language skills and their teachers are selected on the basis of excellence.

In contrast, the curricula of transnational programs are frequently fixed and immutable: regulated by the requirement that they match the parent university's curriculum. The transnational teachers are either local staff or imported teachers who visit as required. Local staff are not provided with the same guidance on teaching expectations and pedagogic principles, although some universities are seeking to provide more substantial support in this area. Few students will be encouraged to explore local complexities, interact with representative experts from their local communities, or indeed, explore their local issues through assessment processes. If their teachers are drawn from Australia, they are likely to be present for a short term only, and to have little or no interaction with the local community. The teachers will often be weary, having travelled considerable distances to reach their teaching destination. Few will have allowed sufficient time to recuperate from the exigencies of travel. They will also be teaching intensively—often over the course of a weekend, or across five nights, before returning to the parent university (Debowski 2005; Gribble and Ziguras 2003). They may not speak the local language and certainly will have very limited insight into the local issues and context. There will be limited or no opportunity to draw these local features into the teaching or activities. Under these conditions, it is apparent that the educational experience is of lower quality.

Further, the students in other nations may come from a very different educational system where learning theory operates from different premises. Asian students, for example, must move from a model where they deeply engage with an authoritative source of guidance, to a more eclectic, inquiry-based model where they should critique and question the theory and its application. In many cases this shift in learning style may not be explained by their teachers, who simply assume they are poorly skilled in learning. Although experienced academics may feel they have a reasonable understanding of transnational student needs through their ongoing association with these students, Gribble and Ziguras (2003) emphasize the critical importance of providing teachers with a more comprehensive understanding of the cultural, political, economic, and legal contexts in which they will be teaching.

Students may also encounter lecturers recruited from their local higher education sector. The resultant hybrid of local and transnational teaching strategies can lead to inconsistent expectations and confusion as to desired outcomes. There may be few strategies in place to provide educational support for local teachers—particularly in promoting the vision and principles of the parent university. In some cases, the students will also be operating through a translator (particularly in China where English is growing in popularity, but is not well established). The quality of teachers, teaching and instructional interaction are therefore major risks that each university must review regularly.

THE STUDENT EXPERIENCE

The transnational student experience is generally poorly addressed by many universities. Offshore students do not receive comparable support to those studying at the parent university. In fact, their successful achievement of a degree is not necessarily strongly assisted by the university and its associated partners at all.

Students who remain in their home country to study are significantly challenged by their ongoing family and work commitments, which must also be accommodated in the study regimen (Davis *et al* 2000). The challenges associated with balancing study and life are further confounded by the intensive instructional blocks commonly employed to reduce costs. They offer little opportunity for reflection, interaction or growth of knowledge (Gribble and Ziguras 2003; Pyvis and Chapman 2004). Students have limited access to their teachers or other aspects of their university (Gribble and Ziguras 2003). The personal circumstances of the students generate a strong desire for streamlined and simplified learning processes—a need that may be in strong conflict with the lecturer's expectations of wider reading, research and exploration (Pyvis and Chapman 2004).

Despite their learning environment, many students will be likely to change and grow as a result of their exposure to university education. Pyvis and Chapman (2004) explore the concept of transnational student identity, noting that many students must reshape their sense of self following their exposure to new forms of learning and novel educational encounters. They relish the opportunity to explore Western thinking, practice and perspectives, and are encouraged to question, debate, and critique current thought: processes that may then transfer to their everyday lives. This transformative learning process is a profound shift in awareness and self-identity. It is best achieved through strong belonging and engagement with the educational community—a difficult accomplishment when studying transnationally. While students build strong peer-based local communities, they are excluded from the more highly desired international association. The provision of alumni events would provide ongoing sustenance of graduates and current students. However, there is little evidence of this form of community engagement in transnational teaching settings. Again, this absence of ongoing association increases the risk of university marginalization from the lives of students and their associates.

Transnational students often experience poor learning conditions (Sheldon 2006). While some universities have established full campuses, many programs are located in hotels, office blocks, and other facilities that are poorly suited to educational functions. However, this issue of facility provision is but the tip of the iceberg for many transnational students. Consider, for example:

- The poor library facilities that are available to transnational students (Sheldon 2006);
- The widespread absence of student services officers with expertise in learning skills, counselling and other forms of specialist guidance;
- The limited interaction between academics and the local community;
- extra curricula activities and interactions are limited or non-existent.

In many offshore programs the university may work with a local partner who provides some of the necessary support services. However, it is hard to argue that this infrastructure is truly comparable to that offered on the main campus. Service evaluation, quality control of enacted policy, and provision of expert staff may be less evident in these settings (Sheldon 2006). University staff may visit rarely, and there will be little in the way of rigorous review process during these visits. The initial partnership agreement may provide for some control over quality of service, but this may be rarely reviewed in practice.

Clearly, the educational risks can be high if these concerns are poorly addressed by a university. The quality of the learning experience for the student will be far less than that gained by those studying on-campus at the home university. There is a risk of student disengagement through an inability to connect with the university community, unsuitable and minimal learning experiences and the limited capacity to fully focus on the program of study, given the modes of instruction offered.

THE STAFF EXPERIENCE

Further issues arise when reviewing the staff experience of working in a transnational program. There are four major issues, which should be considered by a university:

- Workload and remuneration issues;
- Induction, development and evaluation of staff;
- Safety and health of staff;
- Emergency responsiveness.

There are many complexities to be considered when deploying staff to work offshore. Are all academics offered the same opportunities to experience this enriching form of teaching? Is the selection process transparent and equitable? Are staff offered a choice of electing to travel or is it required? Family and other responsibilities may heavily compromise the travel capacity of some academics. More senior staff will be likely to teach offshore, as they will have older families and thus, more capacity to mobilize. However, their absence can impact on the quality of the onshore program, and on their own research students' experience. Further, their more junior colleagues may be expected to pick up additional workload to cover their colleagues' absence. Those who travel will be paid or recompensed for their time away, while their colleagues may not. The sense of inequity may be very high and quite damaging to the teaching community's cohesiveness. Close monitoring of deployment strategies is advisable.

There is widespread recognition that any individual involved in transnational education should be adequately prepared to successfully navigate this different educative role, and embrace an increased span of responsibilities and the added complexities of working in a new cultural setting (AVCC 2002; Dunn and Wallace 2006; Leask 2004). Good preparation of academics who will teach offshore has been strongly encouraged in a number of universities, particularly with respect to promoting greater cross-cultural awareness (Dunn and Wallace 2006; MacKinnon and Manathunga 2003) and providing more guidance on suitable learning strategies, including internationalization of the curriculum (Dunn and Wallace 2006; Edwards *et al* 2003; Gribble and Ziguras 2003). Gribble and Ziguras (2003) advocate the provision of country-specific information to enable more contextualized teaching. However, Pyvis and Chapman (2004) argue that the simple inclusion of 'local content additions' is a limited response and does not fully address the needs of the students. They also suggest the encouragement of communities of practice to encourage teachers to explore their experiences, expertise and insights. However, this form of professional interchange is unlikely unless a facilitator creates the exchange forum, given the additional workloads many transnational teaching staff encounter (Dunn and Wallace 2006; 2007).

Transnational educators do more than teach—they represent the university and its requirements on a number of fronts. In many cases the teacher will also need to provide a range of additional support services to the student cohort. There are many issues which will be raised by students with their current teacher and which need to be explored at that time. Academics working in more isolated settings need to be well versed in university policy and process, student counselling, and the program requirements of the course of study being undertaken by the students. Additional assistance for academics to effectively employ technology in their teaching and associated student relationship management can ensure the online support and interaction with students will be of a high calibre. Staff working with large cohorts of students benefit from ongoing technological guidance, which enriches their teaching. There may also be good justification to review the level of teaching support that is provided to academics who are leading major offshore teaching initiatives.

Universities also employ staff who live and work within the local community. On the one hand, this is a beneficial arrangement as there can be a more stable and enduring teacher presence during the students' study program. Conversely, many local teachers will be sessional or casual appointments with a limited commitment to the university and its goals. They may have limited knowledge of the university's policies and requirements; the standards of assessment; teaching may differ markedly. It is possible that they will not interact with other teachers in the program, and may not be present at examiner meetings or other forms of quality review. As a minimum support strategy, these teachers benefit from a formal induction program into teaching and learning standards and an overview of the program and its outcomes. Additional enhancements could include a meeting with key members of the teaching team, visits to the home university, and feedback on assessment patterns and moderator meetings.

In addition to educational considerations, there is an increasing need to review the safety and health processes that protect staff working transnationally. Certainly, there may be sound policies documenting how the safety of staff will be ensured. However, are those individuals aware of these plans and the requisite processes? The policies may be little reflected in the practice or the preparation of staff for working offshore. Regular forums for staff working offshore can assist in promoting and reviewing existing policy and practice. The establishment of a defined service that provides advice, tips, and support for staff is a potential strategy to consider. As new issues arise, further education of relevant staff will be desirable. Other enhancements could be the provision of a mentor to new staff commencing their role as a transnational worker; the development of a transnational knowledge community, which shares issues, tips, and insights with each other; and the development of a transnational expertise database. These various strategies all assist in promoting a more knowledgeable and informed community, which maintains its awareness of emerging issues and enhanced practice. The issue of staff preparedness is an area that is both complex and largely under-managed.

UNIVERSITY PLANNING AND MANAGEMENT
OF OFFSHORE VENTURES

There have been many examples of universities commencing new ventures only to subsequently declare them financially unviable. Possibly too few stakeholders were involved in assessing the risks and contributing to the planning strategy. Certainly, the embedded costs of developing an educational community are likely to have been insufficiently considered. The likely low market demand during the initial period of establishment and the potential competition from other universities should also be carefully considered during the evaluative phase. The real cost of supporting a campus or presence should be determined. There are numerous aspects of infrastructure that require duplication—just as one would necessarily provide across a multi-campus site within the home country. Student services, library resources, IT support, etc. ... there are considerable high cost services that need to be obtained through local alliances, or provided on the university campus. During the planning phase the commitment to provide a quality education must be foremost in the discussions as well as in later implementation.

Workforce planning is often poorly considered, but of critical importance in creating a sustainable offshore investment. A critical factor is the academic and administrative capacity within the university and offshore to meet the requirements of conducting an offshore program or campus. There will need to be sufficient academics to rotate across the different program offerings, as the travelling takes a toll on each individual. Quality tutors and support staff will need to be identified. Specialist support staff (possibly possessing high-level skills in the local language) will need to be employed.

The effective management of an internationalization strategy requires strong leadership and careful consideration of the best way to manage change and development (Parsons and Fidler 2005). Within the university there will be a number of stakeholders, including faculties, teaching staff, service units, and executives with responsibility for relevant portfolios. The engagement of all of these parties will ensure that most contingencies are identified and addressed. In many past cases the decisions have been primarily drawn from discussions with senior members of the university alone. A wider input is advisable. Reviews of comparable university ventures also provide a very good indication of the problems and challenges that could emerge. The hard-won knowledge of those who have entered the market before is invaluable (Connelly *et al* 2006).

A WIDER VIEW OF TRANSNATIONAL TEACHING

Transnational teaching is a risky business. To be successful there needs to be a strong focus on quality teaching and assurance of good educational practice (Sheldon 2006). Case studies of past ventures point to several factors that can result in failed ventures. Poor choice of offshore partners (Heffernan and Poole 2005), poor planning, inadequate financial costing, limited recognition of the workforce planning requirements, poor quality control, sporadic engagement with the student population and the wider community, and minimal resourcing of the venture and its student support, reduce the efficacy of the offshore strategy. It is clear that in many cases the educational support being offered is a stripped-down model that reduces the commitment to the local student. As time progresses, transnational students are becoming more canny: they know what to expect from a quality international education. Universities will be judged on their quality of transnational service and educational provision—not simply their broader reputation as a higher education provider.

Further consideration might be given to working more collaboratively with other universities seeking a niche in the same market (Sheldon 2006). In some overseas locations there is a plethora of universities vying for students. In Penang, for example, entire streets are lined with university presences, each seeking to establish their ascendance. There are some real possibilities in sharing common services and resources: possible co-badging of some units and building a more integrated approach to transnational teaching. Some potential high cost resource collaborations might, for example, relate to collaborative learning centres, libraries, ICT support and student support services. Joint funding of these centralized agencies would enable a high quality provision for similar costs to those incurred for single institution services. A national strategy to develop a single repository that offers guidance on international political, social, economic and discipline—related contexts as well as sources of expertise—would be a tremendous contribution to those who work transnationally. At present, however, there is little evidence of national leadership of transnational capacity building.

At a more practical level, there are other very simple ways in which quality assurance and risks can be better managed. These include:

- Guidance for academic leaders on maintaining quality assurance of teaching programs;
- Guidelines, induction programs, facilitated communities of practice, and ongoing expert support for teachers involved in transnational teaching;

- Integration of quality assurance strategies throughout the various transnational processes and training of all staff in their application and assessment;
- Recognition of the transnational teaching contribution of academics in promotional and tenure processes to encourage their ongoing engagement;
- Consideration and addressing of risks in a holistic and informed manner, using the knowledge of the many different stakeholders;
- Regular review of partnerships to safeguard the programs (McNicoll *et al* 2005);
- Investment in internationalized curriculum design, assessment and learning strategies to ensure quality outcomes;
- Collaboration with other universities to develop textbooks and associated resources enable contextualized learning;
- Investment in exploring and researching students' needs and issues to enable better calibration of transnational service provision;
- Development of stronger student feedback mechanisms to guide ongoing enhancement of the learning experience and process management—including qualitative evaluations which enable real responses and feedback on local issues (Pyvis and Chapman 2004);
- The construction of key performance indicators that explore process, outcome and practice foci as well as financial/quantitative measures (Sheldon 2006);
- Stronger support for students and their well-being, including more cultural association with their universities and greater contact with teachers and other members of the university.

These are but a few of the logical enhancements that might be made to current approaches to transnational education. It is clear that the minimalist approach applied to date cannot be sustained into the future. Offshore students are more aware of what their student experience should provide. It is now time for universities to seriously review their premises and assumptions about these ventures. They are not a quick source of income. In fact, they are rarely profitable in the short-term. Instead, they should be regarded as long-term commitments to the future of that community. The university likely to succeed in this new and demanding consumer-driven market is one which demonstrates a long-term commitment to educational excellence and quality learning—no matter where the program of study. And that is certainly reasonable; after all, the transnational learning experience should be no different in quality to that provided to others studying at an Australian campus.

REFERENCES

Academic Ranking of World Universities. (2006) Shanghai: Jiao Tong University. Online. Available at: http://ed.sjtu.edu.cn/rank/2006/ARWU-2006Methodology.htm (accessed 30 May 2007).

Australian Education Network. (2006) 'Rankings of Australian Universities'. Online. Available at: http://www.australian-universities.com/rankings/ (accessed 30 May 2007).

Australian Vice Chancellor's Committee. (2002) *Provision of education to international students: Code and guidelines for Australian universities.* Canberra: Australian Vice Chancellor's Committee.

Connelly, S., Garton, S. and Olsen, A. (2006) *Models and types: Guidelines for good practice in transnational education.* London: Observatory on Borderless Higher Education.

Davis, D., Olsen, A., and Bohm, A. (2000) *Transnational education providers, partners and policy: Challenges for Australian institutions offshore.* Canberra, Australia: IDP Education Australia.

Debowski, S. (2005) 'Across the divide: Teaching a transnational MBA in a second language.' *Higher Education Research and Development,* 24 (3): 265–280.

Dunn, L. and Wallace, M. (2006) 'Australian academics and transnational teaching: An exploratory study of their preparedness and experiences.' *Higher Education Research and Development,* 25 (4): 357–369.

Dunn, L. and Wallace, M. (2007) 'Promoting communities of practice in higher education.' In M. Tulloch, S. Relf and P. Ulys (eds.) *Breaking down boundaries: International experience in open, distance and flexible learning: selected papers,* 142–150, Bathurst: Charles Sturt University.

Edwards, R., Crosling, G. Petrovic-Lazarovic, S. and O'Neill, P. (2003) 'Internationalization of business education: Meaning and implementation.' *Higher Education Research and Development,* 22 (3): 183–192.

Gribble, K. and Ziguras, C. (2003) 'Learning to teach offshore: Pre-departure training for lecturers in transnational programs.' *Higher Education Research and Development,* 22 (3): 205–216.

Heffernan, T. and Poole, D. (2005) 'In search of "the vibe": Creating effective international education partnerships.' *Higher Education,* 50 (2): 223–245.

Huang, F. (2003) 'Transnational higher education: A perspective from China.' *Higher Education Research and Development,* 22 (3): 193–203.

Leask, B. (2004) *Transnational education and intercultural learning: Reconstructing the offshore teaching team to enhance internationalization.* Australian Universities' Quality Agency (AUQA) Occasional Paper. Melbourne: AUQA.

MacKinnon, D. and Manathunga, C. (2003) 'Going global with assessment: What to do when the dominant culture's literacy drives assessment.' *Higher Education Research and Development,* 22 (2): 131–144.

McNicoll, Y. R., Clohessy, J. M. and Luff, A. R. (2005) 'Auditing offshore partnerships: Lessons from reviewing nursing and psychology courses offered in Singapore.' *Proceedings of the Australian Universities Quality Forum*: (108 –112), Melbourne: AUQA. Mok, K-H. (2003) 'Globalization and higher education restructuring in Hong Kong,

Taiwan and Mainland China.' *Higher Education Research and Development,* 22 (2): 117–129.

Parsons, C. and Fidler, B. (2005) 'A new theory of educational change—punctuated equilibrium: The case of the internationalization of higher education institutions.' *British Journal of Educational Studies*, 53 (4): 447–465.

Pyvis, D. and Chapman, A. (2004) *Student experiences of offshore higher education: Issues for quality.* Australian Universities' Quality Agency (AUQA) Occasional Publication. Melbourne: AUQA.

Sheldon, S. (2006). 'Diversity in higher education in the Asia-Pacific region, the impact of diversity on international education and on teaching and learning outcomes.' *Proceedings of the Australian Universities Quality Forum*: (28–51), Melbourne: AUQA.

Williams, R. and Van Dyk, N. (2006) 'Discipline ratings for Australian Universities.' Melbourne: Melbourne Institute of Applied Economic and Social Research, Online. Available at: http://www.melbourneinstitute.com/publications/reports/dr_aus_uni/default.html (accessed 30 May 2007).

20 Opportunities and Challenges

Managing Program Quality and Institutional Partnerships in a Transnational Educational Context

Chelsea Blickem and Nick Shackleford

Unitec

INTRODUCTION

The Certificate in Intensive English, which had been operating at a New Zealand tertiary institution since 1991, was made available to Chinese students in Beijing in July 2001 through a co-operation agreement with a Chinese private provider, enabling Chinese students to commence their English studies in China before moving to New Zealand. The Training Centre in Beijing operated for two-and-a-half years before closing in December 2003 because of the disruption of SARS and a general downturn in students from China wanting to come to New Zealand for further study.

This chapter examines the partnership between the New Zealand institution and the private provider, and how the offshore delivery of the program was managed at a time when offshore delivery was relatively new for New Zealand institutions and very few regulatory processes were in place and monitored by the New Zealand Quality Assurance (NZQA) agency.

THE NEW ZEALAND CONTEXT

The reasons for New Zealand education providers to work offshore are similar to other providers around the world. Among them are: 'enhanced profile for the institution; financial benefits; expanded student base; enhanced opportunity for staff and student mobility; development of new curricula; [and] additional research and development opportunities' (McBurnie and Pollock, 2000: 334).

Between April 2002 and November 2005, three stocktakes were conducted by the New Zealand Ministry of Education on the offshore education programs being delivered by tertiary institutions. The final report, 'Offshore Education Stocktake and Analysis' (Catherwood and Associates, 2005), reveals a 53 per cent increase in the number of tertiary institutions engaged in offshore education from 17 in 2001 to 29 in

216

2004. The number of courses and programs offered also increased significantly to 137 but the number of offshore student enrolment numbers is lower, down from 1,472 in 2001 to 1385 in 2004.

The report acknowledges that 'the use of student enrolment numbers alone is not an accurate indicator of offshore education activity,' as students are often enrolled with the offshore partner institution and are not included in the enrolment figures of the New Zealand institution.

The report concludes that 'participation in offshore education by New Zealand providers has been maintained. There has not been any significant increase in offshore education activity, but neither has there been a significant downturn,' but comments that in New Zealand 'offshore education is viewed as a high risk activity.'

The New Zealand Ministry of Education acknowledged in 2004 that the sector generally lacked expertise and experience in international linkages and offshore activity and was behind international competitors (N Z Ministry of Education, 2004).

CHALLENGES AND RISKS

The growth in offshore education has involved significant challenges for institutions, their partners, and the relevant accreditation authorities. Literature documenting the Australian and UK experiences emerged as early as 2000. In New Zealand, experiences have not been as well documented, hence the lack of reference to them here.

In 2002, the UK Quality Assurance Agency expressed concerns at a model of offshore collaboration in China in which they identified 'confusion as to who was responsible for maintaining standards' (The Times Higher Education Supplement online, 4 January 2002). This article identified problems involving the language of the host country, translation problems with quality procedures, the commitment and competence of staff sent to China, and the lack of a secure framework on which the UK institution's programs could develop. Other issues included unregulated admissions standards and overall quality of graduates.

Such problems have been frequent in the UK. Heffernan and Poole (2004: 80) cite Tysome (1996) who reports that

> During 1996, the former Higher Education Quality Council found many offshore partnerships had been established without sufficient information and due diligence. By 2002, the Education Secretary continued to express the fear that some institutions might lower their standards offshore if not for the audit role of the QAA.

Typical quality assurance problems are inferior assessment practices, practices that differ to those at the UK institution, lower entry standards, insufficient supervision of standards, communications failures, and misleading promotional materials.

Australian institutions that have been developing offshore programs have suffered from similar quality issues. The Australian government strengthened the auditing of offshore delivery in 2005 by committing funds and resources to the Australian Quality Assurance Agency for this purpose and for the development of formal relationships with overseas quality assurance agencies, although the impact of these steps has yet to be measured.

Venturing into offshore education brings new risks for tertiary providers: 'financial, reputational, legal, sovereign and physical/personal' (McBurnie and Pollock, 2000: 337), and while quality assurance agencies and institutions may plan for every eventuality, there are still grey areas, so much so that there has been a call for a global quality assurance system for transnational education. Such a move is unlikely, however, when different concerns and priorities exist for different countries.

'QUALITY' AND 'STANDARDS'

Working and delivering offshore involves working and operating in an environment in which language, culture, and practice almost certainly will differ from that of the home institution. The standards that exist in the home institution need to be communicated to the host institution, yet these standards may not be able to be easily enforced due to resourcing, cultural, or structural differences. Equally there needs to be clear communication of expectations about quality and its procedures. What works in the home institution may not transfer or translate to the host institution, or there may be another way to achieve the same goal. However, it is essential for the success of the project that communication of these goals and expectations takes place.

In 2001, the NZQA required the New Zealand institution to collate a description of the facilities in Beijing, the program to be taught, delivery and assessment methods, monitoring processes and staffing, and for the project to have been endorsed by the institution's Academic Board. Coupled with this was a memorandum of understanding detailing the institution's (minimal) financial commitments and expected income from the venture, obligations to staff and quality assurance and how frequently the relationship would be reviewed.

RELATIONSHIPS, INTERNATIONALIZATION AND QUALITY

Heffernan and Poole (2004: 79) point to the 'challenges, difficulties and complexities confronting universities as they internationalize' and emphasize the link between the quality of the program and the quality of the relationship that is established to enable the program delivery to take place. Heffernan and Poole propose that inter-organizational relationships generally consist of five stages.

In the *pre-relationship stage*, the partner is sought and selected. The *early interaction stage* sees the start of serious negotiations about the style and structure of the relationship, a time when a lot of learning takes place and when goals, objectives, expectations, and relationship boundaries are defined. This is followed by the third stage, *relationship growth,* when the 'relationship partners engage in intensive mutual learning and adaptation to the demands of the relationship' (Heffernan and Poole, 2004: 80) when mutual communication, trust and commitment are established. This grows into the *partnership* when the relationship is stable and the agreed goals and outcomes of the partnership are achieved. Finally, the *relationship end* phase occurs when the offshore relationship is discontinued and the contractual obligations cease, often because the costs outweigh the benefits of the relationship.

Heffernan and Poole's (2004) study revealed that the *early interaction* stage when the groundwork for the relationship and the project goals are established is critical to the success of offshore projects.

Heffernan and Poole (2004) undertook 10 studies of relationships between Australian universities and their offshore partners in Asia and from this defined the key factors in the deterioration of offshore relationships. Amongst these was the absence of trust, commitment, and effective communication in the *early interaction* stage. Without a shared vision of the enterprise, or when there is a mismatch in the partners' vision of the project, serious difficulties can occur.

A NEW ZEALAND CASE STUDY

We will now explore the New Zealand institution's experience of the delivery of its English program in Beijing, paying particular attention to questions of quality assurance and the development of the working relationships between the institutions.

Pre-relationship

Early in 2001 the New Zealand institution was approached by a Chinese provider known to the institution to establish a partnership to open an English language training centre in Beijing. The choice of the right partner is a critical decision in the building of a successful offshore venture and institutions are advised to go through a process of due diligence to ensure that the partner institution and its representatives have the capacity to administer and deliver the requirements of the program and that the partnership will enhance the reputation of both institutions.

Early interaction

Heffernan and Poole (2004: 80) maintain that this phase in the relationship is the 'most fragile'. This phase should see the development of negotiated modes of practice and operation between the partners, 'clearly defined in terms of goals, objectives, expectations and relationship boundaries.'

Two visits were made early in 2001 by senior staff to the proposed site in Beijing. These visits determined for both sides what the minimum requirements were to be concerning financial arrangements, classroom spaces, facilities, tutor spaces, resources, and administration. The New Zealand institution entered into a service agreement for the delivery of its program with the partner rather than a partnership that involved capital investment, and also limited the period of co-operation to one year, renewable by mutual agreement. While this agreement limited the institution's influence over the direction of the Training Centre, it also limited the financial risk to which it was exposing itself by entering into the agreement. By June 2001 the institution was satisfied that all of the requirements had all been met and signed a memorandum of understanding with the Chinese partner.

Approval and accreditation

The approval process within the New Zealand institution required documentation as described earlier. At that time the institution worked with NZQA to ensure that all required processes and systems were documented so that offshore delivery was possible. Accreditation was granted by NZQA and the Centre opened in July 2001.

As part of the contractual arrangements, a New Zealand employee was employed within the Centre as a Director of Studies for a minimum period of one year. The Director of Studies was responsible for the quality management of the program and lines of communication to senior staff at the institution in New Zealand were clearly identified. Because there was a shortage of suitable and available teachers in Beijing at that time, New Zealand staff were employed by the Training Centre for short-term, fixed periods to ensure that the standard of delivery of the program was consistent with that of the program being offered at the New Zealand institution.

Relationship growth

During this phase, the 'relationship partners engage in intensive mutual learning and adaptation to the demands of the partnership' (Heffernan and Poole, 2004: 80). The institution and the Training Centre experienced intensive and extensive mutual learning in this phase, which is particularly marked by these issues.

Communication

There were clear lines of communication to the institution for the Director of Studies, but it quickly transpired that there was no such clarity between the Director of Studies' and the partner. The partner had appointed a small team of young, bilingual local staff to run the Training Centre, but that staff lacked management skills and experience, and had no real power to make decisions. While it was clear that the Director of Studies managed the delivery of the English program, responsibility for the management of the Training Centre and its administrative systems was less clear. This led to significant challenges for staff as they tried to work through cross-cultural differences in management practice.

Staff expectations

The Director of Studies and the New Zealand staff came from a culture where they worked five days each week and with regular hours while the local staff were obliged to be at work every day and for extended hours. The situation with the locally employed Chinese teachers was particularly problematic because the Chinese teachers were working under significantly different conditions of employment to the New Zealand institution teachers.

Staff

The New Zealand staff who took up positions at the Training Centre were given the opportunity to participate in an orientation program prior to their departure. Dowling *et al* (1999: 155) see that 'pre-departure training is considered to be...critical...in attempting to ensure the expatriate's effectiveness and success abroad, particularly where the assignment country is considered culturally tough.'

The reaction of the New Zealand staff to their new working conditions varied. While most embraced the experience of working and living in Beijing and benefited both professionally and personally from their stay in China, others experienced pronounced culture shock. As noted in Dowling *et al* (1999: 132), '[cultural adjustment]...the dilemma is that adjustment to a foreign culture is multi-faceted, and individuals vary in terms of their reaction and coping behaviors.' The support and encouragement from staff at the institution in New Zealand became key in enabling staff to continue to work effectively.

On their return, New Zealand staff were asked to provide feedback and suggestions for improvement, which was discussed with the partner.

Quality assurance

The transportation and delivery of an existing program offshore created issues related to quality assurance and maintenance of standards. This was made significantly easier by having a Director of Studies based in the host country. However, there were some instances where enrolment decisions were made for commercial considerations by the local staff, and ran counter to the regulations of the program. With the benefit of hindsight, the early interaction phase of the relationship with the partner and his staff could have focused more explicitly on the administrative processes of the program and included training for the local staff.

Local accreditation

The New Zealand institution entered into the arrangement with the Training Centre having received assurances that the Training Centre had been accredited locally. Being unfamiliar with the complexities of the Chinese accreditation processes and despite having received these assurances, the New Zealand institution later discovered that the accreditation process for the Training Centre was incomplete, causing much embarrassment within the New Zealand institution. Full approval to operate as a Training Centre that employed foreign teachers was granted late in 2001. This delay and the uncertain status of the Training Centre threatened the continuation of the program before it began.

Resources and facilities

Although minimum requirements had been agreed to and largely met, glaring deficits in resources quickly became evident. Fundamental classroom necessities were not available locally and had to be sent from New Zealand. The teaching staff at the Training Centre were questioned as to their use of the photocopier, and necessary faxes from New Zealand could not be sent as there were limits put on fax paper.

Although local English book shops had been visited by the New Zealand staff earlier in the year, it quickly became evident that these shops did not hold the full range of resources required, and that bulk orders of resources led to illegally copied copies of books being supplied. The institution then had to ship fundamental resources to the Training Centre and reached an agreement with the partner to share associated costs.

Whilst the tutor rooms and classrooms were of a high standard, the computer laboratory contained computers that did not have hard drives, and there was no printer. The Language Learning Centre was not adequately staffed to facilitate drop-in learning. Issues such as these were dealt with on an ongoing and ad hoc basis. These problems were not fully anticipated by the New Zealand institution although broad statements about the quality of facilities were included in the original memorandum of understanding.

PROGRAM CHANGES IN RESPONSE TO LOCAL CONTEXT

Despite the undertaking to deliver and assess the English program in China as it is in New Zealand, some changes had to be negotiated between the Director of Studies and the Programme Committee in New Zealand. These changes were often to do with context: how could Chinese students associate with New Zealand culture, weather or customs, for example? How could they relate to many of the Western contexts and concepts that appeared in the textbooks, tasks and assessments? The staff in China worked hard and successfully to adapt their materials and their teaching to the local context and to develop modes of transcultural delivery, some of which has led to ongoing research in specific areas.

The 'cost' of quality

The partner and the local staff soon realized that there were unseen costs associated with quality and the maintenance of quality and standards of the New Zealand institution program. The faxes, phone calls, and photocopying relating to assessment were one example. The strict regulations on entry requirements meant that the partner was turning students away and losing revenue. The explicit guidelines for awarding certificates and student progression within the program was a frequent cause of friction between the institution and the partner, as the partner felt that this process was commercially damaging.

Throughout these discussions, the institution, directly and through the Director of Studies, strived to maintain the standards it had set the program in New Zealand. This was not easy. Although this was made easier with the Director of Studies being present, the Director of Studies himself needed ongoing support from New Zealand, as it was easy for him to be 'captured' by the local context and demands. All this necessitated regular and clear communication between the institution and the Director of Studies.

Partnership

This phase is characterized by 'the establishment of stable social and performance norms, the institutionalization of routines and ongoing achievement of agreed performance outcomes' (Heffernan and Poole, 2004: 80). The venture reached this phase, although it took a considerable amount of time and patience. Institutions entering into off-shore delivery of programs need to acknowledge that successful delivery requires considerable staff commitment and clear management struc-tures at the home institution so that program delivery offshore can be effectively supported.

One of the most positive results of the partnership was the number of students who progressed from the Centre to further their studies at the New Zealand institution. Because of their exposure to the New Zealand teaching methods whilst at the Centre, the students were well prepared for their further study at the institution. Many came with classmates, and thereby avoided the isolation and cultural shock of adjustment that many Chinese students experience on arrival in New Zealand.

The rotation of the New Zealand institution staff through the Train-ing Centre produced mixed results. It meant that New Zealand staff had a valuable opportunity to learn more about a culture which had provided them with challenges in their New Zealand classrooms; it also meant a constant process of (re)establishing local practices and modes of operation, which was particularly difficult for the business partner and his staff, and for the resident Director of Studies.

Performance outcomes

Even during this relatively stable phase, there was reluctance from the business partner to commit to the writing of a business plan which would have described developmental goals for the project and performance out-comes for both parties. This, and other instances, are good illustrations of what Zhu and Downing say (2000) that in China 'practices are quite different from those used in developed and market-economy developing countries, and careful consideration of local idiosyncratic practices is required to operate successfully.'

The institution was unwilling to make a capital investment in the Centre and needed to renegotiate its income from the Centre to ensure that the project was covering costs. This led to the partner's decision to regard the New Zealand institution as only one of the destinations for further study but not necessarily the preferred option. The institution in turn began exploring relationships with Chinese universities, progress-ing its emerging goal of working with overseas universities rather than with private individuals.

Relationship end

This phase often occurs when 'one partner decides that the costs of the relationship exceed its benefits' (Heffernan and Poole, 2004: 80). In early 2003, the strain in the relationship was being felt through the decreased communication between the partner and the newly appointed Director of Studies and teaching staff, and the partner and the institution. There were increasing pressures on the Director of Studies, from the partner, to waive and vary quality assurance processes and program regulations, as there was a gradual decline in enrolments.

The outbreak of SARS in April 2003 brought the delivery to an abrupt temporary end as New Zealand staff were called back to New Zealand. In July, the staff returned to find the enrolment situation precarious. At the same time, the institution was under increased pressure to control costs and produce profits. In the second half of 2003 the relationship between the Centre and the institution deteriorated and by mutual agreement the project finished in December 2003. While there was some discussion about the ownership of some of the resources at the Centre, the institution was able to extract itself from the arrangement with little difficulty as no capital investment or ownership of the Centre had been entered into.

SUMMARY AND CONCLUSION

The offshore delivery of the English program in China between 2001 and 2003 provided the institution with valuable transcultural and transnational experiences at a time when New Zealand government policy and quality assurance mechanisms for offshore delivery of educational programs were relatively undeveloped.

The institution now recognizes that more work could have been undertaken to clarify the goals and underlying assumptions of the project at an early stage of the business relationship and there were many unpredicted factors that had to be managed. However, the New Zealand institution did focus on transporting the program's well established quality assurance policies and procedures into the Chinese context. The institution committed staff to the on-site delivery of the program in Beijing in order to build strong relationships with the Chinese partner and his staff and this resulted in the successful—if short lived—delivery of this program.

Hefferman and Poole's framework for the successful establishment of inter-organizational relationships confirms the importance of defining clear, coherent and reliable quality assurance practice and policy for offshore delivery of programs, together with the importance of establishing clear and culturally appropriate modes of communication. The necessity of defining the goals, expectations, style and structure of the institutional relationship at an early stage in the relationship is of particular importance to the success of any transcultural and transnational educational project. These are key determinants in the success (or failure) of the overseas delivery of educational programs and factors that have been clearly illustrated in the case study of the New Zealand institution's project in China.

REFERENCES

Catherwood, V. and Associates (2005) 'Offshore Education Stocktake and Analysis.' Online. Available at: http://www.educationnz.org.nz/indust/eeip/OffEdFinalRpt281105.pdf (accessed 18 December 2006).

Dowling, P. J., Welch, D. E., Schuler, R. S. (1999) *International Human Resource Management: Managing People in a Multinational Context*, 3rd ed. Cincinnati, Ohio: South Western College Publishing.

Heffernan, T. and Poole, D. (2004) '"Catch Me I'm falling": Key Factors in the Deterioration of Offshore Education Partnerships.' *Journal of Higher Education Policy and Management* 26 (1): 75–90.

Illing, D. (2004) 'Watchdog for Offshore Operations.' *The Australian*, 23 June: 33.

McBurnie, G. and Pollock, A. (2000) 'Opportunity and Risk in Transnational Education—Issues in Planning for International Campus Development: An Australian Perspective.' *Higher Education in Europe* 25 (3): 333–343.

New Zealand Ministry of Education (2004) *Export Education in New Zealand: A Strategic Approach to Developing the Sector*. Online. Available at: http://www.minedu.govt.nz/web/downloadable/d16093_v1/export-education-in-nz-online3.doc (accessed 18 December 2006).

New Zealand Qualification Authority (2005, draft) 'Quality Assurance of the Overseas Delivery and Awarding of Approved Courses and Registered Qualifications.'Online. Available at: http://www.nzqa.govt.nz/ (accessed 30 October 2007).

QAA (2000) *UK Collaborative Links with China: Report of a Scoping Exercise 1999–2000*. Online. Available at: http://www.qaa.ac.uk (accessed 18 December 2006).

The Times Higher Education Supplement (2002) 'QAA Wary of China Ambitions'. 4 January. Online. Available at: http://www.thes.co.uk/search/search_results.aspx?search=China&mode=both&searchYear=2002&searchMonth=1&x=53&y=2 (accessed 18 December 2006).

Zhu, C. J. and Dowling, P. J. (2000). 'Managing Human Resources in State-Owned Enterprises in Transitional Economies: A Case Study in the People's Republic of China', *Research and Practice in Human Resource Management*, 8(1), 63–92.

21 Transnational Education in Mauritius

Quality Assurance for Program Exporters

David Pyvis

Curtin University of Technology

INTRODUCTION

Taking its lead from Dubai, Kuala Lumpur, and especially Singapore, Mauritius is seeking to foster social and economic development by becoming a regional knowledge hub and a center of higher learning. The vision was first enunciated in the New Economic Agenda espoused by the Government in 2000 and was re-affirmed in the 2003/04 Budget Speech (Mauritian Ministry of Education and Scientific Research, 2006).

Critical to this agenda is the construction of a world-class tertiary education sector. Transnational education is regarded by the Ministry (2006: 1v) as a key strategy in achieving this goal. The idea is that the internationalization of the local tertiary education sector through association with reputable overseas universities will generate world-class educational standards and push Mauritius into becoming a knowledge hub and international centre of learning.

Accordingly, in recent years, concerted efforts have been made to attract brand-name overseas universities to set up locally and to partner Mauritian public and private sector tertiary education providers. Most recent available figures show that 9 publicly funded institutions and an estimated 33 private providers associate with some 70 overseas institutions to offer tertiary-level programs to more than 5,000 students, who represent more than 21 per cent of the total tertiary student population in Mauritius (Tertiary Education Commission Report, August 2006).

With the Mauritian Government, and ultimately, the Mauritian people, pinning hopes for social and economic renewal on the capacity of overseas providers to foster quality education in Mauritius, there is a strong obligation on the universities to deliver. The current strategy *presumes* that the entry of reputable overseas institutions into the Mauritian tertiary sector will ensure world-class education standards.

This chapter draws attention to the presence of challenges for overseas providers in the endeavour to provide quality in transnational education programs delivered in Mauritius. The discussion utilizes findings from a study undertaken at a large private higher education institution in Mauritius. The study's aim was to identify challenges to the delivery of quality transnational education in Mauritius, established from the perspectives of those involved in the enterprise. The local provider, the overseas partner, teaching staff and students were identified as 'those involved'.

The host institution maintained partnerships with universities in Europe, South Africa, and Australia, employed more than 70 academics and had almost 1,300 students, most enrolled in programs leading to overseas qualifications. The institution organized transnational education mainly through franchised programs. The franchise program is a common vehicle of transnational education in Mauritius. In a franchised program, an institution delivers a university program of an overseas partner. The partner's academics are not made available to teach in the program, but the partner retains control and carries responsibility for quality. (For more detail on transnational program models see the NTEU, 2004; or, Pyvis and Chapman, 2004).

The focus on perspectives sanctioned a qualitative research methodology (Ezzy, 2002; Crotty, 1998), also endorsed by the importance given to context in the qualitative paradigm (Creswell, 1998; Cassell and Symon, 1994). At the campus, a focus group interview was conducted with 23 undergraduate students studying for various overseas degrees delivered by various 'parent' organizations. Semi-structured interviews were undertaken with 8 students and with 13 academics coordinating and teaching in a variety of overseas undergraduate programs, with the director of the institution, the director of studies, and with a senior invigilator from a major overseas partner. The invigilator oversaw quality control for 8 franchised programs offered at the campus.

The researcher also observed teaching/learning, examined unit material and student work, and accessed more than 40 moderation reports written over the previous two years by academics from overseas partner institutions.

The discussion below draws on the findings of the study to direct attention to the presence of challenges *for overseas providers* in providing 'world-class' transnational education in Mauritius and arguably elsewhere. That is, the discussion uses the study findings to suggest implications relating to the Mauritian context and beyond.

QUALITY CHALLENGES FOR PROGRAM OWNERS: FINDINGS FROM THE STUDY

Recruitment issues

The director of studies advised that the recruitment of staff to teach in transnational programs was achieved 'in cooperation' with overseas partners. To the local provider went the initial responsibility of finding likely candidates and *proposing* them to overseas program coordinators. Sometimes, a single candidate was nominated. At other times, several candidates were offered, and in such circumstances (the director of studies advised), the local provider usually indicated where its preferences lay. After a further period of consultation between academics from both institutions, the overseas partner, usually through the relevant program coordinator, *ruled* on the suitability of the applicant(s). If an applicant was successful, employment was offered with the local provider.

The approach to recruitment described by the director of studies conforms to the standard dictates of franchise arrangements. That is, the university that owns a program ultimately determines who can be recruited to teach it. This is the right and obligation of the overseas university because it carries the responsibility for quality assurance.

In the study, however, it was found that, allowing for some dialogue via email between institutions, the scrutiny of the overseas partner was usually restricted to the electronic analysis of a candidate's curriculum vitae. Typically, candidates were not subjected to any interview process by the body offering the program or award. Instead, job interviews, often formal but also frequently informal, were conducted by the Mauritian partner. According to the director of studies, overseas partners were reluctant to conduct job interviews largely because they were well aware that *they* were not offering employment. (Logistical difficulties, specifically problems associated with communicating over distance, were also suggested as an explanation for the non-involvement of overseas universities in recruitment interviews.) The overseas invigilator remarked of the recruitment process: 'They (the local providers) have to establish personality and commitment. We can only recognize qualifications and experience'.

World-class universities usually require interviews with selected applicants for academic positions, and, as the invigilator suggested, applicants are certainly gauged on commitment (and probably on personality) as part of quality control. It can be argued, therefore, that as interpreted from the study findings, the limited input overseas universities had into the selection of staff to teach in what were *their* programs put quality assurance at risk. The message in this for overseas universities may be that they cannot rely on their control over program content and assessment as the check on quality. The export of program *delivery* also poses a requirement for quality control.

The Mauritian Government requires that transnational educators be 'highly qualified' (Mauritian Ministry of Education and Scientific Research, 2006: iv). The interpretation of 'highly-qualified' is that transnational educators be 'appointed on the same criteria' (Mauritian Ministry of Education and Scientific Research, 2006: 24) as the overseas partner. It can be appreciated that in respect to reputable, overseas, brand name universities, the 'same' criteria translate into masters and preferably doctoral qualifications. This obligation would appear to serve as another check on quality, a further guarantee of 'world-class' provision.

The director of the institution hosting the study acknowledged that policy was being followed and advised that his organization was 'in an ongoing recruitment drive for highly qualified academics to teach in the international programs'. However, he observed that the focus on academic qualifications generated some pedagogical problems. As he described it, there was a dilemma for the local provider, in that in complying with the request to recruit staff with high-level academic qualifications, it risked denying specialized expertise to its existing teaching areas. Transnational programs at the campus were mainly oriented to careers rather than professions. For example, degrees or diplomas were offered in tourism, film and television studies, graphic design, and financial services. The director of studies also acknowledged the dilemma, advising that the institution was occasionally caught in the position of having to 'choose between a job applicant with high academic qualifications but no practical experience in a particular teaching area and an applicant with the professional knowledge and expertise but without the academic qualifications'. The interesting point here is that it was the local provider that recognized and struggled with this problem of professional versus academic qualifications. This is clearly related to quality control and again attests to the need for overseas universities to engage more fully and more directly in staff recruitment into their programs.

Curriculum and syllabus issues

The director of studies advised that most transnational programs delivered at the campus were required to be taught in English. Interviews with the teaching staff revealed that this requirement imposed by 'English-speaking universities', as they were described, was generally considered restrictive and a handicap to learning enhancement. Mauritius is essentially a tri-lingual society, with French, English, and Creole mainly spoken. English, as the international language of business, is the official language. However, French is spoken and read by virtually everyone. It is for many people their first language. Therefore, the requirement that programs be delivered *only* in English transgressed against multilingual practice and often against linguistic preference and facility. It is useful, at this point, to include remarks from the academics to capture the concerns:

> When I taught at the University of Mauritius, it was a bit more flexible, more relaxed. When I talk to the students there in French, I did not have the impression of doing something wrong.

I feel sorry for the students sometimes because you are testing them on their presentation and communication skills and they're being judged on a language that is not their first language. I think it penalizes them and very often I say, can you do this in French and they say, thank you so much, so much easier, because the words don't come in English.

I'm teaching Journalism and there are some things which are not applicable to the local context, so I've had to say I can't do this the (Australian university) way. I do current affairs quizzes in French, based on French newspapers, local newspapers, because it doesn't make sense to do it otherwise, to do it in English.

The invigilator advised that his university had not fully understood the implications of a multi-lingual culture for its educational provision when it had entered into a partnership arrangement with the local institution. The university was now grappling with the question of whether it could 'allow a bilingual partner'. The argument for accepting a 'bilingual component' in program delivery was that parity 'offshore' and 'onshore' could be maintained by requiring the same outcomes. He expressed the argument against bilingual delivery in a question: 'How do our English-speaking academics moderate the assessment results for various tasks in various units in various programs, if tasks are undertaken in French?' The findings of the study clearly suggest that an insistence that a curriculum or syllabus be delivered in the language it is written is not, in itself, necessarily a guarantee of quality. Indeed, the findings indicate that the requirement to teach/learn in the language of the parent organization can threaten the quality of teaching/learning. Perhaps the final word on the subject belongs to one of the academics:

Even if we try to tell them to speak English, even then the French keeps coming. I have a student in a foundation unit and whenever he's writing he'll keep asking 'how do you translate this word to the English one?' I keep telling him to sit next to me and I'll write the English and French ones. We all have English-speaking, but still we are used to thinking and speaking in French, so...

The teacher experience issue

The director of studies advised that most of the academics employed at the institution had French or Mauritian backgrounds. These were the circumstances because teaching staff needed to be proficient in both English and French. Of the 13 academics interviewed, 5 were educated principally in France, 6 in Mauritius and 2 in South Africa.

In the interviews, the academics were united in representing trans-national education as a departure from their previous educational experiences. As lecturers, and indeed, they maintained, even in their earlier lives as students, they were accustomed to what they tended to refer to as the 'theoretical way' of education. The meaning they gave to 'theoretical' was teacher-imparted. That is, their previous, predominant (many argued *exclusive*) educational experiences were of a teacher-centred approach to teaching and learning. For the academics, the 'theoretical way' meant 'only one way direction in communication'. It meant a practice of providing 'one, two or three hour lectures' wherein 'the students were given what they need'. A comment from one lecturer fairly sums up the common recognition of a disjuncture between educational forms: 'Before I taught in the international programs I was used to huge amphitheatres where, you know, you are just a lecturer, detached from the students'.

Not all transnational programs taught by the academics deviated dramatically from the 'theoretical way', but many did, particularly (they said) Australian and English programs. These were the 'interactive programs', not the 'spoon-feeding approach'. For the academics, the requirement to conduct tutorials was the clearest assault on the 'theoretical way' because 'they are discussion-based'. Mostly, the teaching staff welcomed the opportunity (and the obligation) to conduct tutorials, but there was general agreement that 'the difference between a lecture and a tutorial is smaller here than it would be at the parent university overseas'. Class size was the standard reason offered to account for the blurring of the distinction between lecture and tutorial. Most of the transnational units taught had enrolments of 60 students or less. The academics who delivered lectures in a subject that required tutorials also generally conducted all of the tutorials, too. The prevailing perspective was that this had the effect of making the lecture/tutorial division somewhat artificial. As one academic observed: '[W]e have the same people in the lecture and the same people in the tutorial so that it ends up being a repeat really, rather than, you know, different'. Another said: 'I don't really try to split up lectures and tutorials because I am the same person, and they (the students) know that too'.

There were 18 students who reported that they experienced tutorials as a component of their transnational programs. Their attitude to tutorials was positive. Tutorials were distinguished as opportunities 'to make friends', 'to get into groups', 'to talk and discuss', and 'to find out what others think and to get help with things you don't understand' and 'to show what you know'. There was, however, a general belief that there was 'too much teacher-talk' in tutorials.

To accommodate to local conditions, the Mauritian institution had to employ staff fluent in French and English. However, this meant that transnational educators were generally not familiar with key teaching/learning approaches germane to 'English-speaking universities'. An implication from the study findings is that there are potential challenges to quality in exporting educational programs to countries that exhibit (and require) different educational cultures.

The issue of the 'multi-skilled' transnational educator

In the interviews, many of the academics indicated they were teaching across different disciplinary regimes and sometimes outside their areas of speciality. For example, one academic who reported that she had a science background was teaching 'mass communications and I.T.'. Another academic who advised she had been employed to teach business courses was the 'lecturer for tourism' and also was teaching 'two modules of maths'. There was a general view that the transnational programs were often alike in ways that made viable team-teaching and teaching across the curriculum. For example:

> I am teaching Business Communication for one university and (name suppressed) is teaching a communication model in Science for a different university, but we find a lot of things are common. They (the students) have got to do oral presentations, research reports, so there are very similar components and then we share.

The director of studies advised that academics teaching in the transnational programs were 'multi-skilled'. The academics generally agreed, but were emphatic that they wanted to specialize: 'At the moment we wear lots of hats but that's our dream'. Holding back the 'dream' were fluctuations in demand:

> My area of specialization is literature, but that's not an area where there is a great deal of demand, so I end up teaching much more communication, for the time being. Initially, we did offer the literature course from (overseas partner) but there was no demand, only one or two...

The director of studies advised that transnational programs were operational 'when there were sufficient numbers'. That is, the programs ran when the minimum number of enrolments, as determined by the partners, was achieved. This meant that programs were inevitably vulnerable. A small drop in demand and the delivery of a unit or program was no longer viable. As a result of this instability, those academics employed to teach in transnational programs had to be dispersed to where demand was located. Clearly, there are quality concerns imposed by an obligation for educators to 're-invent' themselves as experts in areas foreign to them. The implication for overseas universities is that 'minimum' numbers be set high enough to guard against a reasonable attrition rate.

The communications issue

Under the franchise system in operation at the campus, overseas coordinators had the final say over the locally employed academics on the curriculum and its delivery. Typically, email communications were established prior to delivery and were sustained throughout the life of a unit or program. All of the academics reported that 'teaching by email' was an experience unknown to them prior to their involvement in transnational education. It was common, too, for lecture notes to be emailed and direction given on aims and strategies. The academics reported routinely sending samples of marked assignments and collated grades for overseas scrutiny and moderation. Many had met relevant overseas coordinators, because many overseas partners flew in teams of moderators at least once in a semester. ('Online' units delivered, or, in the more apt description of the academics, *facilitated* by a number of the academics for a university in South Africa constituted the exception. The academics reported 'very little contact at all' with their colleagues in South Africa.) In general, the academics reported positive relationships with overseas program and unit coordinators. This impression is best evidenced through their words:

> I think the perception has been one of team work more than the overseas authority sitting there and dictating things.

> For us, I think we like having that safety net of people in the background.

A small minority of academics indicated that being 'under external control' created morale problems for them and also undermined their authority with students. However, most of the academics were relaxed about the moderation of their assessments of student work and believed their students were also comfortable with this 'double-marking'. Below is a typical example of the majority view:

> The students are happy to know their work is being bench-marked, they are happy to know there is quality control. They are happy to see that (name suppressed) is coming, that their lecturers are being moderated in some way.

Student interviews strongly supported this view. The common agreement was that their programs of study had to be of 'international quality'. As a group, they regarded an international degree as superior to a degree awarded by a local institution. Therefore, they viewed 'external control' of 'local' quality as a positive measure.

What most of the academics really wanted was not freedom from moderation exercises but input into syllabus design. In particular, this view was pressed by academics who were teaching a unit for the second or third time. An example of the common argument is offered below:

> When you are teaching something for the first time, it is fine just to try to teach the content. It is experimental. But when you are teaching it again, you are getting to know what the needs are, what the problems are, what focus you need to put more on for the Mauritian students. Probably, eventually, you need a more active role on the part of the lecturers here whereby we can say, well, you know, we understand the philosophy behind this, the raison d'etre for a particular module, but then, in Mauritius, we believe we should take this out and add this, and put this here…

To be transnational educators, the academics in the study had to teach across a range of disciplines and areas; had to teach, against the grain, in a 'second language' and be sufficiently good teachers to know when to change languages; had to utilize teaching and learning methods outside of their previous experience; had to adapt to seeking and receiving email direction on their classrooms; and had to submit to 'external control'. In the general view, however, the key attributes needed of the transnational educator were humility and a willingness and ability to work as part of a team:

> You can't just get what you need for your module, put your head down and get on with it. You've got to be more approachable in terms of sharing information with others, and getting feedback from others. You've got to be willing to work with others, share with others.

There was also general agreement that teaching/learning would be improved by having exchange programs both for lecturers and for students. The lecturers also desired a particular kind of mentoring experience:

> I think it would be very useful if we were given the opportunities for shadowing with an overseas partner. When you shadow someone else you are exposed to all the realities, all the difficulties and then you can compare it all. Because here, you are limited to your own world.

From the remarks of the participants, it seems fairly clear that the isolation that can be imposed by transnational education practice represents a threat to quality. Email contact is also evidently not sufficient in itself as a bridge to communication. Quality seems to require planned and routine experiences of face-to-face contact.

The student alienation issue

The students who comprised the population for the focus group were sufficiently motivated to discuss their learning experiences and needs that they turned up for the interview at the campus on a public holiday. They generally lauded their teachers and generally complained that more resources were needed. For example, they demanded that the researcher 'inspect the library' where there were 'hardly any useful books or journals'. There were apparently insufficient computers for their learning needs and, for some, not enough equipment in film and television laboratories.

One issue that bothered the students was that they were restricted in the transnational programs from carrying out research. They maintained that they 'learnt how to do research' but could not conduct research 'because the universities won't let you do it without ethical clearances'. Their previous experience, usually in the Mauritian secondary education system, had accustomed them to undertaking surveys and they were unhappy that their current learning was restricted to 'the theoretical'.

The very great concern of the students, however, was that they had 'no contact' with students undertaking the same units and programs of study at the 'parent' universities overseas. They proposed exchange visits, discussion boards and the swapping of email addresses. The same concern re-appeared as strongly in the individual interviews. It was very plain that the students wanted not only to share and compare experiences with peers overseas, but to be part of a greater student community. The short expression for this is that the students wanted to belong. They felt excluded, isolated and marginalized.

The students also were very keen to have lecturers from their overseas programs visit them more often. They reported that 'lecturers from overseas sometimes came and spoke to them' in their classes. (According to teaching staff, these 'lecturers' were usually academics undertaking familiarization or moderation visits.)

Clearly, educational quality is not protected and certainly is not enhanced when students are alienated from their studies. Perusing the promotional literature of overseas universities one day at the campus, the researcher was struck by the images of university architecture and symbols, crowded lecture theatres and groups of cheerful students. In all the literature, the key appeal being made was to belonging, yet from the study findings, a question arises as to how well overseas universities honour their promises of fellowship to transnational students.

CONCLUSION

As a requisite to the transformation of Mauritius from a country dependent on the cane sugar industry to an international knowledge hub and centre of higher learning, the nation has embarked on the strategy of encouraging brand-name universities to set up locally in partnerships with local private and public education providers. The assumption is that the high educational standards of reputable overseas partners will transpose to Mauritian education through transnational practice.

The main aim of this paper has been to draw on study findings to indicate the presence of challenges for overseas universities in providing high quality transnational education in Mauritius, and, by extension, in other markets. What the discussion has tried to make apparent is that educational quality needs to be protected at every step of the enterprise, from acquaintance with the educational culture of a particular market, through the structuring of partnering relationships, through program marketing to students, through recruitment of transnational educators, through curriculum design and articulation and through teaching/learning approaches.

Drawing on the findings of this study, the best advice this discussion has for overseas universities is that they should rid themselves of the cosy notion that their ownership of their transnational programs assures quality. The *export* of programs, no matter how sound those programs are themselves, inevitably produces legion risks to quality that have to be recognized and addressed.

REFERENCES

Cassell, C. and Symon, G. (eds.; 1994) Qualitative methods in organizational research, London: Sage.

Cresswell, J. W. (1994) Research design: Qualitative and quantitative approaches, London: Sage.

Crotty, M. (1998) The foundations of social research: Meaning and perspective in the research process, St Leonards, NSW: Allen and Unwin.

Ezzy, D. (2002) Qualitative analysis: Practice and innovation, Crows Nest, NSW: Allen and Unwin.

Mauritian Ministry of Education and Scientific Research. (2006) Developing Mauritius into a knowledge hub and a centre of higher learning, Mauritius: Ministry of Education and Scientific Research.

NTEU. (2004) Offshore baggage: The experiences of Australian staff involved in the delivery of offshore courses, Melbourne: NTEU.

Pyvis, D. and Chapman, A. P. (2004) Student experiences of offshore higher education: issues for quality, Melbourne: AUQA.

Tertiary Education Commission of Mauritius. (2006) Tertiary education commission report, August 2006, Mauritius: Tertiary Education Commission of Mauritius.

22 Providing Instruction, Orientation and Professional Development for All Staff Involved in Transnational Teaching

Margaret Hicks and Kylie Jarrett

University of South Australia

INTRODUCTION

> In mature markets, any transnational program that does not have high-quality local teaching staff on campus will be very susceptible to competition from those that do... (McBurnie and Ziguras 2007: 59)

In response to the wider need to improve the quality of transnational programs, Australian Education International (AEI)[1] funded a number of 'Offshore Quality Projects' in 2005. The University of South Australia (UniSA) was successful in winning one of these grants to develop a professional development[2] framework for academic staff teaching Australian programs offshore (see Leask, Hicks *et al* 2005). This chapter will outline the findings of this research associated with this project (referred to as the Offshore Quality Project), briefly describe the professional development framework which was developed, and then discuss how the framework has been implemented at UniSA. The key challenge of this implementation process has been negotiating the power dynamics of both professional development and also the transnational education environment in South East Asia. This chapter outlines the approach UniSA has taken in addressing this tension to produce a successful teaching and learning relationship with a transnational partner in Malaysia.

BACKGROUND

Since the commissioning of the Australian Universities Quality Agency (AUQA) to conduct assessments of transnational programs by Australian providers, a major and continuing focus within the field of transnational education is quality assurance. This increased emphasis, together with genuine ethical and educational concerns among some academic staff, is demanding an examination of quality assurance in relation to teaching and learning in transnational programs. As has been argued by Miliszewska and Horwood (2004), the survival of transnational programs in a global educational environment will be dependent on the quality of their educational product, including both the design and delivery of the program. This has paralleled national attention on the quality of teaching and learning as the government has implemented a Learning and Teaching Performance Fund, based on a set of external indicators. More generally, the higher education sector is experiencing greater student diversity, as well as increasing attention being given to internationalization, the use of information and communication technologies, and program quality and evaluation.

Although much of the focus in quality models to date has been on management of the business case within transnational education, focus has begun to shift to pedagogic concerns. Within this shift, professional development of *all* staff involved in transnational partnerships has become a component of a quality regime. The good practice model outlined in The Observatory on Borderless Higher Education report (Connelly, Garton and Olsen 2006: 21) highlights professional development arrangements for both provider and partner organization staff as part of the necessary professional infrastructure within any institution's education plan. The need for professional development is also recognised within AEI's final report on the Outcomes of Universities Transnational Education Good Practice Projects (AEI 2006).

Although the models for offshore delivery vary (e.g. some universities have fully established international campuses while others offer programs through partner relationships), what is typical of this form of education is reliance on a combination of staff who travel from their home university (in Australia) to the offshore location, and local staff employed by the offshore partners (Leask *et al* 2005). From the literature on transnational teaching, it is apparent that teaching in this environment is a complex matter involving multiple people, cultures, roles, settings, programs, and modes of delivery. Yet, while there is a considerable and growing body of literature on the professional development of academic staff generally, less has been theorized and written about professional development for academic staff teaching in transnational programs (see Gribble and Ziguras 2003; Leask 2004, 2006; Dunn and Wallace 2005; Debowski 2003; Dixon and Scott 2003). Even less has been produced on the professional development of local staff based in the offshore location. This is in contrast to the number of transnational programs offered by Australian universities growing rapidly in the last few years (Marginson and McBurnie 2004).

To date, preparation for staff has been seen primarily as a matter of training and access to information. However, this is insufficient, and support for staff involved in these programs requires a multi-dimensional and context sensitive approach which considers the need of the various participants, their knowledges and interactions within the teaching context. Four dominant areas of consideration relating to professional development needs and transnational programs emerged from the literature review associated with the research project:

- the importance of knowing the teaching context;
- developing and adapting the curriculum;
- consideration of teaching and learning issues as they relate to transnational programs, including understanding and interacting with students, supervising postgraduate students, the language of instruction and modes of delivery;
- and, the development of an intercultural stance (Leask *et al* 2005).

These four areas were considered in framing the survey and the interview questions used in developing the framework within the Offshore Quality Project (described in detail in Leask, this volume).

A PROFESSIONAL DEVELOPMENT FRAMEWORK FOR ACADEMIC STAFF TEACHING AUSTRALIAN PROGRAMS OFFSHORE

The research highlighted the complexity of the offshore teaching environment and experience for staff and students. Four themes emerged from the surveys and interviews which were held with both Australian staff teaching offshore and local (offshore) teachers, administrative staff and students. Offshore academic staff need to be:

- Experts in their field: knowledgeable in the discipline within both an international and a local context (where local refers to the offshore context), and both informed about the latest research and able to incorporate it into their teaching;
- Skilled teachers and managers of the learning environment: able to acquit the operational issues involved in teaching offshore effectively and efficiently;
- Efficient intercultural learners: culturally aware and able to teach culturally appropriate materials, using culturally appropriate methods which recognize the critical role played by language and culture in learning and flexible enough to make adjustments in response to student learning needs;
- and Demonstrate particular personal attitudes and attributes: for example, being approachable, patient, encouraging and passionate about what they are teaching (Leask *et al* 2005: 30).

Also, as a result of this research, three guiding principles for the professional development of academic staff were proposed. These were:

- Principle 1: As both Australia-based and local offshore tutors play a critical role in offshore teaching, both groups need to be involved in professional development.
- Principle 2: Offshore teaching is both similar to and different from any other form of teaching activity. The fundamental differences relate to the intercultural space in which it occurs. Thus professional development for academic staff needs to address the intercultural nature of offshore teaching.
- Principle 3: The professional development needs of academic staff will vary according to their role and the stage of their involvement with transnational teaching. Professional development activities and resources need therefore to be flexible and sensitive to the experience, knowledge and situation of the individuals involved (Leask *et al* 2005: 34).

A detailed professional development framework for Australia-based staff and local offshore tutors was developed from the aforementioned themes and principles. The framework captures three distinct career stages for both UniSA and local offshore academics and the needs related to each stage. The framework also provides guidance on the type of content required to satisfy those needs and describes appropriate resources and development opportunities[3]. These resources include, but are not limited to:

- Information pages exploring UniSA's distinctive teaching and learning framework: These pages include an overview of transnational teaching, guides for alternative delivery in case travel is disrupted, managing discussion and group work, student-centred learning, and development of a scholarly approach to teaching.
- A suite of induction materials: This package contains a workshop plan, PowerPoint slides reviewing the University's structure and teaching and learning framework, and group activities to workshop the principles of this framework. These materials are designed to be adapted for particular programs.
- Case study workshops for ongoing professional development and support information: These workshops enable staff, either individually or in teaching teams, to consider, reflect, and propose solutions to complex problems associated with transnational teaching.
- Online workshop relating to research supervision in transnational contexts: This workshop primarily supports UniSA staff involved in the supervision of students based offshore. It provides information

and activities to aid in developing research supervision practice and the capacity to work constructively in an intercultural setting.

An online program called 'Transnational Teaching @ UniSA'—based on the University's compulsory teaching and learning foundation program and the principles of the professional development framework—was also created, both as an induction to UniSA's teaching and learning framework, and the scholarship of teaching. This program requires staff to work through five modules with related reflective activities and submit a short research report based either on an analysis of their own teaching practice, or the needs of their students

In 2006, the focus shifted to the dissemination and implementation of these resources with the appointment of a lecturer in academic development specializing in Transnational Education. This implementation process though has revealed the complexity of professional development in transnational environments. In the remainder of this chapter we discuss these challenges and how UniSA has managed to identify an approach to a successful transnational teaching and learning partnership.

THE FOUNDATION FOR THE UNISA FRAMEWORK

The implementation of this kind of framework is a complicated and delicate process. There is a tension between the need to assure quality and equivalence in transnational education products by ensuring all staff utilize effective teaching methods, and the need to respect local educational cultures and practices. However, the methods to address this tension are unstated within the transnational education field. While advocating for the involvement of local offshore teaching staff in development activities, recent best practice models do not offer any practical advice on how to achieve this. Yet this cannot be a minor consideration in the implementation process. An insensitive approach to professional development in transnational education runs the risk of perpetuating the neocolonial framework of international academic relations where western universities transfer their pedagogic activities and ideals to developing countries, without concern for the cultural milieu in which that teaching is to take place (Kanu 2005).

This effect is underscored in the field of professional development which, as Manathunga (2005) has pointed out, is inherently colonial. It is predicated on the colonial act of 'developing Others' which in the case of transnational education are both disciplinary-based academics and cultural 'Others'. McWilliam (2002: 290) similarly argues that because the idea of development 'is always predicated on the idea that someone is knowledge-able while someone else is knowledge deficient, such communication cannot be a conversation among equals. The developer's knowledge is already assumed to be what leads to progress, not the knowledge of the developee'. These descriptions of professional development as a colonial activity may overstate the case. As Manathunga (2005: 22) also points out, academic developers 'have never really had the epistemological or institutional power to invade or subjugate disciplinary-based academics'. Nevertheless as Said (1994: 9, original emphasis) describes, imperialism today remains in the 'impressive ideological formations that include notions that certain territories and people *require* and beseech domination, as well as forms of knowledge affiliated with domination'. Adopting any implementation framework, which assumed the need and desire for 'remedial' training, in UniSA's particular teaching and learning framework would certainly have perpetuated this form of imperialism.

According to Manathunga (2005: 26), to move out of a colonial framework in professional development 'we need to find ways to display our ambivalence about educational development orthodoxies. We need to engage with our 'Other' colleagues ... in a two-way, reciprocal, intercultural, interdisciplinary exchange'. How to articulate this in practice has been the challenge for UniSA and the role of the lecturer in academic development (Transnational Education) since 2006.

TRANSNATIONAL CONVERSATIONS

What has been identified as most important is a dialogue between UniSA academic staff, including the lecturer in academic development (Transnational Education), and staff in the partner organizations. In these conversations, the teaching and learning development needs of each partner can be expressed, areas of mutual need identified, and initiatives collaboratively developed and implemented. The key is the integration not only of individual local offshore teaching staff into the teaching team, as advocated by Leask (2004), but also the amalgamation of the professional development processes of UniSA and the partner institution's teaching and learning support mechanisms. UniSA has successfully initiated such a dialogue with one partner in Malaysia. With an active and highly engaged teaching and learning support centre, this institution has identified focus areas for professional development and has worked with UniSA staff to develop initiatives to meet those needs. As a responsive engagement, the professional development being implemented here is not an imposition from a more knowledgeable or powerful partner, nor is there the ad hoc method of approaching individual local offshore staff members to encourage engagement with externally determined areas of interest. Instead, the partner organization is treated as an equal partner, able to take ownership and direct the development activities as much as any other arm of the University.

Capacity building around UniSA's teaching and learning framework was identified by the Malaysian partner as a key need at this early stage of the transnational partnership. To support development in this area, UniSA staff have been invited to Malaysia to deliver workshops to local offshore teaching staff on identified topics of interest such as embedding UniSA Graduate Qualities in programs, courses, and teaching practice. The resources produced as part of the professional development framework, including the induction resources, have served as a base for this activity. Some local offshore staff with this partner have also taken up the Transnational Teaching @ UniSA online program through which they are introduced to UniSA's distinctive teaching and learning framework and its relationship with the scholarship of teaching.

Subsequent to undertaking Transnational Teaching @ UniSA, two participants have developed research projects on the implementation of UniSA's student-centred learning approach within the Malaysian teaching context. Along with their local colleagues, the academic developer (Transnational Education) has provided support for the staff undertaking these studies. The findings from this research will form a useful basis for the redevelopment of UniSA courses, as well as serving as a counterpoint in the field of transnational education, which is dominated by studies conducted by academics from provider institutions. UniSA's Division of Business has also invited local offshore academics to visit Australia where they will meet colleagues, experience the Australian teaching environment, be involved in development activities and, importantly, discuss the Malaysian education environment with UniSA staff.

Thus, in the development work we have undertaken together, there have been two kinds of conversational flow. Firstly, there has been the provision of information, resources and activities based around UniSA's teaching and learning framework, and the Offshore Quality Project, but produced as a reply to the partner's request. More significantly, though, there is a growing return flow of information and resources about the teaching and learning environment in our partner institution. This kind of ongoing dialogic interaction is a first step in building a transnational 'community of practice' in which the exchange of ideas can produce new frameworks for action rather than merely falling back on 'imported wisdom' (Wang 2004; Dunn and Wallace 2005).

WHOLE-OF-INSTITUTION STRATEGY

One of the key reasons for the success of this partnership has been the establishment of clear communication lines in the relationship. Pannan's and Gribble's (2005: 7) research into transnational teaching indicates that, for effective cross-partnership teaching and learning engagement to take place, the 'presence of a recognized central liaison person of adequate authority level, in both the provider institution and in the offshore location' is essential. In this case, the partner institution's head of the teaching and learning centre has served as such an anchor point for the relationship with UniSA professional development staff and the organizing hub for the work being conducted locally in Malaysia. She has worked with senior academic development and teaching staff at UniSA to coordinate and organise mutually beneficial initiatives. In many other transnational partnerships there is no such clearly defined liaison or structures and the identification and development of appropriate initiatives has consequently been more difficult.

This implementation process has underscored the need for a whole-of-institution approach for teaching and learning development in transnational education programs. Having the resources to ensure development of staff is vital and this has been achieved at UniSA by the professional development framework and through the position of the academic developer (Transnational Education) role. This is, however, insufficient. It is equally important to have the capacity for this development to be actualised throughout organizational structures.

A commitment to professional development for all staff requires clear contractual obligations within each partnership over the responsibility for teaching and learning development, as well as the adequate communication of those obligations to the relevant bodies. These may be dedicated teaching and learning centres, program directors, program managers or individual teachers. Appropriate contacts need to be identified early within the life of a partnership so that collegial relationships can be developed and a collaborative approach to teaching practice implemented. With this model, induction materials can be produced and delivered in alignment with the institutional goals of both institutions, and incorporating knowledge of the local offshore teaching and learning environment. This places the onus on both organizations for the adequate resourcing of professional development and the timely identification of important staff and student priorities. This requirement may add to the complexities of choosing an appropriate transnational partner and the negotiations of that contract, yet seem necessary if pedagogic quality is to be assured. Within our arrangements with the Malaysian partner institution, UniSA is working towards this framework and the results in relation to development activities are clearly positive.

If professional development activities are to avoid neo-colonialism, the capacity for staff to engage in complex dialogue with their transnational colleagues also becomes essential. This requires more than the exchange of a few pleasantries during a teaching or moderating visit. These relationships require ongoing dialogue so that a substantive understanding of educational diversity can be achieved (Kanu 2005: 495; Wang 2004; Leask this volume). For each academic there may be a need to reconsider their assumed understandings about the nature of effective teaching and to critically reflect on their own cultural understandings. Beyond any personal commitment, this also demands a commitment of time which is at a premium in academic life. This is particularly so in the transnational education environment. The complex work of redeveloping or translating course content for a local setting is often underestimated for all staff involved, as are the costs in terms of research and personal time caused by international travel (NTEU 2004; Debowski 2005, 2003; Mazzarol and Hosie 1997). A whole-of-institution commitment to the development of transnational teachers based in Australia and in local offshore institutions needs not only to value this form of exchange, but also enable it within its policy and processes if quality development activity is to occur.

CONCLUSION

UniSA's focus on development of all staff involved in transnational programs has produced a framework and resources for that development and a process for its implementation. This model incorporates the existing teaching and learning support facilities of the partner organization as another arm of the provider institution and consequently involves those bodies in a dialogue about mutual needs. In the same way as each Division of the University is involved in negotiating professional development projects, so too the partner organization can identify their needs relating to student learning outcomes and staff capacity as scholarly teachers. Through this approach the partner organization can initiate its own projects, and/or be involved in shaping of development activities from the outset. This model involves a shared commitment from all staff involved in transnational programs, including academics, administrators, and program managers, to the need for continual review and development of teaching and learning as part of the quality assurance process. It consequently requires an institutional commitment to enable and ensure a dialogue about teaching and learning along with a demarcation of responsibilities. Such a model will be of increasing significance in an industry environment where quality assurance is a key driver and within which teaching and learning development is increasingly identified as a factor in success.

What is also important about UniSA's implementation approach is that in Manathunga's (2005) terms it displays sensitivity to the practices of professional development and the educational ideals governing the institution's teaching and learning framework. While we remain assured of their value and significance as a model for education, we are also equally assured of their cultural specificity. By negotiating with and including our partner institutions into the aspects of the teaching and learning framework we implement, we ensure that our professional development is a transnational conversation and not merely an imposition of inappropriate educational ideals. We have learned much from this year of engagement with the Malaysian partner and will take these lessons into future development activities with other partners.

NOTES

1. Australian Education International (AEI) in the Department of Education Science and Training (DEST) funded 15 university transnational good practice projects. These projects were administered by the Australian Vice-Chancellors' Committee (AVCC) and the reports were disseminated by the International Education Association of Australia (IEAA). Project details can be accessed at: http://aei.dest.gov.au/AEI/GovernmentActivities/QAAustralianEducationAndTrainingSystem/Grants_GdPract.htm
2. The term 'professional' development is used throughout this chapter to encompass staff, academic and educational development.
3. Full details of the framework and resources can be accessed at: http://www.unisanet.unisa.edu.au/learningconnection/staff/resources/offshorepd.asp

REFERENCES

AEI (2006) 'Outcomes of Universities Transnational Good Practice Projects', report commissioned by Australian Education International in the Department of Education, Science and Training, October. Online. Available at: http://aei.dest.gov.au/AEI/GovernmentActivities/QAAustralianEducationAndTrainingSystem/Outcomes_Unis_pdf.pdf (accessed 22 February 2007).

Connelly, S., Garton, J. and Olsen, A. (2006) *Models and Types: Guidelines for Good Practice in Transnational Education*, The Observatory On Borderless Higher Education. Online. Available at: http://www.obhe.ac.uk/products/reports/ (accessed 14 September 2006).

Debowski, S. (2003) 'Lost in Internationalised Space: The Challenge of Sustaining Academics Teaching Offshore', paper presented at 17th Australian International Education Conference, Sydney, October 2003. Online. Available at: http://www.idp.com/17aiecpapers/program/friday/curriculum/DebowskiFri0900_p.pdf (accessed 9 August 2004).

—— (2005) 'Across the Divide: Teaching a Transnational MBA in a Second Language', *Higher Education Research and Development*, 24 (3): 265–80.

Dixon, K. and Scott, S. (2003) 'The Evaluation of an Offshore Professional Development Programme as Part of a University's Strategic Plan: A Case Study Approach', *Quality in Higher Education*, 9 (3): 287–294.

Dunn, L. and Wallace, M. (2005) 'Promoting Communities of Practice in Transnational Higher Education', paper presented at Open and Distance Learning Association of Australia conference on Breaking Down Boundaries: A conference on the international experience in open, distance and flexible learning, Adelaide, Australia, November 2005.

Gribble, K. and Ziguras, C. (2003) 'Learning to Teach Offshore: Pre-departure Training for Lecturers in Transnational Programs', *Higher Education Research and Development* 22 (2): 205–216.

Kanu, Y. (2005) 'Tensions and Dilemmas of Cross-Cultural Transfer of Knowledge: Post-structural/postcolonial Reflections on an Innovative Teacher Education in Pakistan', *International Journal of Educational Development*, 25: 493–513.

Leask, B. (2004) 'Transnational Education and Intercultural Learning: Reconstructing the Offshore Teaching Team to Enhance Internationalisation', paper presented at the Australian Universities Quality Forum on Quality in a Time of Change, Adelaide, Australia, July 2004.

—— (2006) 'Plagiarism, Cultural Diversity and Metaphor: Implications for Academic Development', *Assessment and Evaluation in Higher Education*, 31 (2): 183–199.

Leask, B., Hicks, M., Kohler, K. and King, B. (2005) *AVCC Offshore Quality Project Report: A Professional Development Framework for Academic Staff Teaching Australian Programs Offshore*. AVCC: University of South Australia.

Manathunga, C. (2005) 'Doing Educational Development Ambivalently: Applying Post-colonial Metaphors to Educational Development', *International Journal for Academic Development*, 11 (1): 19–29.

Marginson, S. and McBurnie, G. (2004) 'Cross-border Post-secondary Education in the Asia-Pacific region', *Internationalisation and Trade in Higher Education: Opportunities and Challenges*, Paris: OECD.

Mazzarol, T. and Hosie, P. (1997) 'Long Distance Teaching: The Impact of Offshore Programs and Information Technology on Academic Work', *Australian Universities' Review* 40 (1): 20–24.

McBurnie, G. and Ziguras, C. (2007) *Transnational Education: Issues and Trends in Offshore Higher Education*, Milton Park, Oxon: Routledge.

McWilliam, E. (2002) 'Against Professional Development', *Educational Philosophy and Theory*, 34 (3): 289–299.

Miliszewska, I. and Horwood, J. (2004) 'Engagement Theory: A Framework for Supporting Cultural Differences in Transnational Education', Higher Education Research Society of Australasia (HERDSA).

NTEU (2004) *Excess Baggage: Australian Staff Involvement in the Delivery of Offshore Courses, research report and case study findings*, NTEU, July.

Pannan, L. and Gribble, C. (2005) 'A Complexity of Influences on Teaching in Transnational Environments: Can We Simplify and Support it?', paper presented at Open and Distance Learning Association of Australia conference on Breaking Down Boundaries: A conference on the international experience in open, distance and flexible learning, Adelaide, Australia, November 2005. Online. Available at: http://www.unisa.edu.au/odlaaconference/PDFs/87%20ODLAA%202005%20-%20Pannan%20&%20Gribble.pdf (accessed 7 February 2007).

Said, E. W. (1994) *Culture and Imperialism*, New York: Vintage Books.

Wang, T. (2004) 'Understanding Chinese Educational Leaders' Conceptions in an International Education Context,' paper presented at AARE International Educational Research Conference, Melbourne, Australia, November 2004. Online. Available at: http://www.aare.edu.au/04pap/wan04028.pdf (accessed 7 February 2007).

23 Intercultural Communities of Practice

Lee Dunn and Michelle Wallace
Southern Cross University

Transnational education holds the possibility of rich and meaningful intercultural encounters among institutions and their staff, teachers, and students, and we have previously explored a way to turn this opportunity into a consistent reality (Dunn and Wallace 2006a). As we have seen, all stakeholders in the transnational educational enterprise desire its success for a combination of financial, educational and other reasons. But while there are many positive stories, all too often dissatisfaction and misunderstanding ensues. The dimensions of the challenge have been shown to be:

- achieving effective communications among institutions, educators, staff and students (e.g. Heffernan and Poole 2005; Leask 2004; Pannan and Gribble 2005)
- arriving at common goals and expectations and negotiating relationships (e.g. Dixon and Scott 2004; Heffernan and Poole 2004: McNicholl, Clohessy and Luff 2005)
- designing and delivering curriculum and assessment for 'localized (yet) international' content and teaching approaches (Leask, this volume; Wallace and Dunn this volume). (See also Carroll 2002; Dunn and Wallace 2006a; Pannan and Gribble 2005.)
- supporting transnational students (Eldridge 2005; Pannan and Gribble 2005; Tickle, Clayton and Hawkins 2003).

The coordination of all groups involved in this setting has been shown to be complex and difficult, so it is not surprising that many of those researching in this field have found communication to be 'the most pervasive issue' confronting those who strive for a holistic approach to transnational education (e.g. Pannan and Gribble 2005: 7). In this chapter we make our case for intentional communities of practice whose first task would be effective intercultural communication between team members who work on authentic teaching, learning and student support tasks. We will then explore the dimensions of the challenge we have identified above, and recommend ways to promote deliberate, nurtured communities of practice in this setting.

CROSS-BORDER COMMUNITIES OF PRACTICE

Professional communities of practice occur naturally when people work together on common tasks or strategies. Wenger (1998) discusses 'situated learning' as learning that is derived from what might be known as professional networking in association with deliberate teamwork. Wenger asserts that institutions should encourage professional communities of practice because the learning that occurs is deeper than that of each individual working alone. We believe that many of the challenges identified above can best be resolved by nurturing broad communities of practice that work to a common goal of internationalization without homogenisation (Risager 1999).

The first guiding principle in 'A Professional Development Framework for Academic Staff Teaching in Australian Programs Offshore' produced for the Australian Vice-Chancellors Committee (AVCC) is: 'As both Australia-based and local tutors play a critical role in offshore teaching, both groups need to be involved in professional development' (Leask, Hicks *et al* 2005: 34). The AVCC project was concerned with academics, and we will propose here that nurtured communities of practice, including administrators, student services staff, librarians, academic skills developers, and IT staff, would complement other forms of professional development.

It is not realistic to suggest that broad, inclusive communities of practice will grow naturally when workload, geography, national borders, and institutional practices intervene. For example, the role descriptions of local tutors in particular programs might not include regular and ongoing participation in curriculum or assessment design, intercultural pedagogy, or identification of student support needs. The desire for successful student learning outcomes, though, and the increasing requirements of national and international quality assurance, provide an opportunity to intentionally build into partnership agreements cross-border communities of practice, professional development initiatives, and professional practice.

We believe that models of inclusive communities of practice can emerge when they are reasonably cost-effective and efficient in terms of workload for all those involved, and when there are tangible benefits. Therefore, as we have argued previously (Dunn and Wallace 2006a), such communities and networks should be nurtured and supported around educational work that is already on the institutional agenda.

COMMUNICATION

Dixon and Scott (2004: 4) found that 'establishing and maintaining excellent communication across and between all levels of the provider institution and the offshore location is central to the success of an off-shore program'.

Our first foray into transnational teaching and learning was as Australian university teachers in one such program in Singapore. On one of our trips we interviewed 23 students of an undergraduate business degree taught in partnership by an Australian university and a Singaporean professional institute (Dunn and Wallace 2004). On our return we interviewed five Australian lecturers in the program. The Australian lecturers encountered difficulties in their communications with their students and the local tutors. The Singaporeans were reticent about how students prefer to learn. One student said: 'We don't like to open up. It's tough for the (Australian) lecturer, asking questions, looking around and nobody answers' (Dunn and Wallace 2004: 297). Pyvis and Chapman (2005) also report that questions formulated by an Australian lecturer to engender both informality and a comfortable group climate had the opposite effect on Singaporean students who, on the contrary, felt exposed and anxious.

In our study, the Australian lecturers, accustomed to robust peer review of their academic work including their teaching, were frustrated when the local tutors were loath to provide feedback that could improve teaching and learning. The Australian lecturers wanted to liaise more closely with their Singaporean colleagues, but were unable to find a way to engender the kind of dialogue that would promote what they considered to be more collegial relationships. An Australian lecturer 'found when he "touches base" with (his) tutor "I just get a nice smile and everything's fine"' (Dunn and Wallace 2004: 298).

All kinds of communication, between partner institutions and their administrative and teaching staff and within the teaching and learning experience itself, are more complex in the transnational setting. Ziguras (2001: 9) notes that, while learning experiences delivered via communication and information technology (C&IT) can promote 'a new way of learning' because students must communicate in well-designed activities such as problem-solving exercises, a reliance on C&IT can reinforce one-way communication (Ziguras 2001: 12).

C&IT has hugely increased the possibility of rapid and frequent communication between colleagues and with students who are geographically distant. However, it has often been shown that it is not a complete substitute for face-to-face meetings in terms of developing trust, goodwill, commitment, and the clear understandings of goals and expectations essential to successful transnational education (Heffernan and Poole 2005; Pannan and Gribble 2005; Dixon and Scott 2004).

RECOMMENDATION

Much of the research reported here shows that effective communication holds the key to success in transnational education. We believe that fruitful intercultural learning will follow when staff of both provider and local institutions are formally recognized as equals in the educational enterprise. That is, when local staff, in the words of one tutor, 'feel like member[s] of the teaching team, as part of the offshore team as well' (Leask *et al* 2005: 32). We recommend that institutions include in partnership agreements and role descriptions regular interactions on authentic pedagogical tasks that will lead to greater trust and understanding across borders and, most importantly, less confusion among students.

GOALS, EXPECTATIONS, AND RELATIONSHIPS

The success of offshore programs depends largely on the quality of the relationships between stakeholders (Heffernan and Poole 2004). Such relationships occur on several levels: at the institutional level; between the academics and support staff of both partners (librarians, student services staff, academic skills advisers, and IT staff); between the academics of the awarding institution and the students and between the local academics and the students.

Educational and commercial goals may not be fully teased out in initial negotiations, thus leading to 'conflicting interests and a mismatch of expectations' between the institutions (McNicoll *et al* 2005: 2). The simultaneous pursuit of educational and commercial goals puts pressure on all stakeholders in these settings (McNicoll *et al* 2005). Partners in transnational educational ventures must satisfy quality assurance benchmarks and guidelines for good educational practice while at the same time ensure the program's financial viability. Operating across borders as they do, the partners might have to negotiate the quality assurance and legislative requirements of two or more countries.

Relations between students and their teachers and between the groups of academics add a complexity that also affects teaching and learning outcomes. It has been shown that students often enrol in a foreign degree to 'experience foreign curricula and teaching styles and acquire international perspectives' (Dixon and Scott 2004: 6). Pyvis and Chapman (2005: 38) also found that one reason the Singaporean students in their study took a transnational program was 'because they were attracted to the idea of an international education'. These students were somewhat disappointed that the program was confined to United States and Australian perspectives. They did not consider this to be truly international. Our survey of Australian academics who teach in transnational programs (Dunn and Wallace 2006b) confirmed the students' perceptions. Australian academics did not change or adapt their teaching and learning styles and materials other than to add local examples. Assessment was rarely changed or adapted in transnational programs.

When we interviewed students for our Singapore study (Dunn and Wallace 2004) we found that the students valued interactions with their Australian lecturers more highly than with their local tutor (possibly because assessment was controlled from Australia). Our recent survey of transnational students (Wallace and Dunn this volume) also reports student concern that local tutors are not fully informed about the Australian university's expectations. They are therefore seen by the students to have a lesser status than the Australian lecturers. These students wanted more contact with the Australian lecturers, but if their local tutors had a stronger role and were better informed about the Australian university's requirements and the Australian teachers' expectations their anxieties could have been allayed.

RECOMMENDATION

Staff of each program could operate as a cross-border team with a team member appointed to be a 'central academic liaison person' (Pannan and Gribble 2005: 9). This person would probably be employed in the provider institution and would work in cooperation with an administrator from the partner organization. He or she would maintain overall records for the program in terms of formal partnership agreements, enrolments, student progression, staffing, workloads, roles of team members, timelines, curriculum, assessment, and student feedback. The role would include liaison across the borders with student administration, library, academic assistance, information technology sections, and other support areas to ensure that they remain 'in the loop'.

CURRICULUM AND PEDAGOGY

Quality assurance guidelines tend to require that transnational programs have equivalent curriculum and similar standards for both onshore and offshore cohorts. We now know it is common for transnational students to take western degrees because they want exposure to international approaches that will stand them in good stead if they need to travel for work, usually in business or information technology. However, there have been examples of unchanged curriculum inappropriately taught in transnational programs. What is the point of a Chinese student learning the Australian industrial relations system? Are western human resource management practices directly translatable to Asian or African settings?

How can provider universities and partner institutions find the most appropriate way to satisfy the needs of all stakeholders?

> [I]t is not sufficient to argue that no change is necessary because science or technology is universal. All knowledge is reinterpreted in particular contexts, and workplaces, customs, industrial laws and the like are far from uniform throughout the world. The location, shape, purpose and scale of a bridge are aesthetic, social and cultural issues, not merely engineering problems, for example. (Curro and McTaggart 2003: 2).

Transnational educators are inevitably caught up in tensions between global modernising trends and local traditional practices and:

> [T]his means coming to understand the way things are done locally before seeking to change them. Western educators can make such decisions about the local practices they understand, but to dismiss local practices in other parts of the world without understanding them is fraught with danger. (Ziguras 2001:16).

RECOMMENDATION

Transnational teachers from provider and local institutions 'have their long held views of teaching and learning challenged' (Leask 2004: 147). Intercultural learning takes place by virtue of the experience of teaching in this setting, but can be formalized and enhanced (by) 'equal' planning and evaluation sessions—sessions in which offshore-based staff and home-based staff work together as a united, egalitarian teaching team (where) all members have a real opportunity to influence the structure and content of the curriculum and the teaching and learning activities' (Leask 2004: 148).

Meetings should be scheduled to include regular input from local tutors. We acknowledge that much of the joint planning must take place using C&IT. Synchronous online audio interactions and videoconferencing could be enriched by face-to-face meetings when staff from the provider institution travel to the local country to teach or for student support or administrative purposes.

ASSESSMENT OF STUDENT LEARNING

Assessment is the culmination of the learning experience for students and of the teaching experience for academics. Assessment drives learning (Biggs 2003) and in its design we show students what we want them to learn and how we want them to learn it. Assessment is hard enough when students are accustomed to the same educational system as their teachers; when assessment tasks are clear and inclusively designed; when students are not over-assessed; when assessment tasks are pitched at the appropriate level; when requirements are explicit; and so on. How much more difficult is it when teachers and students are separated by diverse prior experiences of all these things?

Pyvis and Chapman (2005) found that transnational students suffer from culture shock similarly to international students who travel to study in another country. They experience a foreign education system (including foreign assessment practices) imported with the transnational program. Lecturers and students need to learn about each other—students need to 'have the cultural knowledge' of what the lecturer wants them to do (Pyvis and Chapman 2005: 32).

In recent times there has been much concern in academic circles about a perceived conflict of values between education as a 'commodity' and the 'maintenance of academic standards (which is) the foundation upon which an institution's reputation is built' (Morgan *et al* 2004: 67). The argument goes that fee-paying students are treated as 'customers' who, having paid for their degree, may, for financial reasons, be awarded grades higher than their performance warrants. Proponents of this argument assert that academic standards are lowered as a result.

In becoming 'preoccupied' with standards, academics might lose sight of the principle 'that inclusive assessment ought to be a primary consideration in the development of assessment strategies' (Morgan *et al* 2004: 48). Assessment should be pitched at an appropriate level of difficulty and take account of the diversity of the student population.

Assessment is both a science and an art. We suspect that the challenges of getting assessment right are not confined to for-profit programs. It has been shown that individual markers apply different interpretations of marking rubrics when marking student performances on any assessment task. It has also been shown that different markers may not agree on a result for the same student's work (Brown *et al* 1994).

If marking and grading are to be fair and consistent, assessment practices should be moderated during the assessment process. Particularly, problems can arise when multiple markers do not have the opportunity for collegial discussion and support to negotiate how to interpret marking rubrics.

RECOMMENDATION

There is a strong argument for establishing collegial agreement in transnational programs regarding academic standards, the level and fairness of assessment tasks, academic integrity, and the reliability of student results. This is a vexed area and includes different understandings within teams of academics who operate in the same location. Fairness and consistency is more difficult to achieve across borders. In addition to including assessment in planning and evaluation sessions as suggested above, moderation meetings should be held to ensure that students and the partner institutions can rely upon the results as a true record of student performance. Much of this work can be done via C&IT augmented with face-to-face communication during normal visits.

SUPPORT

Librarians, IT staff, academic skills advisers, and student administration staff are as involved in the cross-border intercultural education experience as are their academic colleagues. In their study of undergraduate programmes in Vietnam and Africa, Pannan and Gribble (2005: 6) found 'the availability and capacity of offshore infrastructure to supply, for example electricity, information and communication technology, and textbooks, have a major influence on the resources and facilities that may be available in the offshore location'. Tickle et al (2003) recommend that students receive advice about enrolment, including their study workload. They also suggest the establishment of procedures to 'check ordering and receipt of learning resource materials and set texts' (Tickle et al 2003: 77).

> Student support needs were observed to be multi-faceted, occurring in independent learning skills; cultural integration of new educational experiences; information and IT literacy; ongoing English language enhancement being vital in programs delivered in English offshore while the students remain immersed in their local language and culture. (Pannan and Gribble 2005: 9)

The relative newness and complexity of transnational education makes it necessary for institutions to re-evaluate their approaches to administering these courses and supporting offshore students (Eldridge 2005).

RECOMMENDATION

It is important that academic staff be aware of the kind of support (especially academic skills advice, library and IT) available to students in their local institution and that they avoid incorrect 'assumptions' (Dautermann 2005: 141) about what technology is available to students. Support people also need to know whether offshore students can navigate around systems and what communication, technical, or academic difficulties might arise. Relevant academic skills advisers, librarians, IT support people, and student administrators should be included in cross-border teams to enable them to become integral to the intercultural community of practice.

CONCLUSION

We agree with those who argue that internationalization, including transnational education, needs a 'whole of institution approach'. (e.g. Castle and Kelly 2004; Leask *et al* this volume). This chapter has focused upon a means of integrating educational operations across the academic, support, and administrative structures of the institutions involved in the transnational educational enterprise.

Communities of practice will develop naturally as people work together (Wenger 1998), but the experience of transnational education has shown that these communities are not inclusive: that is, they do not cross the borders (Dunn and Wallace 2006b). The complexity of this new form of education demands that inclusive intercultural communities of practice be nurtured and not be left to serendipitous chance. While our focus has been at the level of educational delivery we know that our recommendations will not be implemented unless they are embedded in agreements between the parties to these programs and, very importantly, in policy and guidelines for practice.

REFERENCES

Biggs, J. (2003) *Teaching for Quality Learning at University* 2nd edition, Buckingham, UK: Society for Research in Higher Education and Open University Press.

Brown, S., Rust, C. and Gibbs, G. (1994) *Strategies for Diversifying Assessment*, UK: Oxford Centre for Staff Development.

Carroll, J. (2002) *A Handbook for Deterring Plagiarism in Higher Education*, UK: Oxford Centre for Staff and Learning Development.

Castle, R. and Kelly, D. (2004) 'Internationalisation: A Whole-of-Institution Approach', *Proceedings of the Australian Universities Quality Forum*, AUQA Occasional Publication.

Curro, G., and McTaggart, R. (2003) 'Supporting the Pedagogy of Internationalisation', *Paper presented at the 17th IDP Australian Education Conference*, Melbourne, Australia.

Dautermann, J. (2005) 'Teaching Business and Technical Writing in China: Confronting Assumptions and Practices at Home and Abroad', *Technical Communication Quarterly* Spring, 14 (2): 141–160.

Dixon, K. and Scott, S. (2004) 'Professional Development Programs for International Lecturers: Perspectives and Experiences Related to Teaching and Learning', *Proceedings of IDP Australian International Education Conference, Sydney*. Online. Available at: http://www.idp.com/aiec/past-papers/wed%20-%20Dixon%20&%20Scott.pdf (accessed 18 October 2007).

Dunn, L. and Wallace, M. (2006a) 'Promoting Communities of Practice in Transnational Higher Education', ch. 16 in *Breaking Down Boundaries: International Experience in Open, Distance and Flexible Learning.* Selected Papers, Charles Sturt University, Bathurst, Australia: ODLAA.

Dunn, L. and Wallace, M. (2006b) 'Australian Academics and Transnational Teaching: An Exploratory Study of Their Preparedness and Experiences', *Higher Education Research and Development,* 25 (4): 357–370.

Dunn, L. and Wallace, M. (2004) 'Australian Academics Teaching in Singapore: Striving for Cultural Empathy', *Innovations in Education and Teaching International,* August 41 (3): 291–304.

Eldridge, K. (2005) 'Value Dilemmas in the Administration of Offshore Delivery: Finding the Road to Absolution', *Proceedings of the IDP Australian International Education Conference,* Gold Coast. Online. Available at: http://www.idp.edu.au/aiec/programme/Fri%201050%20Kaye%20Eldridge.pdf

Heffernan, T. and Poole, D. (2005) 'In Search of "The Vibe": Creating Effective International Education Partnerships', *Higher Education,* 50: 223–245.

Heffernan, T. and Poole, D. (2004) '"Catch Me I'm Falling": Key Factors in the Deterioration of Offshore Education Partnerships', *Journal of Higher Education Policy and Management,* March 26 (1): 75–90.

Leask, B. (2004) 'Transnational Education and Intercultural Learning: Reconstructing the Offshore Teaching Team to Enhance Internationalisation', *Proceedings of the Australian Universities Quality Forum,* Adelaide: AUQA Occasional Publication.

Leask, B., Hicks, M., Kohler, M. and King, B. (2005) *AVCC Offshore Quality Project Report: A Professional Development Framework for Academic Staff Teaching Australian Programs Offshore,* June: University of South Australia for the AVCC.

McNicoll, Y. R., Clohessy, J. M. and Luff, A. R. (2005) 'Auditing Offshore Partnerships: Lessons from Reviewing Nursing and Psychology Courses Offered in Singapore', *Proceedings of Australian Universities Quality Forum,* Sydney, Australia. Online. Available at: http://www.auqa.edu.au/auqf/2005/program/papers/session_e3.pdf

Morgan, C., Dunn, L., Parry, S. and O'Reilly, M. (2004) *The Student Assessment Handbook: New Directions in Traditional and Online Assessment.* London: Routledge.

Pannan, L. and Gribble, C. (2005) 'A Complexity of Influences on Teaching in Transnational Environments: Can We Simplify and Support It?' *Paper presented at: Breaking down boundaries: international experience in open, distance and flexible learning,* Adelaide, Australia, October ODLAA Online. Available at: http://www.odlaa.org/events/2005conf/ref/ODLAA-2005PannanGribble.pdf

Pyvis, D. and Chapman, A. (2005) 'Culture Shock and the International Student "Offshore"', *Journal of Research in International Education,* 4; 23–42.

Risager, K. (1999) 'Globalisation or Internationalisation: Friends or , in *Sprogforum* no. 13, vol. 5, 7–12. Available at http://inet.dpb.dpu.dk/infodok/sprogforum/Espr13/risager.html

Tickle, K., Clayton, D. and Hawkins, K. (2003) 'Quality Management Models for International Campuses and Operations: A Case Study of a Regional Experience', *Proceedings of the Australian Universities Quality Forum 2003.* AUQA Occasional Publication.

Wenger, E. (1998) *Communities of Practice: Learning, Meaning and Identity*, Cambridge, UK: Cambridge University Press.

Ziguras, C. (2001) 'Educational Technology in Transnational Higher Education in South East Asia: The Cultural Politics of Flexible Learning', *Educational Technology and Society* 4 (4): 8–18.

Index